KU-161-366

The Right to Childhoods

Critical Perspectives
on Rights, Difference and
Knowledge in a Transient World

Dimitra Hartas

continuum

Continuum International Publishing Group

The Tower Building	80 Maiden Lane
11 York Road	Suite 704
London SE1 7NX	New York, NY 10038

www.continuumbooks.com

© Dimitra Hartas 2008

First published 2008
This paperback edition published 2011

All rights reserved. No part of this publication may be reproduced or transmitted in any form or by any means, electronic or mechanical, including photocopying, recording, or any information storage or retrieval system, without prior permission in writing from the publishers.

Dimitra Hartas has asserted her right under the Copyright, Designs and Patents Act, 1988, to be identified as Author of this work.

British Library Cataloguing-in-Publication Data
A catalogue record for this book is available from the British Library.

ISBN: 9780826495686 (hardcover)
9781441176424 (paperback)

Library of Congress Cataloging-in-Publication Data
Hartas, Dimitra, 1966–
The right to childhoods : critical perspectives on rights, difference and knowledge in a transient world / Dimitra Hartas. – 1st ed.
   p. cm.
Includes bibliographical references and index.
ISBN: 978-1-4411-7642-4 (paperback)
ISBN: 978-0-8264-9568-6 (hardcover)
1. Children–Social conditions. 2. Youth–Social conditions.
3. Children's rights. I. Title.

HQ767.9.H39 2010
305.23–dc22

2010029219

Typeset by Newgen Imaging Systems Pvt Ltd, Chennai, India

Contents

Contents

Part IV: Knowledge for Rights and Democracy

Preface

To organize scholarship in the field of childhood is to attempt to tackle the multiplicity and plurality of childhood, the ecologies of children's life, the current frameworks of children's rights and children's education for citizenship and a viable future. And this is a vast area to negotiate. The terrain of childhood and children's development is polyphonic, encompassing many perspectives and voices, some complementary and some contradictory. Mapping this terrain carries a great deal of responsibility and emotional commitment in that issues regarding children's well-being tend to receive a range of emotive responses from parents, teachers, politicians and the media. To address constructions of childhood (children as objects of concern, citizens or resources with enterprising qualities), the transient ecology of children, children's rights, voice and participation and knowledge for democracy is to embrace the life chances of children. Childhood, as a site of critique, has not just surfaced as the current media focus may suggest. Issues about children's well-being, rights and citizenship have a diachronic quality, requiring us to combine retrospective views about child development with new modes of inter-disciplinary knowledge to understand the children's experiences of growing up in the 21st century.

The principles that guided the writing of this book include a critical attitude towards the abstract and universal basis of current frameworks of children's rights; a rejection of dualistic approaches, e.g. nature vs. nurture, regarding interpretations of children's development by positioning childhood at the interplay between biology and culture; an advocacy for a relational framework of children's rights, i.e., the right to childhoods, that reflects the many childhoods shaped by diversity and difference; a commitment to a civic education and learning for rights and democracy; and most of all the welcoming of 'children as young citizens, equal stakeholders with adults' (Moss and Petrie, 2002: 40).

There are four major strands, namely, rights, transience, difference and knowledge that run through this book. First, children's rights and their competing discourses are discussed, observing that the current children's rights frameworks do not always account for the plurality and diversity in children's life and the major societal changes they face. An alternative framework, i.e., the right to childhoods, is discussed, underpinned by the principles of plurality, dialectical and relational approaches to rights, respect for difference, voice and participation in civic life and responsiveness to the impact of transience on children's quality of life.

The second strand, i.e., transience, encompasses the major changes in children's spatial, social and economic reality, and their implications on the attainment of happiness in children. Globalization, individualization and technology have changed children's natural and social world at a pace that is unprecedented in the history of human evolution. More and more children are growing up in transient neighbourhoods due to residential mobility, and community disintegration and gentrification. Families and human relationships also change, with parenthood and childhood moving into the public domain. The implications of growing up in a fast-changing world are not always understood. Some children's life consists of fragments where relationships are provisional, and identities are negotiated continually in an attempt to construct cohesive narratives of their life.

The third strand, i.e., difference, is an organizing principle in young people's life. Childhood is heterogeneous, diverse, encapsulating the lived experiences of children from diverse ethnic and linguistic backgrounds, who encounter challenges and present multiple possibilities. The discourses on difference appear to be absent in the discussions of children's rights and the constructions of childhood. The right to be different and the right to be the same are not (and should not) be in conflict. The current frameworks of children's rights do not account for the ways in which difference shapes young people's lives. The commonly-held assumptions about normalcy, disability, ethnic and linguistic variations construe difference as inferiority. What is advocated, instead, is an emancipatory conception of human dignity, based on acknowledging the different cultural facets of young people's lives.

The fourth strand, i.e., knowledge, has stimulated discussions on the nature and purpose of knowledge in a knowledge-based society where the shifting boundaries of nation-states and welfare policies have changed the face of democracy as we know it. Knowledge and what is to be known have undergone major transformations as we enter an era of radical doubt. The changing nature of knowledge raises questions about the type of education and learning that is required to prepare young people function in future societies. A new form of criticality is valued that does not confine itself to an exercise of reason only, but enables young people to engage critically with the big issues that affect their life and community. In this c ontext, knowledge emerges as being relational and situated within ethics and a sense of obligation.

To understand the influences of rights, transience, difference and knowledge on children's quality of life requires new approaches and lines of argument. Current sociological and psychological theories of children's development and pedagogies cannot address entirely what it means to be a child in the 21st century. Also, although current policy and practice in early years education has alluded to the children's rights and the diversity in society, the most fundamental issue, that of the right to childhoods, is rarely debated. Do children, especially those who are different or experience adversity and disadvantage, ascertain their right to not be treated as a single entity? Are the polyphony and diversity of children's experiences and the circumstances that surround their lives acknowledged? The dominance of the market economies, consumerism, poverty and the increasing individualization entice new forms of children's exploitation and victimization that, ultimately, deny their right to citizenship and compromise their well-being.

At times, the views offered in this book may appear incompatible, entailing competing discourses and highlighting tensions. This book does not attempt to reconcile the tensions that emanate from the discourses on childhood and its place in time. The right to childhood*s*, and not the right to childhood, is the right to acknowledge human variation and the diversity and plurality that are inherent in children's experiences. The right to childhoods advocates for children's rights to become living rights, relevant to the circumstances that surround their life. Transforming human rights from an abstract code of conduct into a living reality for children and their families is a project not yet complete.

Dimitra Hartas
University of Warwick, UK
March 2008

Acknowledgements

This is a research-based book, drawing upon research findings from the Needs Analysis study that was carried out at the University of Warwick (Hartas and Lindsay, 2007), and from the Young People's Social Attitudes (YPSA) survey (2003). I would like to thank the young people and the organizers from various youth centres in the Midlands, who generously gave their time and offered views about issues that matter to their life and the life of the people they care for, within the context of the Needs Analysis study. Also, I am grateful to having been given access to the YPSA dataset by the UK Data Archive at the University of Essex.

This book is dedicated to all children and, among them, Pavlos and Victor, whose experience of early childhood has given me a glimpse into what a child is in the 21st century, enabling me to articulate the multiplicity and plurality of their lives, and also re-examine the wider issues that affect their well-being in a fast-changing society. Parental anxiety has also been the impetus behind this book which, I hope, will provoke further debates on current trends towards an increasing fragmentation and social engineering of children's lives. Finally, this book calls for redressing the balance between regulation and creating the conditions that would support the right to childhoods by recognizing children as a social group on its own right and advocating their rights and citizenship.

Introduction

In recent times, the debates on childhood and the society's role in rearing children[1] have moved from the academic circles to the media domain. Numerous articles have appeared in newspapers, debating issues regarding the state of childhood and the mounting concerns about children's happiness and well-being. Al Aynsley-Green, the children's commissioner for England, described 2007 as 'a year of unparalleled focus on children and young people's lives', a year of 'unprecedented debate' on childhood and how, as a society, we nurture children and young people (Aynsley-Green, 2007). The Labour Government has formed the Department for Children, Schools and Family in an attempt to place children and young people at the centre of public policy, and make the United Kingdom, as the Secretary of State for children, Ed Balls, aspires, a country that is the 'best place in the world' to be a child.

In 2007, the UNICEF commissioned a report and the Children's Society undertook the Good Childhood Inquiry to shed light into the experiences of children growing up in the United Kingdom. The report described Britain – the fifth richest country in the world – at the bottom of a league table for child well-being across 21 industrialized countries. The United Kingdom and the United States of America found themselves at the bottom third of the rankings for five of the six dimensions (i.e., material well-being, health and safety, educational well-being, family and peer relationships, behaviours and risks and subjective well-being) reviewed. The Good Childhood Inquiry has also provided evidence regarding the shrinking of children's spaces and the limited opportunities that children have to play with their peers away from adults' supervision and regulation (Children's Society, 2007).

The Big Issues

Childhood is an ambivalent reality (Jans, 2004), but so is adulthood. Childhood has become a site of critique, not just for children but also for adults to engage with the big issues that affect the quality of their life in a fundamental way. The big issues that we face as a society are the erosion of adults' and children's quality of life as a result of globalization, civic disengagement and community decline, market-driven societal values, and the experience of growing up in a transient world. In a society where children are caught in a cycle of risk, i.e., children are in danger but they are also perceived as being dangerous, their rights, well-being and social positioning are compromised. The erosion of the quality in the life of children and their families is perpetuated by the widening poverty gap and community decline, especially the disintegration of children's physical and social spaces. These issues have not been dominant in current discourse and debates on childhood and early years education and care. Nor are our reflections on the state of adulthood.

The same forces that reduce the quality of life in adults and the sustainability of their communities also diminish children's quality of life and their capacity to exercise their rights. Taking into consideration the demographics worldwide, proportionately, a large number of children are born to families with no formal education who live in non-egalitarian societies and who experience poverty in the form of community disintegration, lack of resources and socio-economic disadvantage. Moreover, a large number of women and children in non-egalitarian societies are treated as second-class citizens, being denied their fundamental rights (Csikszentmihalyi, 2006).

The concerns about the diminishing quality of children's life have been mutated into a panic over modern childhood, which has been described as 'toxic' and 'in crisis'. The adults' responses range from moral panic and hysteria to over-regulation (Brooks, 2006). The real risks, however, that our society poses on both children and their families result from the manipulation of parental anxiety, a reduced spatial integrity and social trust and commercialization of neighbourhood space, civic disengagement and over-regulation in the form of a nanny state. And, above all, the biggest risk is limiting people's awareness that other possibilities for a better quality of life might exist.

The erosion of parents' life

Concerns over parenting, mostly articulated in the form of insecurity and contempt towards parenthood, are widespread. Currently, politicians and the media send the message that a large number of parents do not have adequate parenting skills, as portrayed in reality television programmes where professionals offer advice and guidance on how to be a good parent.

However, poverty and reduced opportunities for employment place a significant strain on parents, especially mothers, to exercise their parenting skills. As Michael Rutter commented 'good parenting requires certain permitting circumstances. There must be the necessary life opportunities and facilities. Where these are lacking even the best parents may find it difficult to exercise their skills' (Rutter, 1994 as cited in Utting, 1995: 33). According to a report for the Women's Budget Group, a disproportionate number of women in the United Kingdom live in poverty, and the strain of poverty has a direct impact on women's and their children's well-being (Lister, 2005; WBG, 2005). Moreover, the rise of a workaholic culture and parents' inflexible working hours contribute to parental anxiety, and in some parents to difficulties in forming emotional bonds with their children.

The changes in the culture of parenting are reflected in the UK government's newly launched National Academy for Parenting Practitioners. Although it aims at reversing contempt for parents and families, concerns are raised about the extent to which the state should interfere with family life, which has traditionally been a private domain. It also raises questions as to whether a state intervention targets the real factors, e.g., poverty, disadvantage, work pressure, that affect parents' capacity to be good parents.

Market-driven ideologies and values

Neoliberalism[2] has constructed the free market as the organizing framework in life, 'the ultimate arbiter of political decisions' where the role of nation-states is diminishing, and education and cultural achievements are given a price but not a value (Csikszentmihalyi, 2006). Market ideologies have taken precedence over any other value, and their destructive power has an impact on the environment, the traditions and ways of life in indigenous communities and social equality. Most crucially, its impact is an intellectual and cultural one that permeates the very quality of children's and adults' life. As Seabrook argues, 'a generation has grown, formed within, by and for the market rather than by and for society' (2007).

Moreover, global commerce and business operate according to the market values of competition and individualization. The disappearing face of democracy, or as Csikszentmihalyi describes it, the rise of anti-democratic forces, has reconfigured rights and citizenship (2006). A new economic and social order emerges from the gradual replacement of nation-states with multinational structures propelled by globalization and cross-border commerce that shift the economic boundaries between countries. The influences that nation-states have exerted on domains of public life are gradually diminishing. Current issues, such as the movement of populations, trade and business, environmental concerns, terrorism, security, health outbreaks, can no longer be resolved within the boundaries of nation-states.

The challenge is to reverse this new order and prepare young people for the prospect of a civic society. One may ask, however, what the landscape of a civic society is, considering that the role of governments has been reduced to regulating rather than governing, and citizenship has been shaped by the values of the market. The market cannot support a civic society because it diverts thinking from important issues such as health, education, community infrastructure, poverty, human rights (including children's rights), and public safety, towards profit to sustain the interests of the few. Market ideologies have not only undermined democratic processes but, most crucially, people's relations and social trust, resulting in fractured communities and a society where obligation, care and responsibility have no position in a technocratic rationality (Marquand, 2003).

A technocratic rationality personalizes social crisis, poverty and the inequality gap, and reinforces assumptions of deficit in individuals and communities. The discourse on responsibilization has shifted the boundaries between social and personal/moral crisis, directing blame towards the individual without accounting for the impact of social/political processes and institutional structures on their life. Responsibilization, a neoliberal strategy, constitutes the self as being entirely responsible for success or failure, and encourages 'action on the self by the self' (Bragg, 2007: 345). Against this notion of selfhood, difficulties are transferred from a societal to a personal level, whereas, at the same time, the 'technologies of the self' rather than community consensus and mutual dependency, are offered for individuals to reinvent themselves (Foucault, 1997).

In this book, a four-part structure offers a framework to discuss a wide range of issues that reflect the complex landscape of childhood. The first part focuses on constructions and the positionality of childhood and the purposes they serve in terms of social control, social engineering and discriminatory practices towards children's lives. The second part discusses issues of transience and change in the ecologies of children (e.g., family, community, peers, cyberspace), stressing the importance of peer interactions and friendships for children's happiness. The third part engages with the debates on the relevance and applicability of children's rights to children's lives. Considering that a large number of children are growing up in non-egalitarian societies, children's rights require new thinking to ascertain children's protection, survival (biowelfare) and, the most neglected area of all, participation. Finally, the fourth part presents debates on the nature of knowledge for democracy and rights, and offers civic education as a model to prepare young people to exercise a criticality that is shaped by reason, ethics and a relational understanding.

Part I Constructions and Positionality of Childhood: Multiplicity, Difference and Enterprise

In Part I, constructions of childhood and the positionality of children are explored, stressing the multiplicity, diversity and difference that childhood entails, encapsulated in the notion of the 'heterogenized' child. The discourse on the heterogenized childhood acknowledges that children's different experiences are shaped by power inequality and poverty. Children, especially those who experience multiple forms of disadvantage are likely to propel the transformation into 'other', reinforcing marginalization and social exclusion.

Childhood is becoming increasingly politicized; family, parenthood and child-rearing practices are moving into the public arena with the economics of childhood (e.g. children as an investment, human capital) being repositioned. Children as a resource is discussed, where the 'enterprise' child emerges as a fresh energy that will offer creative solutions to major problems that the globalized world faces.

The positionality of children in an adult world is discussed by critiquing the concept of 'protected space'. Childhood as a protected space has functioned as a tool for social control in that it reinforces separateness between children's and adults' worlds as a means of marginalizing children. At the same time, this positionality has failed to protect children in that violations of their 'protected space' occur within zones of war and violence, consumerist cultures, fundamentalism and other contexts within which children are forced to face society's ills.

Fundamentalism, be it religious or secular, blurs the boundaries between childhood and adulthood, and plays on young people's and their parents' insecurity by offering them a 'secure' space where children do not have to figure out things themselves. Moral authority is situated within the context of religion or state interventionism, and is likely to restrict opportunities for children to engage with the debates about right and wrong and make moral judgment (Law, 2006). Diversity is unsettling, and thus fundamentalism offers certainty in the form of a dogma that is accepted axiomatically.

Consumerism also blurs the child/adult divide; children, through the consumption of products, images and lifestyles, gain access to the adult world. Children have become commodities themselves in many ways. In the absence of any other source of ideology, through consumerism, children form identities as consumers of products and services. Young people's identity, in terms of selfhood, notions of femininity/masculinity, beauty, attractiveness, is often formed according to stereotypes shaped by consumerism, and functions as a means towards social inclusion in that, through accessing products and images, children gain access to peer cultures.

Part II The Ecologies of Childhood in the 21st Century

In Part II, children's experiences of growing up are explored through discussions of transience, change and uncertainty and their implications on community coherence, children's play and enjoyment, and the physical, social and critical spaces they occupy. The changing face of family and the politics of care have brought new challenges to children and their parents. A disproportionate number of children grow up in polarized and segregated communities, with their spatial and civic integrity being compromised. Children's ecologies are shifting; childhood has become both individualized and institutionalized, and this shift bears significant implications regarding children's attainment of happiness.

The experience of transience has defined the physical, social and cultural parameters of children's lives. Children grow up in transient neighbourhoods mainly due to ethnic tensions or neighbourhood disintegration, all having a negative impact on community cohesion. Increasing urbanization and the destruction of the environment compromise the quality of children's places. Socially, transience renders relationships with both peers and adults provisional, with children's socialization being reduced to theme-park interactions and virtual-zone encounters. Culturally, children's play and enjoyment of leisure have changed, becoming more adult-structured and offering fewer opportunities for children to construct their own fantasy worlds.

Over the last two decades, the physical space occupied by children has started to shrink and, with it, their social and critical spaces. The lack of public spaces where children can go and be safe puts limits in their social interactions with peers and the conversations, conflict resolution and social problem solving they entail (Gill, 2007). Children's spaces are not neutral; they reflect power structures and relationships. Children are increasingly spending more time in virtual environments. The cyberspace is perceived as a continuation of the physical space, and children's language use in virtual zones tends to be very similar to the one used in more conventional interactions.

Be they virtual or conventional, friendships play an important role in young people's life. The nature of friendship is changing; increasingly, it shares many features with networking. Traditionally, friendships have been based on emotional closeness, disclosure, intimacy and a sense of belonging. The types of friendship that young people form currently in the virtual space are characterized by expansion; children report a large number of friends, rather than a few in-depth relationships. Peer acceptance and friendships are central to children's happiness, and define their experience of schooling. Many children approach schools as places where they meet with their peers, friendships are formed or dissolved and understandings of social subtleties are gained. Bullying causes a great deal of distress in young people's life; but at the same time, questions are raised about the different shades of bullying, and the opportunities that children are offered to show resilience and exercise agency during peer interactions.

Part III The Right to Childhoods

In Part III, the adequacy of current frameworks of children's rights to support children's rights for survival, protection and participation and, most crucially, the right to be treated as equal citizens is debated. In this part, I argue that children's rights, as they currently stand, suffer from a crisis of legitimacy in that they are abstract codes that do not always reflect children's living reality, especially for children who are at the margins of a society. Worldwide, young people occupy social and cultural borderlands where their rights and citizenship are not always recognized. Many children around the world are treated as a minority group with limited participatory rights and a reduced social and moral status (Mayall, 2002). In many societies, there is a gap between the right to survival and protection and the right to participation in a political and civic life, with the latter being rarely recognized and met.

There is a growing interest in young people's participation, occurring at a time when children's public presence is not always desirable. Participation is thought to have educational and social benefits in terms of young people functioning as resources for the betterment of their communities as well as personal development. The politics of participation are debated, challenging tokenistic and exploitative assumptions regarding children's participation. Research evidence on young people's participation as service users is also discussed. Although the instrumental nature of a service-led participation has been critiqued extensively, research has highlighted deep-seated concerns in young people regarding the limited influence they exert on decision making, service access and delivery at a macro level (Hartas and Lindsay, 2007).[3]

The current challenges in children's rights have been articulated through a critique of

- rights as abstract codes based on reason, offering ahistorical and apolitical views, not acknowledging transience in children's life and not translating into living rights;
- needs as construed within power structures with the needs of young people being defined by those in power, encapsulating an element of philanthropy and not entitlement;
- obligation, which implies that the exercise of rights should be linked to corresponding duties. The notions of obligation and responsibility imply that rights should be granted to those who are in a position to exercise rights and accept responsibilities, offering a restricted social contact; and
- equality and difference, advocating that the right to be the same and the right to be different should not be in conflict.

An alternative framework of children's rights, i.e., the right to childhoods, is discussed. The right to childhoods takes an ethical and relational approach to children's rights, and encompasses the right for a social and moral status. It is underpinned by an ethical praxis that defines rights along the lines of care, responsibility, mutual dependency and obligation towards the other. Against this background, it stresses the relational nature of rights by transforming them into a living reality that accounts for the particularities of children's life. Finally, the right to childhoods encapsulates the right of children to be treated as citizens. To follow rules handed to them by legislators in a top-down manner reduces young people's rights and citizenship, being no longer desirable. Preparing young people to recognize and ascertain their rights and act as citizens, especially in an era of uncertainty and radical doubt, would require education that has a strong civic basis.

Part IV: Knowledge for Rights and Democracy

The Part IV starts with two important questions. The first question refers to the type of knowledge that is required to develop young people's capabilities to exercise rights and citizenship. The second question revolves around the type of education and pedagogy that young people require for a viable future. The main premise in this part is that the nature of knowledge and morality is changing as we move towards an era of a radical doubt. The reconfiguration of knowledge in a knowledge-based society is likely to stimulate changes in education to enable young people to develop the intellectual and emotional capacity to engage in critical thinking and develop an understanding of their communities and place in the world.

Many education systems across the developed and developing world are in crisis. At present, education is defined by measurable outputs, consumer responsiveness, service efficiency, public inspection, being framed by a culture of managerialism, audit and profitability. Schools, as they currently operate, have not been responsive to the dramatic changes in the nature of knowledge, its epistemology and ontology. There is a growing dissatisfaction with the role of education and schools, and its contribution to producing children who suffer from stress and have not acquired sufficient knowledge about the things that matter to them (Schank, 2006). A large number of children have become disaffected and unmotivated, and the skills they acquire, assessed through controversial tests, do not often equip them to cope with the requirements of complex societies. Worldwide, intellectual property has been accumulated in the hands of a small technological elite, and large numbers of children are left without any access to formal education. Those who access education perceive schools as places for socialization mainly and not as sites that stimulate critical thinking and creativity.

One may ask what the purpose of learning is, learning for economic growth, as it is argued in the context of a corporate education, or learning for personal development and community cohesion, as it is presented within a civic education model. In this book, I argue that education should prepare young people to engage with a new form of criticality that is relational, not a mere exercise of reason, and promotes ethics and obligation towards the other. This may be achieved through pedagogies that are based on ethics, diversity and difference that offer young people the tools to validate non-dominant forms of knowledge and the little narratives that emanate from their lived experiences. Finally, the formation of communities of practice that are based on forms of social and cultural capital generated through the involvement of parents in schools and young people as researchers are expected to support children and their families to exercise rights and citizenship.

There is a growing realization that science, as an abstract universal body of knowledge, has not met its original promise to liberate individuals, and the principle of thinking for yourself has created autonomous individuals who do not operate within what Readings called 'a network of obligation' (1996). Abstract truths reflect power structures within which the narratives of those in power are legitimated and presented as objective truths, stressing the need for a relational knowledge that is contextual and inclusive of all young people's narratives and lived experiences. To question the epistemology of science and accept doubt and uncertainty are signs of intellectual and emotional maturity; however, replacing one grand narrative with another will achieve no more than replacing one authority with another.

The existence of clashing epistemologies is not a new phenomenon. Galileo's cosmological views clashed with those held by the Church, and Darwin's views about human evolution challenged religious accounts of how the first man appeared on earth. However, the clashing epistemologies should not be accounted for the challenges, mainly driven by economics, young people face in the 21st century. Instead, the changing or disappearing face of democracy and the rise of neoliberal ideologies, with the resulting poverty gap, have brought unprecedented challenges to humankind.

Knowledge for rights and democracy shifts the focus from a corporate towards a civic and cosmopolitan type of education to enable children and their families to exercise their rights and citizenship. A civic education has the potential to prepare young people to face the challenges that knowledge-based societies bring because it is not restricted by spatial or temporal arrangements, and can be located within communities of practice whose boundaries are porous. These communities are formed in a bottom-up manner by harnessing the social and cultural capital that already exists in families and communities.

Communities of practice have the potential to shift perspectives held on knowledge by those in power, be they an intellectual or a technocratic elite, by legitimizing the role that young people's groupings and local cultures play. It is often the case that local communities are respected by those who have formed them, with their local voices and narratives not always being heard by those in power. Communities of practice have the potential to expand young people's physical, social and virtual spaces, offering them a new forum to develop critical thinking that is not necessarily bounded by educational establishments. A new criticality may be achieved through conversations and narratives, which convert facts and information (raw material/resources) into knowledge that is meaningful and relevant to people and their communities, and thus likely to increase their quality of life.

Readings argued that the replacement of nation-states with multinational structures, in what he described as a host-historical era, has removed the context within which ideology often flourishes (1996). Nation-states offer the structures and the impetus to delineate cultural references and the ideologies that define a nation. With the decline of ideology, the purpose and function of education and pedagogy have changed from supporting the nation-state ideologies to offering a technicist knowledge required for market economies. The view of education as a process to gain knowledge for the purpose of cultivating character and ethos, a view that is mainly located within the German idealism movement, is no longer the case. What has emerged instead is a technocratic notion of excellence, which has become the organizing principle of pedagogic institutions (Readings, 1996). Against this background, failure to achieve excellence and become responsive towards the needs that market economies create is synonymous to marginalization and social exclusion.

Epilogue

There is a wide pessimism when it comes to children's experiences and well-being, and a defeatism in the belief that public engagement with policy can make a positive difference in children's lives. The quality of life for both adults and children has been eroded, and their democratic rights have been violated. But, is it all doom and gloom? With this book, I wanted to challenge the view that because there is a universal legal framework for children's rights, children actually have a right to childhoods. At the same time, I believe that other possibilities do exist. However, we need the freedom of thought, the cornerstone of democracy, to explore these possibilities. Young people's ideas and attitudes have an impact on their life and thus complacency is not an option. With a framework that transforms children's rights into a living reality, and a new form of criticality, flourishing within communities of practice where doubt is encouraged, young people may be better equipped to face future challenges on their very sense of being human.

Notes

[1] The United Nation convention defines children as aged between 0 and 18. In this book, the terms children and young people are used interchangeably.
[2] A view that society is organized around the market in which the role of state is reduced to regulating instead of governing. The onus is thus on individuals to ensure that they function, through employment mainly, in a way that meets the demands of a market-driven society. The guiding principles of neoliberalism are moralization and responsibilization of individuals. In this context, social,

economic or political crises become personal ones, and individuals who fail to achieve an optimum functioning, according to market requirements, have themselves to blame.

[3] This is a research-based book. Information on the Needs Analysis study and the Young People Social Attitudes (YPSA) dataset that was used for the quantitative analysis of young people's views about an array of issues, e.g., family structures, roles and responsibilities, friendships, social capital, can be found in the Appendix. It is important to note that although this book discusses issues on childhood, such as children's rights and well-being, that bear a global significance, the data used were collected within the UK context. Nevertheless, the UK data were discussed and placed within the context of international research studies, drawing links between the local and the global.

The Needs Analysis Study (referred to throughout this book) was conducted by Hartas and Lindsay (2008) to examine young people's decision making on issues that affect their life such as bullying and involvement in evaluating the availability and effectiveness of services for young carers, young people with disabilities and their families. The aim of this study was to offer young people a platform to evaluate access to existing services and make recommendations towards their improvement, as well as to discuss issues such as bullying, access to public spaces that affect the quality of their daily life (detailed information about the methodology of the study is provided in the appendix). The findings from the Needs Analysis Study are illuminating, especially with regard to young people's agency in evaluating and negotiating services and offering suggestions for their improvement within the context of their family, schools and peers. Agency was reflected in their capacity to act with intent and awareness in taking initiatives, offering solutions and influencing action within the constraints of their social settings. The young people showed determination and were active in making recommendations thought to increase the quality of their experience at school and their community. They emphasised the importance of accessing services of a practical nature such as learning / homework support, transportation and access to physical spaces in their communities. Young people are expected to exercise democratic responsibilities as citizens; however, it is crucial they are nurtured to develop the intellectual, social and emotional maturity to participate in decision making actively. Schools and other institutions need to make the process of participation and decision making transparent, and become accountable for the ways they support young people's voice.

Part I

Constructions and Positionality of Childhood: Multiplicity, Difference and Enterprise

Childhood has been understood and discussed differently across time and place. In the mediaeval times, children were seen as miniature adults, and with the advent of the era of the Enlightenment, they were perceived as being in the need for reform. In the 18th century, diverse views about how children should be raised and educated were voiced, mainly through the religious canon. These views ranged from those of John Wesley, a Methodist, who believed that parents have to discipline children to uproot the 'evil' and reform them so they abide by God's will, to those of Rousseau who, in his book *Emile* (1979), presented childhood as being full of innocence and goodness (the natural child), ascribing childhood a place of its own that is separate from the adult world. The concept of the original sin was dominant in the 17th century, with the *Evangelical Magazine* (1799) referring to children as 'sinful polluted creatures', who have 'a corrupt nature and evil disposition' (Hendrick, 1997, as cited in Smidt, 2006).

Towards the end of the 18th century, in the industrial era, the children of the poor were perceived as being denied their childhood by engaging into the harsh world of industrial labour. A century later, state intervention and welfare were seen as essential to raise the quality of life in all children, especially those of the poor (Jans, 2004). In the early 20th century, the advent of mass education and regulation of child labour reconfigured children's positionality in an adults' world. The separation between childhood and adulthood increased along with the rise of the 'precious' child. As Jans observes, a significant shift in the position of children occurred: from being heavily involved in society, mainly through child labour, and having limited protection during the 18th and 19th centuries, to having a limited social participation with a strong emphasis on child protection in the 20th century (2004).

Although this shift captures the positionality of children with clarity, I argue that the emphasis on protection, as encapsulated in the concept of a 'protected space', has failed to deliver its promise and, instead, has served to marginalize children. Children's and adults' worlds have been kept separate, as a means of reducing the visibility of childhood in the public arena, and converge when children are forced to face a society's ills (e.g., war, fundamentalism, poverty). It appears that the degree of a cross over between the adults' and children's worlds is determined by the economics and political considerations of a globalized world.

To acknowledge the heterogeneity and diversity that shape children's life, the childhoods of difference are discussed. Several discourses on difference are presented and views about 'celebrating' or 'tolerating' difference are critiqued, stressing the need to respect difference and accept it as an integral part of human nature. Children are different; however, for some, difference propels their transformation into the 'other' and thus social exclusion. The interplay between disability and difference is critiqued, questioning the assumptions that underpin disability as difference (ability/disability as a social phenomenon, in a similar vein as ethnicity is), and difference as disability (ability – or lack of it – as being normally distributed). The ideological battles on children's plural worlds and their shifting identities are likely to define the debates on childhood in particular and human nature in general for the 21st century.

Our society goes through major transformations that have been triggered by globalization, individualization and information as mediated by technology. New types of learning and the capacity for reinvention are necessary to prepare young people to compete within international economies. Against this background, the rise of the entrepreneurial child, who is viewed as a resource and an investment, is discussed delineating the shifting landscape of young people's citizenship, especially in an era that the human nature is being redefined.

Chapter 1

The Multiplicity and Positionality
of Childhood

Childhood is multi-dimensional and multi-faceted, constructed through the interplay of nature and nurture, biology and culture. The multi-dimensionality in childhood reflects fluidity, border crossing, diversity and difference. Over the years, childhood has been 'differently understood, institutionalized and regulated in different societies' (Woodhead, 2006: 15). The many childhoods are reflected in the lives of boys and girls from different social and geographical locations whose identity is shaped by ethnicity, poverty and ability/disability.

In this chapter, the multiplicity and positionality of childhood is discussed by exploring the contradictory nature of the notion of 'protected space', and the separation as well as convergence of adults' and children's worlds. I argue that the construction of childhood as a protected space serves a social control function. In the name of protection, it reinforces a separation between children's and adults' worlds, resulting in institutionalized and, under certain circumstances, marginalized childhoods where children's experiences are fragmented and their relationships are provisional. At the same time, this separation has not delivered what it promised to deliver, i.e., to protect the children and enhance their well-being. Children's and adults' worlds converge when faced with society's ills; children have not been spared violence, war, poverty, religious and secular fundamentalism, consumption or commodification.

The Separateness of Childhood and Adulthood

The romanticized concept of childhood as a protected space should be discussed in the context of political and historical changes, such as the advent of the welfare system, mass education, industrialization, globalization and technology. Childhood as a protected space, a time of innocence and wonder, a time to be loved without condition, is a fairly recent phenomenon and the product of affluent societies where children are construed as precious commodities. For the economically disadvantaged children, however, their everyday reality has been shaped by the impact of post-industrialization and the rise of neoliberal ideologies (Smidt, 2006).

The manipulation of children's protected space has been reinforced by neoliberal ideologies and practices that have contributed to fractured communities, adults' long working hours and poverty. In a pre-industrial era, children's and adults' worlds intersected, in that employment was mainly contained within family and community settings, and parents did not have to spend long hours away from their family. In a post-industrial society, however, family responsibility and spending time with children have become secondary to productivity, despite the governmental rhetoric of family-friendly work policies. The divide between adults and children has been accentuated by current structures of employment and the increasing institutionalization of children. In contrast, war and adversity, technology and consumption have made children's and adults' worlds to converge.

The nature and purpose of the separateness between children's and adults' worlds have been debated extensively, with childhood as a protected space being partly responsible for perpetuating this separation. The temporal and spatial differentiation between adults and children has been described as 'insularisation', presenting it as a form of social control (Zeiher, 2001a; 2001b). Childhood as a protected space has an emotive and ethological basis, and has been used to marginalize children as a social group. What seems to define the boundaries between children and adults or children and the rest of the society are economics and exploitation rather than community consensus and mutual dependency, impacting on both adults' and children's rights and well-being.

The need to protect the young, to create a second womb, has strong ethological roots in our evolutionary history to ensure the survival of the species. However, in contemporary societies, parents' biologically wired tendency or instinct to protect their young and maximize their survival has been mutated into a mechanism of oppression and social control. To understand this, we need to differentiate between the notion of a protected space as a biologically rooted response, and protected space as a social construction. The former can be empowering in that it offers a space for children's evolving capacities to flourish, whereas the latter has served to subordinate children and young people by reinforcing vulnerability, containment and exclusion.

Perceiving children to be vulnerable, with limited powers for representation, participation and citizenship marginalizes them. It also marginalizes adults who, in a climate of increasing anxiety and paranoia, are afraid to approach other people's children and volunteer in the community. Jenni Russell argues that in a society where raising children should be everybody's responsibility, adults are not allowed to interact with other people's children. The responsibility for their care falls on the family, friends or the professionals, but not on the society as a whole. The assumption that underpins this shift is that 'any adult can legitimately be considered a threat to any child'. This is an 'unprecedented way' of rearing children with the society at large 'retreating from socializing the young' (2005: 32).

A growing moral panic has shifted the public emphasis from the real to perceived dangers and risks, resulting in regulating rather than protecting and respecting children. The 'stranger hysteria', a widespread fear for strangers, prevails in our society despite a lack of criminal evidence to justify this fear. The number of children that are abused and killed by strangers each year is very small compared to that of children being killed by family members and friends (see UN report 2008). The stranger hysteria reinforces further the separation between children and adult worlds with the pretext of protecting children.

The vacuum left from a society failing to care for children is filled with regulatory legislation. In the United Kingdom, the Safeguarding Vulnerable Groups Bill makes it compulsory for all adults who work with young people to undergo a criminal record check. Although the motive behind this bill is to ensure that unsuitable adults are not given any responsibility to look after children, it sends the message that social trust can only be achieved through police or state intervention and regulation. It also sidetracks the emphasis on the real dangers that emanate from irresponsible driving, consumption, a culture of disengagement and apathy, violence, restricted physical and social spaces and a target-driven society.

Public fears about imaginary dangers are reinforced through attempts to regulate children's access to popular culture (e.g., TV watching, internet access). However, violence that emanates from the act of living in an increasingly segregated world, where difference brings indifference, has the potential to destroy the very sense of being human in both adults and children. The violence that children experience is an institutionalized violence, perpetuated by the state machine, war, conflict and displacement, and the increasing over-regulation of family and children's life. Some children and adults experience violence of the most devastating type that arises from being denied a basic social contract, and not violence from strangers or paedophiles as the popular culture claims.

A cycle of risk is observed in how society views young people and the spaces they occupy. On the one hand, children and young people are understood as being vulnerable and exposed to the dangers of the society. On the other hand, the term 'youth' has grown to have a negative connotation, with young people being increasingly perceived as posing a threat to others. These conflicting views reflect adults' ambivalence with regard to children's social and moral status, as well as theirs, and their capacity to cope with an increasingly diverse and complex society.

Social inequality, insecurity about children's place in the world and a lack of social trust and respect are breeding grounds for anti-social behaviour. Children who perceive adults other than their immediate family as the 'other' are likely to be disaffected. The UK government's respect agenda, e.g., ASBOs (Anti-Social Behaviour Orders), is a manifestation of over-regulation that does not account for disadvantage and the ways in which it breeds alienation in young people. Currently, the national preoccupation with youth crime and anti-social behaviour diverts the focus from the real problems young people face, especially those with family members with disabling conditions and in the need of care, such as depression, bullying and disadvantage. To maximize children's welfare, policies should have a positive impact on both children and families. This may be achieved by accounting for the local parameters of children's life, and invigorating social networks and the principles of mutuality and social reciprocation (Dench, Gavron and Young, 2007).

The separateness between adults and children is also a symptom of a culture of contempt for parenthood and young people in our society. Bunting refers to 'natalism' to describe the growing aversion towards parents with young children (2006), and Kraemer observes that 'after sexism and racism, we still have to confront childism' (1999: 285). O'Neill discusses the systematic separation between children and adults through the use of technology to monitor young people's movement in schools and streets (2006). In some city centres, for example, technological devices, e.g., mosquito nets, which emit sounds of a certain frequency that is painful to young people's ears, have been installed to deter them from going to these places. The message sent to young people is that they are a threat to society and that being on the streets is synonymous to committing crime. Some do fulfil this prophecy, with statistical figures showing that 65 per cent of the crime in city centres is committed by young people (Social Inclusion Index, by Booth and Ainscow, 2000).

The ambivalence towards parenthood and childhood further reinforces this separation. A fundamental question, however, is not whether adulthood is (or should be) separate from childhood, but who decides about this separation, what and whose purposes it serves, and how access to these separate worlds is negotiated. The nature of separateness, be it the outcome of negotiation between children and their parents/communities or an externally imposed separation that marginalizes children, needs to be understood better.

The separateness between adulthood and childhood, perpetuated through the discourses of vulnerability and protected space, has contributed to construe children as a minority group, with limited rights and political participation. There are degrees of separation, mainly manifested in terms of a systematic physical, social and cultural segregation. Adulthood and childhood have become distinct, not necessarily due to their different developmental needs but, most crucially, as a result of a view of children as a minority group that is not an integral part of a society. There are many 'innocent' cultural practices that seem to reinforce this separateness; for example, children's birthday parties are for children only where adults are there to organize and regulate and not to engage in joint celebrations with the children.

I would like to distinguish between an institutionalized and a children-initiated separateness. An institutionalized separateness, expressed in terms of a physical, social, cultural and political separation, has been imposed to subordinate young people by violating theirs and their families' rights and removing their participatory power. On the contrary, a child-initiated separateness has always been portrayed as a desirable aspect of a childhood life, where children construct their own worlds away from parental or adult authority. There are plenty of examples in children's literature where children view separateness as a platform, a space free from adult interference, to engage with their adventures. In Enid Blyton's *Famous Five* and J.K. Rowling's *Harry Potter*, children's adventures with their peer group occur away from parental authority where they enjoy independence and exercise agency. More recently, through the use of information technologies such as the internet, children construct a virtual world that is fairly free from adult authority.

Childhood as an institutionalized entity

An institutionalization of childhood is 'a process by which organized arrangements, chiefly the school system, influence children's lives and organize their days' (Frones, 1994: 150). The rise of a childcare institution is a relatively new phenomenon. Historically, schools were the first institutions to draw a line between children's and adults' worlds; however, recently, early-care and after-school clubs are likely to reposition this separation.

Children spend increasingly more hours in institutionalized settings, characterized by the spatial and temporal control as exercised by teachers and childcare workers (Nasman, 1994).

Children have moved from the context of their families and immediate communities to the public domain and its overarching ideology based on children's rights (protection, survival, participation), on the one hand, and the economics of childhood (e.g., child as investment, human capital) on the other. Childhood is becoming increasingly politicized, with family and child rearing practices moving into the public arena, resulting in significant changes in the spatial and social/critical framework of childhood (see Chapters 4 and 5 for a discussion on the changing face of family and children's physical and social spaces). These new 'institutional geographies of childhood' intensify the adulthood/childhood division in that children's places are separate from adult spaces with very limited opportunities for interaction (Philo, 2000: 251).

Moss argues that the 'institutionalization of childhood can offer new possibilities – for children, for families and for communities', especially when institutions are understood as children's spaces.

> Institutions understood as children's spaces are emancipatory in the sense that they create possibilities for individuals to think for themselves through creating knowledges, identities and values and by challenging dominant discourses. They are also relational. As places of encounter, their possibilities are realized through relationships between children and adults. As public spaces, they offer opportunities for relationships between the individual and the group, so forging new forms of solidarity which do not deny individuality yet recognize that individuality is dependent on others. (1999)

However, we should engage with the risks and challenges brought by the fact that children spend less time with their primary caregivers and parents, likely to affect the building of intimacy and attachment bonds. With this in mind, it is important to explore the physical, social and psychological characteristics of institutions, and understand how they shape children's everyday experiences. There has been some criticism that spaces in childcare institutions do not flow naturally, being rather compartmentalized and planned based on certain pedagogical understandings, or adults' views of what children enjoy. Childcare institutions are characterized by hierarchical structures that dictate children's movement, conversational and socializing patterns. Children have limited opportunities to choose their activities and alter the spatial and temporal arrangements accordingly (e.g., Smith and Barker, 2000).

Schools, and especially after-school spaces, have become increasingly controlled and structured in ways that promote and reproduce formal and hierarchical relationships between children and adults (Alderson, 2000; Burgess, 1986). Some after-school places exercise social control by offering children an artificial choice between alternatives set by the care workers. The control of the temporal and spatial arrangements of childcare places is likely to become internalized by the play workers and the children them-selves, in a process of 'self subjectification' (Robinson, 2000). Children are aware of the hierarchical structures of educational settings and are likely to reproduce power relationships. Some know how to negotiate and challenge boundaries, instead of being passive recipients of care, whereas others may show obedience to adults. Children exert influences informally by their spontaneous behaviour displayed in the setting and, formally, during their interactions with childcare workers who encourage children's participation in decision making.

Some children experience out-of-school clubs as places for play and enjoyment, and challenge an educational emphasis exerted by policy mak-ers and parents (Smith and Barker, 2000). This bears important implications when considering children's views about after-school places. In the Needs Analysis study (Hartas and Lindsay, 2007) children expressed an interest in joining after-school schemes or clubs. However, they stressed the impor-tance of engaging in activities that are relevant to their interests, different from educational activities based on the curriculum.

The institutionalization of children in terms of the physical and temporal arrangements that organize their day away from their family draws a clear line between children's and adults' worlds. In contrast, acts of war and the rise of fundamentalism and consumerist cultures blur the boundaries between these two worlds.

The Convergence of Childhood and Adulthood

On the institutionalized separateness/convergence continuum, the manip-ulation of the notion of a protected space has a selective function: it separates children from adults to marginalize them but brings them together, without children's consent, to face the fraught that characterizes the adults' world, in the form of war, fundamentalism and a rampaging consumerism. Clearly, constructing childhood as a territory that is separate from adults' to protect the children has not worked. On the contrary, it has

LIVERPOOL JOHN MOORES UNIVERSITY
LEARNING SERVICES

blurred the boundaries between family and institutions, and has sanctioned images of children growing up in an era of fundamentalism, consumerism, violence and war.

Growing up in an era of fundamentalism

Both religious and secular fundamentalism are on the rise, manifested in the form of extremism and the politics of fear, e.g., 'war on terror', as well as the political chaos and social upheaval in many parts of the world. Children are growing up experiencing multiple wars, from an actual to a 'cultural war' between liberals and fundamentalists, 'a war for children's minds' (Law, 2006: 100). Law articulated the goal of a culture war as an attempt to 'rescue the next generation from the poisonous relativism of the liberal elite and reground children in traditional values' through moral and religious education (ibid.: 100).

Fundamentalism fills the vacuum left by moral relativism and a reduced capacity for moral judgement that characterize consumerist societies. Fundamentalism exerts psychological control over children and their families, prescribing only one route and no alternatives. It suggests that moral authority has meaning within the context of religion only, and thus, it does not offer opportunities for children to engage with debates about right and wrong and express judgement. Fundamentalism plays on young people's insecurity in that it offers a secure space where they do not have to figure out things themselves. Diversity is unsettling, whereas fundamentalism offers certainty in the form of a dogma; when rationality, emotional maturity and capacity for critical reflection are removed, dogma fills the gap (Law, 2006).

A dogma is appealing, especially in an era of uncertainty, because it embodies certainty. It is not only a property of religion; many secular views are dogma-based. Neoliberalism, for example, where the market needs supersede social needs, has become an all pervasive ideology using the naturalizing discourses of free markets, e.g., economic growth, to address social issues with regard to public services, social inequality and poverty. A secular dogmatism can take the form of over-regulation of children's lives, through the creation of a 'nanny state', resulting from the failure of governments to govern. Within this mindset, social order and respect are giving away to a 'culture that is calculating rather than rule-abiding' (Lawson, 2006: 10). The legitimacy of the state as an instrument of regulation and moral authority in the lives of children and families, as well as the boundaries between the state and the market should be interrogated.

LIVERPOOL JOHN MOORES UNIVERSITY
LEARNING SERVICES

Children as consumers and commodities

Postmodern constructions of childhood entail images of children as consumers who, through consumption, gain access to 'adult worlds' (Robinson and Diaz, 2006). Children have been positioned at the centre of a consumerist culture without having contributed to the debates on the politics of globalization that has produced it in the first place (Fass, 2003). Markets have created a plethora of 'needs' and products for children, with the parents being coerced into buying them as a means of ascertaining their care and love (Kasturi, 2002). Children are able to access goods across physical and virtual settings, being portrayed in advertisements as having a buying power to join adults in consumerist ventures. Commercial companies, especially in the cyberspace, have created shopping spaces that do not differentiate between adults and children.

Consumption defines children's physical and social spaces. Social interactions are positioned around consumption, in that shopping centres have become loci for socialization for young people, blurring the boundaries between the material world and social connectedness. Being a consumer also offers a participatory identity in children, enabling them to negotiate their peer status. Possessing the latest mobile or iPod and the 'right' pair of trainers enables children to situate themselves within the popular culture and gain access to their peer groups. Through consumerism, children generate social and cultural capital, which in turn, may increase their popularity with their peers. Consumerism has also been seen as being responsible for children's desire to grow fast to enter the adult world, with some teachers raising concerns that childhood is becoming 'uncool', because children place too much emphasis on the material culture, rather than on games or conversations with their peers.

In early industrial societies, children accessed the adult world by actively participating in the production of goods as child labourers. In a knowledge-based society, the shift from 'production to consumption' has become 'the norm of achieving integration in society' with both children and adults exercising a buying power (Hengst, 2000: 71–72). The increasing privatization of public services, such as education and health services, has created another commercial niche for children. For those parents who can access children's services, the services have become 'technologised', offering pre-specified, objective outcomes to be achieved within market-driven contexts (Moss and Petrie, 2002).

Growing up in consumerist cultures, some children become commodities themselves. The process whereby children become a commodity varies according to the social and cultural capital of their family, as well as the historical and political circumstances of children's place and time. In modern societies, life in itself has become a commodity; even the way language is used reflects economic transactions (e.g., patients become clients and students become customers). In this context, the new morality is greed, maximization of profit and individualization, and 'everything has a price and nothing has a value' (Buxton, 2007).

Children's identities as consumers and commodities have removed the boundaries between adults' and children's worlds. The commodification of children works in implicit and explicit ways. Some children define their selfhood according to the images that the corporate world offers to them. Some internalize the images and the products they acquire, and develop corporate values of beauty and norms of acceptance/inclusion. Commodification homogenizes childhood because it sets prescriptive ideals of beauty, femininity/masculinity and acceptable behaviour. It also defines the ideal parenthood along the lines of acquisition of children's products. Children and their families who experience socio-economic disadvantage are most likely to be victimized by an economic order that does not differentiate between products and children as resources that embody social capital.

The commodification of childhood involves the deliberate manipulation and exploitation of the social and cultural capital that childhood as a protected space entails. Views of childhood as being a 'sacred place' or a 'mythical realm', untouched by the evils of the adult world, have been harnessed to maximize the impact of conflict and violence by provoking strong feelings when the final frontier, i.e., children's innocence, is conquered. A deliberate destruction of children sends a powerful message to the world. An article titled 'Ahmed's Gift of Life', stimulated a debate on the killing of children in war-torn areas and the transformation/symbolization of their death as a form of human sacrifice. Ahmed, a Palestinian boy, was killed during an Israeli–Palestinian conflict. His parents decided to donate his organs to an Israeli person. This act was described by the media as a 'noble gesture', a human sacrifice to the God of war to appease his furry. 'Maybe one Israeli will decide not to shoot again', his parents said.

As this example illustrates, the cultural and moral significance of killing children is used to maximize the impact of institutionalized violence on children and their families. Children are used in conflict to 'harvest' the cultural and social/capital embodied in childhood. This view of children highlights the dangers of 'capitalization', and its negative impact on the decisions we make about children's well-being. As Cohen and Prusak have commented, not everything of a value should be called a 'capital' (2001: 9) because capitalization reinforces an understanding of childhood as a commodity and skews our decisions towards the economic.

Growing up in zones of war and adversity

Before the Second World War, conflict occurred in the battlefields away from children and their communities. With the advent of a modern warfare, the separation between adults and children diminishes, with children becoming the victims of war, conflict and social unrest. In today's conflicts, almost 90 per cent of the victims are civilians (e.g., women and children) whereas in the First World War, 5 per cent of the casualties were civilians (Hyder, 2005). War threatens children's survival, damages their development and violates their rights as set by United Nations Convention on the Rights of the Child (UNCRC).

> Children are not spared. It is estimated that 500,000 under-five year olds died as a result of armed conflicts in 1992 alone. In Chechnya, between February and May 1995, children made up an appalling 40% of all civilian casualties; Red Cross workers found that children's bodies bore marks of having been systematically executed with a bullet through the temple. In Sarajevo in Bosnia and Herzegovina, almost one child in four has been wounded.(UNICEF, 1996 as cited in Hyder, 2005)

The Amnesty International offers a view about the ways in which war threatens children's survival, including 'nutritional deprivation (structures and methods for food production and distribution are destroyed); spread of diseases (food and water supplies are damaged and health services are limited); disability; loss of education; child soldiers; child abduction, torture and slavery, and violence against girls' (1999: 32). In a report published in September 2006 by the charity Save the Children, 43 million children living in countries destroyed by war and armed conflict were left without the chance to go to school. Countries torn by war face multiple disadvantages beyond the immediate consequences of war; destruction extends to the future generation through the devastating consequences of armed conflict on education, the destruction of the infrastructure, the killing of teachers and the making of child soldiers.

The victimization of children in war-torn areas has entered the vocabulary of war. The killing of children and the growing number of those with serious mental health problems due to war-related trauma have been documented extensively. Montgomery et al., (1992) have delineated the consequences in children who have experienced armed conflict, in terms of

- physical or psychosomatic symptoms in terms of headaches, stomach aches, loss of appetite, insomnia and disturbed sleep;
- psychological in terms of becoming depressed, and socially withdrawn, daydreaming, feelings of guilt, blaming parents;
- cognitive in terms of concentration, poor memory and poor listening skills.

In a more recent study, Raundalen and colleagues conducted a study on Iraqi children's health and well-being. They interviewed about 100 children by the International Study Team, and found that pre-school children were able to articulate with chilling details the devastation and violence perpetrated by war. Specifically, around 62 per cent of the children said thoughts of war intruded even when they tried to think of other things, and 83 per cent said they had waves of strong feelings about the war, namely fear and anger. 'One five-year-old said there would be cold and hot air, and we will burn from the bomb after it destroys our house' (Raundalen et al., 2003: 28).

Apart from the obvious destruction of children through injuries and killing, there are other, less direct ways whereby children's well-being is compromised in zones of adversity. The chaos and uncertainty that war brings upon communities destroy the very fabric of trust and social cohesion. Conflict forces people to re-examine their priorities, rights and responsibilities, and this is often externalized through a display of extreme behaviours and power abuse to which children become victims, especially when systems of child protection and support are non-existent.

The boundaries between childhood and adulthood are also blurred when considering the harsh reality of child labour. In Western countries, the lack of a legislative framework for access to employment for children is perceived by some as another obstacle towards claiming the adult world (Kouvonen, 2002). However, for children in the developing countries, especially in the Asia/Pacific region (122 million working children) and in Sub-Saharan Africa (49 million working children), child labour threatens their survival and well-being. Around 126 million children work in hazardous conditions, and an equally large number of children work as agricultural workers and domestic servants (ILO, 2006).

The images of children as consumers and commodities, or victims of war and fundamentalism raise ethical concerns with regard to the separateness of children's and adults' worlds. The boundaries between the two worlds are porous and can be easily crossed, especially under circumstances of violence, power inequality and violation of children's rights. Both an institutionalized separateness and a forced convergence of children's and adults' worlds may set the scence for children's exploitation. The former marginalizes children, whereas the latter positions children at the centre of a society's ills, both contributing to inequality and violation of children's rights. In contrast, a child-initiated separateness may have emancipatory potential in terms of cultivating agency and promoting a social status in children. The fundamental issue is not separateness or convergence per se but the extent to which they function as tools for social control, posing restrictions upon articulations of the multiplicity and plurality of childhood. What should be at the heart of the debates on childhood as a protected space is diversity and difference, to account for the influences of culture and the social/political circumstances on children's well-being.

Chapter 2

Childhoods of Difference and Diversity

Childhood is not a unitary entity; it is embedded in place and time and shaped by biology, society/culture and their interplay. Childhood is hetero-geneous and diverse, encapsulating the lived experiences of boys and girls from diverse ethnic backgrounds, with various degrees of ability, disability and possibilities. Heterogeneity is expressed in the childhoods of immi-grant, refugee and displaced children, and the childhoods of the poor and the rich.

To approach childhood as being heterogeneous, multiple and diverse is to account for the reality of children's life. This has implications in terms of respecting difference and testing the assumptions we make about what con-stitutes a good quality of life for children across different cultures. Over the years, the discourses on difference have moved from sociological critiques (Tomlinson, 1982), to legal perspectives (Minow, 1990; Santos, 2001) and philosophical approaches (Nussbaum, 2004). They all have challenged assumptions about normalcy, sameness, ability and disability that construe difference as inferiority, raising dilemmas about access, support, rights and inclusion.

Diversity and Difference: The Heterogenized Child

When we speak about children's developmental similarities and differences, we always exercise a judgement. Children's universal characteristics are understood in relation to the value and meaning of their communities, in that the expression of their inherited abilities is shaped by the tools of their culture (Concu and Gaskins, 2006). Children's experiences of growing up in the sub-Saharan Africa are not the same as those of children growing up in the United Kingdom. At the same time, independent of geography and cultural and political circumstances, children share many characteristics and attributes. These include inquisitiveness, playfulness, the capacity to construct meaning and learn at an increased pace, dependency on warm

and secure relationships with caregivers and being susceptible to adults' views (Concu and Gaskins, 2006; Jans, 2004).

The trajectories in children's development which are common across cultural and ethnic groups point to the importance of accepting both the universality and particularity of children's lives. Universal characteristics are not essentialist in that how they manifest themselves differ from culture to culture and from one historical period to another. The commonalties and differences in children and adults are the product of the intersection between biology and culture, and reflect degrees of human variation, manifested in children's physical, mental, social and emotional functioning, as being distinct from that of older children and adults (Woodhead, 2006). What is common and different in all children can be delineated in ways that balance universal and particular understandings of children's development and well-being.

Traditional psychological and sociological models and theories of child development (e.g., Theories of Piaget, Vygotsky or Chomsky) have made important contributions to delineating what is common and what is different in children, albeit their focus has been on individuals and groups within the Western societies. The notion of a developmental niche has been offered to articulate progression and change in children's language, thought and other socio-cognitive competencies, which, in turn, are shaped by their surroundings. A developmental niche is more appropriate than a developmental phase to bring together the physical, social and cultural dimensions of the settings children inhabit without denying the importance of maturational patterns and biological predispositions in children (Super and Harkness, 1986; Woodhead, 2006).

The heterogeneity of childhood is not bounded by dichotomous views about universal and particular characteristics in children's development. Early development can be understood and discussed in universal terms, and also be linked to contextual factors such as ethnicity, culture and the socio-political circumstances of children's lives. For example, play is a universal activity in humans with unique developmental outcomes which may not be similar in all contexts of childhood. Specifically, Western societies tend to attribute more significance to children's expression of pretense and imagination during play, whereas other cultures place more emphasis on rough-and-tumble play (Concu and Gaskins, 2006).

Nussbaum stresses the importance of focusing on 'what is common to all humans, rather than on differences . . . and to see some capabilities and functions as more central, more at the core of human life, than others' (2004: 54). Other theorists have debated the social and historical influences on children's lived experiences, and the particularities of their contexts (e.g., Mayall, 2002). Regardless of whether we focus on children's commonalities or differences, it is important not to overlook developmental psychology perspectives, and the findings from genetics and brain imaging research on children's cognitive and social functioning. Mono-disciplinary perspectives are not adequate to capture the changing nature and polyphony of childhood, keep the discourses of difference alive and counteract cultural relativism and essentialism.

Mono-perspectival approaches to children's development and experiences are likely to reduce child development into 'common sense' beliefs, resulting in naturalizing and normalizing children's dispositions and attributes and use them to define children as a group. To keep the discourses of difference alive, we should focus on the whole child rather than on essentialist interpretations about certain visible characteristics (stereotypes) of children's identity, presented as being representative of the whole child. Along these lines, distinguishing between difference/diversity and cultural relativism has important implications for children's well-being in terms of mitigating against harmful practices, such as female mutilation, child brides, ritual child killings, on children around the world.

The debates on heterogenizing childhood take the view that children's different experiences are shaped by power inequality and poverty, stressing that childhood does not only exist as a domain of the rich (Smidt, 2006). Diversity and difference are inherent in the experience of growing up and respecting difference is likely to set the scene for respecting the 'other'. Childhoods of difference encompass the children of the poor and the rich, and of boys and girls of different ethnic backgrounds and languages.

Current practices around diversity and difference reflect a normative understanding of children and their families. The contradictions and complexities that surround diversity, especially in early childhood settings, can be resolved by responding ethically to difference. Ethical responses acknowledge and are likely to challenge social inequality, and 'deconstruct the barriers that currently exist that prevent the full inclusion of socio-cultural 'Others' (Robinson and Diaz, 2006: 169). As discussed in Part IV, educating young people for rights and democracy would require a reflexive approach to diversity and difference. This may be achieved by positioning young people at the centre of civic life and support them to engage in inquiry as researchers.

Researching difference is expected to offer the platform for young people to deconstruct stereotypical understandings of 'tolerance' towards difference 'in order to refocus more on the discourse of respect' (Robinson and Diaz, 2006: 169). This is likely to shift the focus from 'celebrating' or 'tolerating' difference, to the discourses of respect, care and citizenship based on a well-articulated framework of rights and responsibilities. The concept of tolerance is constraining because it resonates power relationships and hierarchies in people's rights, and construes difference as being inferior. It is also arbitrary, in that children who have visible markers of difference (e.g., ethnicity, religion) may be more or less tolerated, depending on the circumstances of their life. In contrast, the notion of respect resonates an understanding that plurality and diversity are essential, and that there are multiple 'ways of being, knowing and doing' (ibid., 2006: 169).

Recognition of difference should be embedded into our understanding of the fluidity of human nature, realizing that differences exist not only 'between individuals and social groups, but also within the self' (Tronto, 1993: 60). In many societies and educational systems, there has always been a drive to turn otherness into sameness, and marginalize the other for not fitting into conceptions of normativity. Keeping the discourse of difference alive, would require us to respect the distance between the self and the other, and at the same time, find ways to connect with the Other without violating its alterity, 'respect for the Other . . . but on absolute and infinite responsibility for the Other' (Dahlberg and Moss, 2005: 79). This notion counteracts current tokenistic views of the other as diversity to be celebrated.

Diversity has been found to be a troubling concept for many young people. In the Needs Analysis study, young people with diverse profiles and requirements (e.g., young carers, looked-after children) presented their life as being 'average', not different from their peers', because difference, in this case, would have meant 'problem' or 'inferiority'. This attitude was evident during discussions with young carers about their caring responsibilities and their impact on their social and school life. Many said that they 'feel that their life is normal', not much different from the lives of other carers and non-carers they know. Likewise, around half of the young people from the bullying and LDD (Learning Disability/Difficulty) groups also described their life as being 'normal and average'.

They engaged in normalizing discourses, presenting their experiences as 'common sense', and offered restricted representations of their identities and subjectivities. Although they displayed capacity for agency at a micro level, they were less reflexive in deconstructing their views by 'unpacking' the circumstances in their life, their needs and capacity to access services. A limited critical examination of their values and assumptions did not help them to articulate how particular ways of doing and thinking have shaped their lived experiences and thus, they did not challenge them because they represented a 'natural order of things' (see Chapter 8 for details on young people's access to services). Young people's tendency towards normalcy has also been observed in a recent research study into poverty and education funded by the Joseph Rowntree Foundation, involving 8- to 13-year-olds, mostly White, from both economically better-off and worse-off backgrounds. Both better-off and worse-off young people perceived themselves as being 'average'.

Being Different: Poverty and Disadvantage

A report for the Sutton Trust showed that social mobility in the United Kingdom, compared to other developed countries, has not improved over the last 30 years, suggesting that class divisions in the United Kingdom remain as wide as they were in 1970s. By the age of three, the average middle-class child has a 1,100-word vocabulary, whereas the average working-class child uses 525 words. Bright children who are born in poor households drop in cognitive performance from the 88th centile at the age of 3 to 65th centile at the age of 5. The least-able children from well-off households move from 15th at the age of 3 to 45th at the age of 5. These results confirm that poverty and disadvantage have a negative impact on children's academic performance (Blanden and Machin, 2007).

In the UNICEF report titled 'Child Well-being in Rich Countries', the United Kingdom was ranked bottom of the league tables among rich countries with regard to young people's well-being, painting a troubled picture of the experience of growing up in the United Kingdom (2007). As a response, the UNICEF UK formulated a Declaration of 'Principles and Priorities' to give impetus to eradicate poverty, and foster a culture where children are at its centre. The Declaration builds on the views expressed by young people focusing on issues such as eradicating child poverty, offering resources and support to participate in civic life, creating spaces that are safe for young people to learn, play and enjoy childhood.

As the UNICEF report suggests, poverty cuts across the developed/developing world divide. Oxley et al., (2000) in an OECD study found that of the 17 developed countries they examined, 12 showed a growing inequality between the children of the poor and the rich. Indeed, new evidence suggests that the poverty gap in developed countries increases, creating poles of advantage and disadvantage. The bell curve scenario is no longer the case, in that the average is shrinking and the gap between the rich and poor is widening (ibid., 2000). Geography determines destiny in that where children live correlates highly with the quality of their education and health, as well as with exposure to violence and crime.

Poverty is a major factor that affects children's well-being through a combination of limited resources, marginalization and social stigma. Public attitudes towards children who live in poverty tend to be those of stigma and marginalization (Lister, 2004). Poverty is a multi-dimensional construct that should not be equated with economic or material poverty alone; it also encompasses social and cultural deprivation, limited access to resources and services, and restricted opportunities to participate fully in life. The growing inequalities and segregation in communities have shifted views about childhood as being diverse and different, with difference being interpreted as deficit. For a large number of children and their families who live in poverty, the dismantling of welfare and public services accentuates their disadvantage.

Women's poverty has been found to have serious implications with regard to their physical and mental health, as well as their children's well-being. In the absence of community/family/social networks and adequate public services, women try to manage limited resources, poor housing and the social strain from living in run-down communities. They rely on their personal resourcefulness to find solutions and mitigate against everyday strain, and also have to cope with guilt and social stigma that are generated through the responsibiliation[1] rhetoric that constitutes them responsible for their difficult circumstances (Lister, 2005; WBG, 2005). By presenting a social crisis as an individual one, the important role that social, political structures play in children's lives is diminished. For example, the World Bank's African early childhood development programme has attributed difficulties in children's early life and experiences to parents' limited capacity and understanding about children's development, concluding that developmental difficulties and malnourishment is 'largely due to inappropriate child feeding practices, high morbidity, and poor child caring practices' (Penn, 2002: 126).

Moreover, the peer pressure for children who live in poverty to 'fit in' the social groups by possessing resources and materials (e.g., fashionable clothing, technological devices/gadgets) accentuates the guilt felt by their parents. On the one hand, women who experience poverty try to meet their children's needs for social and peer acceptance and 'shield' them from marginalization. On the other hand, they experience shame if they use scarce resources for accessing materials that are deemed to have a popular culture appeal (Lister, 2005). In Part IV, the discussion on cultural/social capital that parents possess is empowering because it acknowledges that parents, regardless of SES (Socio-Economic Status), are resourceful and have important skills to contribute. Although poverty makes it more difficult for parents to become involved with their children (Utting, 1995), respecting parental contributions is likely to alleviate feelings of guilt and shame, and the social stigma attached to poverty.

Becoming the 'Other'

Worldwide, children who experience disadvantage constitute a minority group who lack voice and powers of representation. Multiple layers of disadvantage push individuals into the category of the 'other', reinforcing marginalization and social exclusion. The 'other' is constructed by removing children's citizenship and participatory rights, and also through dualisms in our thinking or the 'cultural binary opposition of us/them'. These reinforce the fear of the 'other', as well as the process of 'creating social-cultural others by placing different values on the language, dialects and values that define children's diverse lives' (Robinson and Diaz, 2006: 2).

Within current discourses in the field of disability and critical studies, 'otherness' is either feared or forced to become 'sameness' (Robinson and Diaz, 2006). In Western societies, despite an ongoing movement of populations and 'mixing' of cultures, ethnic and linguistic differences are perceived as deficit. Bi- or multi-lingual children who bring languages in the classroom other than the dominant one are not necessarily seen as possessing an asset or a cultural capital. What is valued instead is their capacity to assimilate in 'English only' classrooms through minimizing their cultural and linguistic differences. Although it has been recognized in the SEN Code of Practice that speaking a language other than English does not equate with special educational needs (DfES, 2001), the discourses on needs and learning support bear potential for discrimination.

This raises the need to reposition the 'other' by focusing on the discourses of respect, care and citizenship, and transforming children's services and institutions into 'loci of ethical practices' (Dahlberg and Moss, 2005). Within 'loci of ethical practices' the other may become a borderland open to the cultural exchanges between people from either side, characterized by negotiation and assimilation. This borderland may also become a 'frontier' which involves openness to strangers, opportunism and the capacity to reshape traditions (Santos, 2001). The notion of the 'other' as a frontier is likely to empower children, especially those who cross cultures and negotiate multiple identities.

Children do not remain in one culture but move between 'cultural borderlands' (Rosaldo, 1989) or 'simultaneous worlds' where they become members of more than one cultural group. Children may occupy the borders, the periphery or the centre of their communities depending on their and their family's cultural and social capital. Cultural borderlands require shifting identities or multiple identities, for children to adapt to the complexity and changes in their lives. A constant rewriting of the self takes place, especially for children who cross cultural and linguistic borders. Refugee children, for example, are expected to acquire multiple and complex identities to accommodate different and, possibly, clashing cultures, i.e., theirs and that of the adoptive country. Children require support to construct their identity within a shared culture, and to shift their identity when exposed to different cultural and linguistic codes. Moreover, they should be equipped to engage in a critical analysis of a dominant culture's views of difference, and articulate how being different in terms of language, ethnicity and religion impacts on their life.

Difference as Disability or Disability as Difference?

Historically, difference and disability have had an uneasy relationship, reflected in paradigms shifts and various theoretical understandings of disability. The functionalist and structuralist paradigms of disability have reduced difference to deficit, which is located within the individual or in the societal structures. The functionalistic paradigm approaches disability as an objective, inherent pathology that can be diagnosed and, in some cases, cured. Within this mindset, disability is depicted as a 'thing', an objective condition rather than an integral part of the human nature (Gallagher, 2007). Moreover, disability is seen as something that exists and can be measured objectively, an attribute that is intrinsic to individuals; a person has a disability regardless of how we think about it or interpret it. This view is grounded in the logic that ability is normally distributed (e.g., Kavale and Forness, 1996).

The structuralist paradigm views disability as a subjectivity that relies on interpretations of processes or relations within class and social structures. Disability is seen as being reproduced through unequal power structures and social injustice. Focusing on the spaces between subjectivity and objectivity is important to examine the physical body and the symbolic meaning/representations and interpretations of it, mainly located within discourses of oppression, disablement and social injustice (Gabel and Peters, 2004).

Both the medical and social models of disability have not been adequate to explain the nature of human variation and what we make of it. Where do we draw the line between impairment understood as an objective differ-ence and impairment as a social construction, a judgement or a symbolic representation of difference? Gallagher argues that the 'the very act of observing difference is to make an interpretation, there is no line to be drawn between ostensive versus subjective aspects of difference and disabil-ity' (2007: 518).

Constructing disability as a lack of ability relies on normative views of abil-ity and normalcy, and reinforces arbitrary decisions about the types of human variation that constitute vulnerability. Also, disability as a socially constructed difference neglects the impact of genetics and biology. Although children with disability are likely to become the 'other', disability should not be placed under the general umbrella of diversity and differ-ence (e.g., gender, ethnicity) in that, by focusing on disability as a social phenomenon only, we may reduce the complexity of human variation. Nei-ther should disability be equated with difference, nor should difference be equated with disability. Disability is an integral part of one's personhood, a part of human nature and a manifestation of human variation. Shakespeare and Watson stated that 'disability is not a singular identity but a multiplicity and plurality, that is situated in the intersection of biology and society, of agency and structure' (2001: 19).

Heshusius (2004) and Nussbaum (2004) refer to an 'exclusionary fear', the fear for what we consider to be abnormal when encountering human variation. This fear emanates from a desire to preserve traits and attributes that we consider them to have a value, which in turn propels an anxiety towards others that do not fit into our image of the good and standard. The act of constructing a person who possesses characteristics and functionings that do not fit with those we value as disabled helps us to define ourselves as non-disabled (Heshusius, 2004). Nussbaum has also offered a similar view on our anxieties and fears about the vulnerability of the human nature, and the trouble of being human. She argued for the need to 'shift from the idea of the normal citizen . . . the image of a citizen as productive worker, able to pay for the benefits he receives by the contributions he makes' (2004: 176–177).

Disability is not an objective category or a singular identity, in that, depending on the values that a society holds, the same physical/mental impairment may be seen as being disabling or not disabling (Kudlick, 2003).

Children with disability construct their social persona (how they appear to others) and their self-identity (how they appear to the self) while they negotiate their visible or invisible markers and territories of disability. Some argue that reconceptualizing disability may give us new tools for thinking about social order, in that, through the lens of disability, notions of art, law, philosophy, aesthetics, religion are redefined (ibid.). Human variation and difference are likely to offer a framework for the ideological battles in the 21st century that may reconceptualize childhood, identity, pluralism, citizenship and inclusion.

Chapter 3

Children as a Resource:
The Rise of the Entrepreneurial Child

Our society goes through major transformations at an economic, cultural and societal level. The processes that underlie these transformations are globalization, individualization and information which are mediated by rapid advances in technology. In a knowledge-based society, the raw material is not goods per se but information and knowledge. Processing and managing information require flexibility, capacity for reinvention and creativity and the ability to face uncertainty. They also require adaptation to continual change and acceptance of its transience and provisionality, as well as 'the capacity for learning and the capacity for enterprise' (Masschelein, 2001: 4).

The Making of the Entrepreneurial Child

In a knowledge-based society, young people are seen as an enterprise, a critical resource that is likely to offer creative solutions to major problems, such as the destruction of the environment, fragmentation of communities, the gradual receding of public services and welfare that the globalized world faces. The terms enterprise and entrepreneurial originate in the business sector. The notion of a self-enterprising individual emerges from Frederic von Hayek's theory[2] of the *Homo Economicus,* defined as a person who is capable of adapting to and contributing to the market competition. Taking this view, within market structures, human agency mutates into an economic agency which has the potential to maximize public resources (Ong, 2006).

Young people who encompass the 'spirit of enterprise' are those who are likely to draw connections between learning and the requirements of the knowledge society. Children as entrepreneurial citizens are expected to meet the needs of the market (European Commission, 2003). The Scottish Government, one of the many examples of enterprise learning in the

United Kingdom, emphasizes the exposure of primary school teachers to enterprise education schemes and programmes in an attempt to develop a school ethos that is conducive to enterprise. The National Swedish Board for Industrial and Technical Development has also transferred and adapted enterprise into the school context, stating 'to be entrepreneurial or enterprising means utilizing opportunities and changes and having the ability to carry out activities aimed at improving, developing and creating values that may be social, personal, cultural or economic' (NUTEK, 2000: 78). Entrepreneurship in schools has come to mean 'all forms of work that stimulate students' self-confidence, self-knowledge, creativity, energy and ability to cooperate and communicate' (ibid.: 47).

Traditionally, enterprise learning has taken place within the context of families or small groups in the community. Its nature was hierarchical, and it was geared towards a model of apprenticeship where the apprentice follows the steps of the master, maintaining the status quo (Leffler and Svedberg, 2005). This model is no longer useful because the uncertainty that characterizes a knowledge economy requires new artefacts and knowledge to be created continuously. At present, the entrepreneurial child is more likely to operate within middle-class contexts that offer the resources and the capacity for choice and voice necessary for participation and initiative (Bragg, 2007). A new normativity emerges that differentiates between children as a resource and those who are not; and children who participate and those who cannot or choose not to participate. This is likely to create new power structures and potential zones of exclusion, especially for young people who, for various reasons (e.g., disability), are not part of this new normativity.

To adapt to and benefit from the learning society, young people need to become entrepreneurial and self-regulating by being proactive and responsive to the requirements of the market and other societal needs (Dieleman and Lankshear, 1996 as cited in Masschelein, 2001). The entrepreneurial child is a problem solver who applies creativity to offer solutions, and engages critically and reflexively with the shifting individual and collective needs. The entrepreneurial child is also capable of learning to learn, in terms of 'acquiring skills of cognitive self-regulation which involves choice of ends according to different ends, choice of activities fitting these ends, mobilizing means, control of one's own concentration, motivation, working methods and results' (Masschelein, 2001: 12).

The rationality of science and technicist approaches to learning offer a view of pedagogy that is restricted to train and retrain individuals to become a flexible workforce, responsive to the shifting demands of a knowledge-based society. Learning is the organizing principle of a learning society (Ranson, 1998), and is triggered by needs and demands, and not necessarily by a desire for exploration and discovery. In this context, learning entails problem solving and processing and managing information, assessed not according to the knowledge it generates per se but by the 'fit between needs and activities and environment' (ibid.: 13). Learning is thus needs-driven, and its quality is defined by the extent to which it meets pre-specified economic targets. Young people's reluctance to engage with this type of learning often results in social exclusion. Masschelein contests the discourses of a learning society that perpetuate the 'threat of being excluded from the community or from society, that is we have to learn permanently because our survival is at stake' (2001: 3).

The shifts in learning have important implications for educating young people to become life-long learners and active in deciding what, how and where to learn. Life-long learning requires a significant reorganization of schooling and other forms of education, and a rethinking of the capacity and possibilities of young people and the subcultures they form. Life-long learning also requires commitment, motivation and agency in terms of being actively involved in constructing meaning and making sense of shifting realities.

Agency is reflected in individuals' capacity to act with intent and awareness of the self and social relationships (Robinson and Diaz, 2006). It is a process of forming a sense of selfhood that involves the capacity to exercise choice and determination. This notion of agency can be linked to Foucault's concept of 'technologies of self' which is understood 'as the practices and techniques through which individuals actively fashion their own identities' (McNay, 2000: 8). This concept reflects individual resilience, reflexivity and problem solving, but also raises important questions about collective responsibility and the role of individuals as active agents (Hall, 2004).

A cultural shift from a welfare dependency to the making of an entrepreneurial self has taken place by 'reconstructing culture in terms of enterprise' and by 'remodelling public institutions along commercial lines as corporations' (Peters, 2001: 60). Education has also been remodelled according to the principle of investing in children, which is underpinned by 'investing in the self at crucial points in the life cycle', to create an entrepreneurial self (ibid.: 61). The view that the money poured into education and social services should maximize children's future capital may reinforce the commodification of children. The recent children's plan introduced by the UK government shifts the focus from this managerialist framework of education towards children's well-being and happiness.

From an economic point of view, life-long learning and enterprise are seen as a response to counteract unemployment and meet the market demands of a knowledge-based society, where the new industry's raw material are information, ideas and creativity. Against this background, enterprise learning has an instrumental value, employed to solve societal problems through engineering young people's attitudes and 'transferring the problems from a societal to an individual plane' (Leffler and Svedberg, 2005: 225). Similar critiques have been articulated by Dahlberg and Moss, who observe that

A foregrounding of technical practice connected to a highly instrumental rationality is nothing new. It is the product of a mindset or paradigm that has been influential for more than two centuries, and which has often seen children as redemptive agents, ideal subjects for technical practice, through which we will fix problems without having to address their structural causes. (2005:11)

The Ethicopolitics of Enterprise and the Entrepreneurial Self

In the discourses that construe children as resources or enterprise, major ethical shifts have occurred. Investment in children's human capital is at the centre of ECCE (Early Childhood Care and Education) policy, through its linkage with an instrumental view of young children as a natural resource to be harnessed (Woodhead, 2006). Constructing children as a resource or a human capital is likely to shift the values we attribute to childhood; capitalization has its dangers, especially when operating within managerialist frameworks of children's development. The construction of children as an investment and as a resource reflects a hegemonic economic approach towards children's education where teaching and learning are for preparing a productive and flexible workforce for the future. It also offers an instrumental view of children's experiences and needs, and opens up possibilities for exploitation. Moreover, the rise of an entrepreneurial self will fundamentally shift the ethics of citizenship, as governing becomes concerned less with the social management of the population (biopolitics) than with individual self-governing (ethicopolitics) (Rose, 1999a).

Within a neoliberal ideology, the problem is not the 'anti-social effects of the economic market, but the anti-competitive effects of society' (Gordon, 1991: 42). Thus, individuals who do not present a competitive edge are likely to be perceived as problems, having failed to function as autonomous, choice making, rational and responsible individuals. This reflects a wider tendency to place the responsibility for governance and decision making on individual capabilities and dispositions, rather than on society (Rose, 1996). The notion of an individual enterprise thus becomes particularly important, because human disposition, motivation and capabilities are conceived within an economic model. Within this rationality, the entrepreneurial child is expected to be competitive with the potential to function as a resource or investment. Against this background, personhood and self-worth are articulated in economic terms, i.e., accumulating capital and blaming the self when experiencing failure.

The rhetoric of individualization for children and their families has implications with regard to the 'ethicopolitics' of care (Rose, 1999a). Individualization removes schools' and other civic institutions' responsibility for providing for children. In a context where family, community and other institutions are receding, the individual becomes 'the reproduction unit for the social in the life world' (Beck, 1992: 130). Individuals are compelled to become the makers of their own 'livelihoods', a 'D-I-Y project', shaped by the forces of the market (ibid.: 135). One may ask whether 'the public virtues of caring for those unable to care for themselves, survive in this new order' (Heap and Ross, 1992: 1). The emphasis on individuals to be entirely responsible for shaping their future through voice and choice reinforces social inequalities and victimization, because those who do not manage to become agents of change would have themselves to blame (Bragg, 2007).

This notion of individualization is distinct from individualism, and has an economic rather than a humanistic basis. It can function as a tool of oppression that defines identity along the lines of a rational, responsible individual who is preparing the self to become a flexible resource. The 'duty to the self – its simultaneous responsibilization as a moral agent and its construction as a calculative rational choice actor – becomes the basis for a series of investment decisions concerning one's health, education, security, employability, and retirement' (O'Malley, 1996: 200). It can also function as a device for social control and engineering towards the development of an enterprise culture that prepares children to compete within an international economy. Being distinct from individualism, individualization does not encourage a balance between individuals' capacity to shape their own livelihoods and the constraints of institutional and market demands.

Within this context, Beck's notion of a 'tragic individualism' emerges: individuals are given choice and responsibility to manage risk and its outcomes, especially in the absence of other systems of support, such as family, community or national governments. This type of individualism is tragic because individuals are expected to exercise choice and make decisions about situations and outcomes that they cannot predict (e.g., the consequences of genetic modification or nanotechnology on their life, choices of food and drugs). It is also paradoxical because it brings together individual decision making and institutional dependency, or what Beck describes as the 'contradictory double face of institutionally dependent individual situations' (1992: 130). On the one hand, young people are considered to be responsible for their own life and future and, on the other hand, they are dependent upon institutional and social structures, such as access to education and health care, imposed by the market.

Increasingly, families play a pivotal role in the creation of responsible young people, capable of making the right choices within an economic model. However, families and young people who do not adapt to this model are at-risk (Kelly, 2001). Risk[3] becomes individualized rather than an entity generated by institutional structures (Beck, 1992). Withers and Batten have focused on two competing discourses on youth at-risk (1995). The first discourse is characterized by a 'humanistic intention', and involves debates on the nature of care and the impact of disintegrating communities on children's well-being, sense of belonging and social networks. The second discourse has an 'economic intention' within which the costs and benefits regarding the identification and management of risk are paramount to ensure that, through intervention, young people will overcome risk and enter a productive workforce.

The humanistic and economic intentions are competing with each other, with the economic becoming more prominent in current discussions of children's well-being and socialization (ibid.: 5–6). The view of young people's future, as shaped through individualization and standardization, assumes that there is a 'universal moral consensus' with regard to people's values, motivation and aspiration (Rose, 1999b: 490). It also assumes that an assemblage of science, technology and education will bring an economic growth and international competition without challenging poverty, the unequal distribution of resources, and the increasing invisibility and marginalization of young people (Peters, 2001).

Finally, the image of children as an enterprise reflects the ambivalent world that childhood occupies. On the one hand, childhood is perceived as a protected space with children requiring care and protection and, on the other hand, as a resource capable of making a significant contribution to their communities. The entrepreneurial child offers a view of childhood that is strong, independent, autonomous and competent. This view exudes a powerful allure because it counteracts constructions of children as being vulnerable and in the need for protection. However, the responsibility is on the individual child to be reflexive, creative, and capable of maximizing opportunities and turning learning into functionings that are valued in a market-driven society. This form of responsibilization is likely to create new zones of exclusion and manipulation, shifting rather than removing power structures and inequalities.

Disability and the Entrepreneurial Self

Within industrial societies, the majority of individuals with disability had experienced disadvantage and exclusion from the economic and civic life. The systematic exclusion of disabled people from paid work under industrial capitalism has made inclusion a priority for disabled people's organizations in recent decades (Gleeson, 1999). At the same time, neoliberalism's privileging of paid work as a marker of citizenship has intensified the costs associated with failing to access the workplace (McDowell, 2004). Limited access to paid work does not only mean lack of contribution to communities but, most crucially, exclusion and non-citizenship.

Rose argues that current critiques of the post-war social citizenship have given rise to new ways of understanding individuals as 'subjects of freedom', where freedom refers to the capacity/responsibility of the autonomous individual to 'determine the course of one's own existence through acts of choice' (1999a: 84). Paid work plays a fundamental role in facilitating social inclusion, or a type of social inclusion that requires its subjects to reinvent themselves as abled disabled.

Market-driven societies aim at supporting individuals, including those with disabilities, to enter or re-enter the job market (Hall, 2004). At first glance, this is liberating in that individuals with disability are likely to move from dependency to autonomy. However, one of the dangers is to fail to account for inclusionary practices that may generate exclusion (Titchkosky, 2003). Inclusionary practices rely on assumptions that disability requires remedy or that individuals with disability are excluded because of their disability. As Judith Butler argues, disabled people have been made to matter as excluded and marginalized, as victims of not only biology but also society (1993).

Normalcy and normativity require the existence of the 'abnormal' or the 'other' against which these terms are defined. Bauman (2000) argues that the individual has become a project in that the self needs to be 'made up' in order to be able to respond to challenges and changes. We witness the rise of an 'enforced individuality as a fate' which is very different from 'individuality as the practical and realistic capacity for self-assertion' (ibid., 2000: 34). To view individuals as being responsible for their problems and their solutions raises ethical implications for those with disability. Individuals with disability may be forced to find solutions to 'manage and even overcome' their problems in order to become included (Titchkosky, 2003: 525).

Actualizing the self as a project is underpinned by an enforced individuality which requires young people to constantly reinvent themselves, rather than an individuality as a realistic capacity for self-actualization. Individuals with disability are integrated/included in the society either in the form of employment or education once, through remedial programmes, they manage to erase disability (Stiker, 1997). This reality constructs disability as a 'thing' that is not part of an individual's personhood (Titchkosky, 2003: 537). To become included, individuals with disability are required to separate disability from personhood and reinvent the self.

However, one may question the nature of inclusion that requires individuals to acknowledge that they possess a type of functioning that deviates from normalcy, a 'thing' that they need to manage and, possibly, overcome by 'making up' the self. Genuine inclusion and participation are likely to emerge from a view of disability as a possibility, a space for a critical inquiry of culture and societal norms and practices. Reconceptualizing disability as a space for critical inquiry is likely to trigger debates on every field of human endeavour from aesthetics to social policy and economics. This is important, especially within market economies that strive to promote a certain social order, where any deviation from the mindset imposed is likely to be construed as deficit.

Citizenship or Sheer Survival?

The principles that underpin market-driven societies such as flexibility, mobility and entrepreneurialism have become the ideal qualities of citizenship. However, they are likely to undermine the democratic achievements of the American liberalism based on the ideals of equal rights and equal opportunities (Ong, 2003). The global markets induce such activities, so that 'flexibility, migration and relocations, instead of being coerced or resisted, have become practices to strive for rather than stability' (Ong, 1999: 19). The synergy between global capitalism and commercialized citizenship creates milieus where market-based values articulate the norms of citizenship and human rights (Ong, 2006). In this context, the entrepreneurial child occupies a shifting terrain of citizenship. A 'flexible citizenship' fits the civic requirements of an entrepreneurial citizen who responds fluidly and opportunistically to dynamic borderless market conditions (ibid., 2006).

A large number of young people from countries that have embraced an aggressive mode of capitalism and market citizenship, as well as from the Western countries that have been affected by the economic shift from the West to the East, have been pushed into an 'uncivil civil society' (Santos, 2001). In emerging economies, in particular, 'the embrace of self-enterprising values has made citizenship rights and benefits contingent upon individual market performance' (Ong, 2006: 503).

Citizenship is no longer defined by nation-states but by sites where displaced and excluded children and their families fight to claim their rights by engaging with the human rights discourses or applying neoliberal criteria (Ong and Collier, 2005). Displaced and marginalized individuals understand that citizenship, as an abstract concept, cannot guarantee them a social contract in terms of accessing the bare minimum resources to meet their needs for protection and survival. In certain places, female migrant workers experience severe exploitation and, even loss of life. Feminist NGOs fight not for human rights but for something more basic, biological survival, or 'biowelfare' on behalf of these workers (Ong, 2006). Children's biowelfare is also at stake, especially as citizenship rights do not often accompany displaced children as they cross borders.

For many young people and their families, 'the goal is no longer Utopia but simply survival' and 'learning to survive' (Ainley, 1998: 48, 50). Some young people live under a situation of a permanent threat, mainly emerging from technology and its unintended outcomes, and the widening poverty gap. We seem to be in a constant state of a struggle for survival, not only as species but also as organizations and civic institutions. To survive, we need to become 'reflexive' learners and problem solvers capable of offering rational solutions by focusing on 'the fit between what is offered by the environment and the various different and changing needs' (Masschelein, 2001: 14). An appropriate balance between the market demands and the individuals' needs should set the starting point for this type of learning.

Masschelein argues that learning in a learning society does not always maximize the possibilities for social inclusion and citizenship; it may lead to a greater individualization. The purpose of learning is to enable young people to engage in enterprise, and not necessarily 'to continue a particular culture or tradition' (2001: 15). The content of learning is not important; it varies, and this flexibility is crucial because applying diverse skills to process diverse contents maximizes adaptation and survival. The social or political problems are no longer formulated in terms of 'guiding the process, of defining goals and norms for that process' (ibid.: 15). They are conceptualized in terms of whether individuals are active or passive, included or excluded. There is a limited emphasis given on the meaningfulness and validity of the process, and there is no place for 'real critique' either (ibid.: 16). Thus, the capacity to participate and respond to change and uncertainty is more valued than the content and nature of the knowledge per se. Social inclusion has gained new meanings; it is not about thinking and deciding the process itself or critiquing whether the process is indeed inclusive; it is about participating in the process.

Children are growing up in a society where the very sense of what it means to be human is being redefined. The advances in biotechnologies (e.g., genomics) will create 'a new space of hope and fear . . . around genetic and somatic individuality' (Rose and Novas, 2003: 39). The human body has become the ground for exploration and discovery, where individuals through choice can extend or enhance the self. The self as a project in making requires a new form of citizenship that is borderless (not tied to a national identity or ideology), and not dependent on the social citizenship of a welfare state. The young people's bio-well-being is also likely to be challenged by the use of technology to modify/enhance the human body. The possibility for human enhancement is the Pandora's box, with consequences that cannot be predicted, pointing to a new form of biological citizenship. In this context, a 'political economy of hope' is emerging in terms of constructing the self as an entity with 'biovalue'. The genetic manipulation of the human body has the potential to increase its health and capabilities and thus the economic productivity and value that a market society ascribes to it (ibid., 2003).

This raises important ethical dilemmas in that some young people, due to a limited choice and access to genetic manipulation, may have less biovalue than others. It will also shift the importance we place on the 'bare life' of human beings in terms of identity formation and human rights (Agamben, 1998). Young people would be required to know not only their cultural heritage but also their genetic histories, and who they are would be shaped by race, ethnicity, religion or language and also by their genetic make up. Identity is likely to be constructed along images and a vocabulary from biomedicine in terms of the strengths and limitations of the human body and its inclination or predisposition to diseases (Rose and Novas, 2003).

The dilemmas about the possibilities and vulnerabilities of human beings and their fluid identities are framed by current debates of citizenship and human rights. Increasingly, it becomes particularly difficult to distinguish nature from artifice, biology from politics and morality. Technology and politics shape the human body and influence the debates on normalcy, abnormalcy and artificiality. What human dignity and human rights would mean in this new genetic and technological reconfiguration of human body remains to be seen.

Is It All Doom and Gloom?

So, what is the alternative to Beck's tragic individualism and a market society that cannot guarantee some children's rights to survival and protection? A new form of collectivity emerges that may enable individuals to respond to challenges that the global society create and offer solutions through border-crossing activism. Gould refers to a 'cosmopolitan intersociation' and Beck to 'transnational interdependencies' to capture the inter-connectivity of people's life at a global level. The gradual receding of nation- states stimulates a new form of subpolitics whereby political groups and NGOs propel activism at a global level, that are facilitated by the use of the internet and other communication technologies. In the cyberspace, citizens become nitizens and use internet-mediated communication as a means of gaining information and exercising rights through protests. In China, for example, some young people use the internet to express dissatisfaction about the accountability of the Chinese government and expose instances of exploitation and violence perpetrated by the state machine. The cyberspace allows for political activism and voices to be heard that perhaps would not have been possible in a more conventional political space (Ong, 2006).

The use of communication technologies and the reshaping of a conventional citizenship into a digital citizenship have made the ground fertile for protests against violations of human rights. More interestingly, the language of human rights is being calibrated to reflect the ethics, values and cultural practices of specific regions. The universalism that characterizes current human rights discourses is not applicable to places that do not operate within the Western notions of liberalism. The discourse of human rights has been hybridized to reflect the social and political realities of the populations and regions they serve. Situated ethics is a hybrid of Western concepts of human rights in a language that reflects a particular culture and secular and religious beliefs.

NGOs and human rights groups tend to calibrate their own language and ethics to make claims to corporations or the state. For example, in Indonesia, humanitarian, non-violent, and women's groups protested against state brutality, especially articulated through the violence inflicted on the human body (military instigated women's rape) (Ong, 2006). In Southeast Asian countries, women's groups and religious NGOs have articulated state-instigated violence as 'violations of humanity, as understood in local religious terms of compassion, reciprocity and forgiveness'. In Malaysia, a NGO Sisters-in-Islam articulated women's rights in terms of Muslim precepts, pointing to situated ethic (ibid., 2006). This illustrates Gould's concept of concrete universalism that situates universal views of rights into a local milieu.

The richness of children's capacities and understandings is expressed in accounts of children's participatory powers, repositioning themselves and their shifting identities to make sense of their rapidly changing world (Moss and Petrie, 2002; Paley, 2004). The image of the rich and competent child however is different from that of children as enterprise or entrepreneurial citizens. The entrepreneurial child can become Malaguzzi's 'rich' child if we place him/her within a relational framework, where social interactions and the conversations and the narratives that people construct as part of a lived experience shape their civic participation and learning. Instead of an entrepreneurial self, what is advocated is an image of childhood that is relational and situated within communities of learning (Fleer, Anning and Cullen, 2004).

Enterprise, as defined within communities of practice, is not shaped by the responsibilization and moralization discourses but by a network of ethics regarding children's well-being. In this context, children's well-being is promoted through participation, rights, recognition of achievement, respect of personal and moral values and respect of difference, rather than through self-reliance. This well-being framework should be at the centre of policies and legislation and, most crucially, be part of a major culture shift by moving the discourses on needs to discourses on care and ethics. The holistic child is a rich child and not an accumulation of social, health or educational needs.

Notes

[1] Responsibilization is achieved through the shifting of blame for risk from institutions and social/political structures to the individual. Responsibilization is the result of viewing life through the lens of risk discourses (Hunt, 2003: 186). Beck understands responsibilization along the lines of cynicism of the failure of institutions to support the well-being of individuals collectively (2008). In this context, social problems become individual problems that cannot be solved through collective action.

[2] Hayekian order: This phrase reflects the outcome of the economic theories of Frederick von Hayek. A Hayekian order supports (and perpetuates) the free market as being the organizing principle of society.

[3] Risk is the defining characteristic of postmodern society. It is a systematic way of dealing with hazards induced and introduced by modernization (Beck, 1992). Personal decision making becomes the basis of social decision making, and individuals are expected to be self-reflective and self-evaluative to manage risk in order to survive. Wells argues that 'this notion of risk justifies new kinds of regulatory interventions, legitimizes new types of problematization and embroils whole new populations in systems of control. A preoccupation with risk as a rationale for enforcement also challenges the notion of a simple distinction between the moral and the immoral, the member of the respectable majority and the deviant minority. Such a 'respectable' identity is, it is proposed, under considerable challenge in a society where risk is increasingly being used as a justification for the problematization of its citizens' (2007: 1–2)

Part II

The Ecologies of Childhood in the 21st Century

As we journey in the 21st century, the ecology of childhood is changing rapidly. Market-driven economies pose restrictions to welfare states, offering choice and freedom to individuals. With the welfare state shrinking and state intervention gaining in dominance, the social, economic and spatial reality of children's everyday life is changing. Childhood has become both individualized and institutionalized, being framed by competing discourses that construe children as objects of public intervention (childhood as a concern); as future investment (childhood as a project); and as a social group that should exist on its own right (children's rights).

Worldwide, change and uncertainty are redrawing the map of children's experiences of growing up. In the United Kingdom, although, recently, the Labour Government has formed a Department for Children, Schools and Family, to stress the prominence of children's issues, public policy has not placed children and young people at its centre, neglecting their experiences, and the physical, social and cultural geographies they occupy. Both in public discourses and the subsequent welfare policy making, the emphasis has shifted to economic factors regarding welfare provision and management for children and their families. In this transient world, an interesting paradox emerges, in that as globalization increases, a tendency towards a global homogenization based on Western ideas, values, artefacts and images becomes apparent. In a globalized world, it is challenging for societies and cultures to define their boundaries, and difference and diversity become difficult to sustain.

In this part, images of childhood in transience are presented by focusing on the changing face of family and care relationships; changes in children's physical and social spaces and the increasing fragmentation of their communities; and changes in children's play culture and enjoyment. The impact of peer interactions and friendships, real and virtual, on young people's happiness is discussed. Moreover, the growing worries about young people's mental health have stimulated a discussion on the role of education to prepare young people for public and personal life.

Chapter 4

Transient Childhoods:
The Politics of Change and Uncertainty

Children grow up in an era of radical doubt where the certainties of tradition are rejected and knowledge is interrogated and contested (Parker, 1997). Doubt stimulates experimentation and fresh approaches but also brings insecurities and conflicting perspectives on parenthood and children's well-being. The parents' growing anxiety about children's socialization in a 'risk' society is exploited by the media and the state intervention machine which, through the implementation of governmental policies and initiatives, has put children and their families under public scrutiny.

Transience has defined both the physical and social parameters of children's life. Increasingly, children grow up in transient neighbourhoods, mainly due to residential mobility and neighbourhood disintegration or gentrification, experiencing limited social cohesion. We tend to travel much further to work, shop and enjoy leisure opportunities that are located less and less in the physical and social context of a neighbourhood. Moreover, the destruction of the natural environment and the limited non-commercial space that is left for families and children to socialize have damaged people's 'spatial integrity'[1] (Putnam, 1995), with children growing up experiencing 'theme-park' type of interactions and virtual-zone encounters.

Transience has also become a feature of human relationships, manifested in the changing face of families and fracture of civic communities,[2] and children's socialization and friendships. The experience of childhood and parenthood is reduced to a 'lifestyle' shaped by a consumerist culture and civic disengagement. The increasing individualization and the lack of long-term commitment exert an adverse effect on the structure of family and personal life. In a fast-changing world, children do not have the chance to develop 'a narrative of identity in a society composed of episodes and fragments' (Sennett, 1998: 27).

Growing Up in an Era of Civic Disengagement: The Fractured Experience of Childhood

Children's lives are shaped by individualized experiences, mainly mediated by the media and virtual social networks. Within communities, civic disengagement[3] and lack of social trust have a profound effect on children developing as social and moral beings, and, most crucially, on their capacity to exercise rights and responsibilities. Views and norms about morality and well-being are shaped within cohesive communities with well-defined traditions and patterns of interaction. However, in fragmented societies, relationships become instrumental, a means to an end. Gray comments that 'by privileging individual choice over any common good it tends to make relationships revocable and provisional . . . All relationships become consumer goods' (1999: 37).

Michael Young argued that market economies would fragment relationships in families and communities, with disastrous effects on our physical and emotional well-being, and the very sense of being human (Dench, Gavron and Young, 2007). Social networks and close-knit communities offer a collective mutuality and co-dependency that prepare children for participation, building capacity for self-reliance, communication and problem solving. In transient and fractured neighbourhoods and communities, people are less likely to reach a consensus or have a shared code of behaviour and culture to unite them on issues of children's well-being and care. A lack of common assumptions with regard to youth socialization and care accentuates fears for what we perceive to be the 'other', with youth socialization becoming the responsibility of a handful, trustworthy individuals.

To illustrate the relationship between state regulatory functions and civic engagement, Santos distinguishes between three types of civil society, namely, the intimate civil society, the strange civil society and the uncivil civil society (2001). The intimate civil society comprises the circle closest to the state and includes individuals and social groups who enjoy the 'three generations of human rights, i.e., civic–political, socio-economic and cultural' (ibid., 2001). These groups operate within the forces of the market which encourages state privatization. The strange civil society involves individuals and social groups who experience both inclusion and exclusion in varying degrees, and who exercise civic and political rights with, however, limited opportunities to exercise socio-economic and cultural rights. Finally, the uncivil civil society involves social groups who have been excluded from the dominant civic structures and discourses, being socially invisible and situated at the margins of a society.

Santos reflects on the implications of the formation of an uncivil society by referring to the emergence of a social fascism, a form of a social apartheid, which has divided communities, spatially and socially, to 'civilized and savage zones'. The savage zones are kept separate from the civilized ones through a 'neo-feudal system of gated communities and private spaces' (2001: 186). The lack of democratic practices is mostly felt in the savage communities where a social contract, of any type, is no longer applicable. Santos argues that neoliberal ideologies have forced many individuals to move into the uncivil civil society, with their communities becoming more polarized and segregated, due to the widening gap between the poor and the rich.

The transience at a society level translates into changes in the everyday experiences of children with their families and peers, and in the cultures of care, play and enjoyment.

The Changing Face of Families

There have been considerable changes in the nature and structure of family life over the last decades, with families becoming smaller and more isolated, leading to a reduction of social networks and diminished opportunities for social cohesion and civic involvement. The proportion of lone-parent households with dependent children has doubled, with nearly a quarter of children living in a lone-parent family (Social Trends, 2004). With the families becoming smaller and communities more transient, the socialization of young people is left in the hands of their parents, in many cases a lone-parent, and the professionals.

During the 20th century, family life was kept separate from the world, private and untouched by state regulation and intervention. This is no longer the case; families, as social institutions, have opened up to regulation and scrutiny, and anxieties about child rearing, childcare and parents' employment have entered the public domain. Public policy focuses on the effects of parenting on children, stressing the responsibilization of adults, i.e., parents and their immediate community, with regard to child rearing. In the early 1980s, Hilary Clinton stressed the importance of a 'village' and a community in raising children, moving the debate away from child rearing as being the sole responsibility of the nuclear family. Although approaching child rearing and well-being as a communal responsibility is empowering, it is important to differentiate between communal involvement and state intervention. Traditionally, state interventionist approaches to child rearing have been underpinned by notions of responsibility deficit in children's families and communities. Deficit assumptions are reflected in family compensation models, whose aim is to remedy the parents and the community through professional intervention. Communal systems of mutual support have been undermined by policies and initiatives that portray parents as the problem, in need of intervention, and the professionals as the solution (see Chapter 12 for a discussion on parental involvement as a form of social capital).

It is widely accepted that parents and families have a greater impact on childhood development and life chances than any other factor (e.g., Mayall, 2002; Walberg, 1984). Recent findings, stated in the report An Overview of Child Well-being in Rich Countries, revealed that children, in general, do not see material goods and leisure activities as a top priority (UNICEF, 2007). Instead, the relationships with family members and peers were rated as being particularly crucial for their life and enjoyment.

The spread of market economies worldwide and the resulting rapidly changing patterns of paid work among women have influenced traditional ways of rearing children, forcing families to reorganize their functions and relationships around paid work. In some cases, adults' inflexible work arrangements have transformed family interactions into a luxury, where time to spend with family members is a highly priced commodity, a bonus. Time pressure, especially in two-career families, reduces opportunities for interacting and building social and emotional bonds between parents and children, as well as with the extended family, impacting on care, relationships, communication and involvement in public fora. Dahlberg and Moss argue that the 'hegemony of paid work has to be challenged, its stranglehold on time loosened' to alleviate its ramifications on individuals and communities (2005: 188). This raises the need to reconsider the merits of leisure, especially for parents with young children, and to recognize that the dilemmas faced by families with regard to the impact of paid work on their well-being are not personal but political, and should be debated publicly.

Dealing with the stresses of balancing work and family life tends to be presented as a personal dilemma; thus, making collective choices becomes neither feasible nor desirable (Diamond et al., 2004). However, alternative employment structures that would allow people to take time off from paid work to raise children, look after the elderly and engage in democratic fora to sustain civic engagement should be considered. Beck discusses the notion of 'public work', as 'a new focus of activity and identity that will revitalize the democratic way of life', to stimulate the development of 'new foci of political action and identity formation' (Beck, 1998: 60). Taking time off employment to engage in public/community affairs has the potential to activate democratic practices and social responsibility towards the care of children and the elderly. Moreover, for parents who choose to do paid work, a flexible and good quality of childcare system is necessary and, most crucially, the need for parent-friendly workplaces that respect and support the twin priorities of working parents (Diamond et al., 2004).

Data form the Young People's Social Attitudes (YPSA, 2003, see Appendix) survey have captured young people's views about the impact of female paid work, gender roles and responsibilities and family structures on relationships and care. Regarding female paid work, their views were examined through the lens of ethnic background, social/occupational class and gender. Young people, especially boys, believed that family life suffers if a woman has a full-time job. Boys with parents who hold lower educational qualifications (e.g., O level) were less certain that working mums are capable of establishing warm relationships with their children. In contrast, boys and girls whose parents hold higher educational qualifications disagreed that female paid work gets in the way of establishing emotional bonds between mothers and their children.

Moreover, boys' and girls' views about working mothers' emotional availability were found to differ depending on their ethnic background. Specifically, Black boys of African and Caribbean origin, as well as boys of Asian origin disagreed that working mums can establish warm relationships with children. These results suggest that the pressures of a paid work are felt differently across ethnic and social groups; the impact of female paid job is felt more strongly in households from certain ethnic background (i.e., Asian, Black Caribbean and Black African), and in families where parents hold low-paid jobs.

Young people also offered interesting views about gender roles within families and the job market. These views differed between boys and girls of various ethnic origins. Specifically, Asian girls disagreed with the survey statement 'man's job is to earn money and women's to look after children', whereas boys from the same ethnic background agreed strongly. Similar views were expressed by Asian and Black Caribbean boys, whereas White boys expressed less traditional views about gender roles within families. Furthermore, views about gender roles were influenced by social class and parents' degree qualification. Boys from households with high income and parents who hold a higher education degree expressed more liberal views about gender roles, compared to the views held by boys in households where adults had limited educational qualifications as well as in households with low income.

In the YPSA study, young people's views about family structures, roles and responsibilities differed by gender and occupational class. Overall, girls

from middle-income households, were found to agree more than did boys
with statements such as 'one parent can bring up a child as well as two parents', suggesting that boys are likely to hold more traditional views about
child rearing practices and family structures. In contrast, girls from very
low-income households (e.g., income less than 3,999 pounds per year) disagreed more than did boys from similar households that one parent is
adequate to raise a child. Moreover, both boys and girls from households of
a higher occupational class offered traditional views about family structures,
agreeing that one parent cannot bring up a child as well as two parents.
Girls who attended fee paying private schools, in particular, disagreed
strongly about a lone parent's capacity to raise children. It appears that raising children as a lone-parent is not perceived favourably by young people at
the higher end of household income. Girls from either side of the income
divide, expressed strong views against lone parenthood, whereas girls from
middle-income households agreed with the adequacy of a lone parent. Boys
from higher- and middle- income households expressed more traditional
views about lone parenthood, whereas boys from very low-income households agreed with the adequacy of lone parenthood.

Young people's views about family roles and responsibilities were further
diversified when ethnic background was considered. Specifically, compared
to Black young people, Asian and European boys and girls disagreed about
the adequacy of one-parent families with regard to raising children. These
ethnic differences reflect different historical and social realities that have
shaped the structures and roles of families in these ethnic groups, as well as
young people's normalization of these structures. The current results are
interesting considering that the proportion of households consisting of a
couple and their dependent children has fallen to over a fifth in 2003.

Moreover, young people's views with regard to less traditional family
structures, such as couple living together and not marry, were found to differ significantly depending on their ethnic background and gender.
Compared to boys from the same ethnic background, Black girls of Caribbean origin did not accept that it is 'all right for couples to live together and
not marry'. The opposite was found for girls of a mixed origin who agreed
more than did boys with this view. Regarding other ethnic groups (e.g.,
Asian, European), the majority of the responses were found to be neutral,
possibly suggesting a wider acceptance of less conventional lifestyles by both
boys and girls.

Girls from households with adults holding educational qualifications at a
degree level, e.g., A-level and O-level, disagreed strongly with the statement
'parents should stay together if they have child/children', compared

with boys from similar households. These results may suggest that girls are embracing less traditional family roles and expectations, especially those with parents who hold relatively high educational qualifications. In contrast, girls with parents who hold CSE or equivalent educational qualifications, agreed more than did boys on parents staying together to raise their children, embracing more traditional family values.

Consistently, these results suggest that young people's views about gender roles, female paid work and family structures differ considerably as a function of social and occupational class, gender and ethnicity. Compared to the views of young people from less well-off households, both boys and girls with parents who hold higher qualifications embraced less traditional views about gender roles in the family and the impact of female paid work on child rearing. With regard to parenthood and gender roles, girls from both sides of the income divide offered more traditional views (e.g., one parent cannot bring up a child as well as two parents), compared to girls from the middle ranges of income (e.g., with parents who hold educational qualification at A-level). Boys from middle- and higher-income households, offered more traditional views regarding lone parenthood. Interestingly, although boys from these households agreed that one parent alone is not enough to raise children, those with parents who hold CSE or equivalent qualifications, as well as those from low-income households, disagreed with the statement that parents should stay together if they have children and agreed with lone parenthood. Although young people offer less traditional views about female paid work and gender roles, many do not agree with the adequacy of lone parenthood.

Regarding female paid work, boys from certain ethnic backgrounds, e.g., Black of African and Caribbean origin and Asian, disagreed that working mothers can establish emotional bonds with their children. Although they expressed more traditional views about gender roles in the family (e.g., a man's job is to earn money . . .), boys of Black and Caribbean origin agreed with the adequacy of one-parent families to raise children, and with the statement 'it is all right for couple to live together and not marry'. Overall, boys of a European origin held less traditional views about gender roles and parenthood. These results illustrate the influences that ethnic background exerts on young people's views about the structure of the family, gender roles and parental capacity/responsibility.

Fairly polarized views about gender roles in the family and the impact of female paid work on child rearing were expressed by young people, especially boys, from households that operate at the end of the class divide. At the higher end of income, both boys and girls expressed more liberal views about gender roles and more traditional views about lone parenthood, and disagreed that female employment has a negative impact on child rearing and family relationships. The liberal views may be explained by systems of support that are likely to be in place in well-off households to counter the effects of women's paid work on child rearing.

Among girls, from either end of the income divide, a consensus on lone parenthood was found, possibly for different reasons. Poverty has a differential gender effect, with girls and women being more likely to function as 'shock absorbers' to reduce the effects of poverty on their family, with significant physical and mental health consequences regarding their well-being (Lister, 2005). The impact of lone parenthood in less well-off households is felt more strongly by girls and not by boys. Moreover, girls and boys from well-off households were found to disagree about the adequacy of lone parenthood, possibly because they attribute more value to traditional family structures in terms of their capacity to generate the social and cultural capital that is required to raise children and offer them access to opportunities.

The Politics and Ethics of Care

Recently, the debates on the nature and provision of care have entered the political arena. At the same time, the provision of care has been framed as a personal rather than a political dilemma, requiring a new thinking about the redistribution of domestic work and support for children and the elderly. In an achievement-orientated culture, care is changing, being placed 'below and above' politics (Tronto, 1993). Paid care work is normally taken up by low-paid care providers, highlighting its low position within current welfare states. The low position of care is also illustrated in the Needs Analysis study (see Appendix) where, although young carers were expected to cover the 'care deficit' by making a significant contribution to their families and communities, they were not encouraged to participate in decisions regarding service provision. If we are to bring care into the children's rights discourse, we need to engage with the ethics and politics that underpin it. The dilemma of viewing care with impartiality and professionalism, on the one hand, and with a sense of empathy, relational understanding and emotional involvement, on the other, is at the centre of the politics of care. This dilemma is further accentuated by the current care deficit that both the developed and developing world experiences, albeit for different reasons.

The discourses of care are mainly situated within the post-colonial feminist ethics, although I would like to differentiate between 'feminist ethics of care' and 'ethics of care' to avoid the misconception that care is relevant to women's life only. Ethics is an elusive concept in that it means different things, ranging from a philosophical study of morality to a set of moral values that reflect daily practices in a society. For Habermas (1990), morality refers to principles that are universal and carry a cross-cultural force, whereas ethics refer to values and conceptions of a good life embedded in particular cultures, pointing to a universalism/particularism continuum. Post-colonial feminist ethics do not accept the universality of care, and approach it as a reality that is influenced by the power structures and the different circumstances that surround the life of children and their families. From this perspective, identity, power inequality and social class define care and its manifestation within family contexts.

Care is a relational construct that is removed from the realm of a moral certainty to a social and political judgement, with family and cultural structures influencing values, ethics and obligation (Mohanty, 2003). The context of care is defined by the physical, social and critical parameters, and the hierarchical and power structures that reflect the particularities of children's life. For post-colonial feminism, 'the ethical significance of context is two-fold: first, because it affects the meaning of a particular right, value or principle; second, because it affects the way in which the effects of measures promoting particular values and principles are experienced' (Hutchings, 2007: 91).

Traditionally, the provision of care has aligned itself to the nature of women's work. What women do at home in the form of unpaid labour and what public services the state offers are likely to reposition care. The shifts between paid and unpaid work are not new. However, what is new now is that, within certain social classes, women's unpaid labour is replaced by work carried out by migrant care workers, whereas the welfare state is receding from the responsibility of offering support in the form of public services.

Responsive care has become a scarce commodity, with families and communities across the developed and developing world experiencing a form of care deficit. There is a growing tendency to 'sub-contract' or 'outsource' family support and care for children and the elderly. In two-career families in the developed world, some parents who do not have the time to offer care 'buy care' for their children. Ehrenreich and Hochschild have coined the phrase 'emotional imperialism' to describe the process whereby the work-orientated developed world does not offer a space for care, patience and emotional bonding in families; instead, it imports them from the developing world (2003). Care is assigned to individuals, from the developing world, mainly women who leave their own children and families behind to fill the care gap, which has become a huge challenge for welfare states in many Western countries. Filling the care gap has also proven to be a challenge to children and the elderly in the developing world who experience 'care drain' (Ehrenreich and Hochschild, 2003).

Care drain is not a new phenomenon. During the industrial era, in many parts of the developing world without an established industrial economy, parents were leaving their children with the extended family to migrate to industrialized nations to find work, in factories mainly. What is different now is that, in post-industrial economies, the care deficit in Western countries due to changes in family and employment structures has created a care market that offers employment to individuals from the developing world.

Jody Heymann (2006) explored the effects of globalization and market economies on family structures, especially for the families of care providers. The changing conditions of the care market have threatened children and the elderly in the developing world. The distribution of care work can no longer be addressed within state boundaries because it has a global impact. Heymann and colleagues researched hundreds of families in countries across the world, from Botswana to Vietnam and Mexico, where childcare is limited or nonexistent and employment rights in terms of maternity/paternity leave are restricted. Of the families they interviewed, 36 per cent admitted they had had to leave young children at home alone, 39 per cent had left a sick child at home alone and 27 per cent had left a child in the care of another child.

The distribution of care is unequal across the developing/developed world divide, and has become, as Ehrenreich and Hochschild observe, the last 'commodity frontier' that is traded with dire consequences to both care providers and care receivers (2003). There is a higher need for care in many developing countries; the ratio of children and elderly to working-aged adults is more than 50 per cent higher than that in the developed world. Also, considering that illness rates are higher and the lack of medical provision is acute, especially in Sub-Saharan Africa with the Aids epidemic and the rising number of orphans, the need for care is increased dramatically. The provision of care, and children's rights to protection and provision are inter-connected, stressing the need to position care at the heart of children's rights.

The Changing Culture of Children's Play and Enjoyment

Children's play reflects the political, cultural and ideological trends of a society. Their toys and games encompass cultural artefacts, rituals, customs and norms that formulate the 'psychography', or 'civilization sign' of a culture. Children's cultures of play are changing, with children engaging in limited unstructured and self-initiated play in the name of safety. The current shifts in children's enjoyment and use of leisure time should be approached diachronically to appreciate that certain issues, such as the role of play in children's enjoyment have been addressed throughout history.

In ancient Greece, the terms 'youth' and 'education' had a common root, denoting that education and enjoyment were seen as overlapping entities capable of shaping young people's lives (Lazos, 2002). Playing in ancient times was placed on a continuum from entertainment, rivalry, spirituality to education, playing a strong social, religious and civic role in children's development and experience of childhood. In Latin, the word 'ludus' means entertainment and schooling, suggesting a semiotic extension from play to education or to teaching and learning through play which, according to Plato's *Dialogues*, forms the basis for a person to function as a citizen. Through play, children participate in social activities and develop the capacity for decision making, constructing and following rules and understanding the implications (win or lose). Plato advised parents to let their children play as a preparation for becoming citizens in a democratic society. When children engage in child-initiated activities, skills such as volition, decision making, capacity for judgement, leadership qualities, teamwork and a critical stand towards oneself and others develop.

In the era of the Enlightenment, Rousseau in *Emile* (1762) viewed play as an essential platform for children's development, referring to 'play with a purpose', and raised concerns about the impact of technology and society on children's nature (Hyder, 2005: 14). Moreover, within developmental psychology, play has been ascribed a function towards the development of children's cognitive, linguistic and emotional needs. Vygotsky placed play in the social and cultural context of their lives, and observed that children's play take into consideration the norms and values of their communities. Bruner also viewed play as a vehicle for learning, which stresses the importance on encouraging children to engage in play as an avenue for exploration and learning.

Hutt and colleagues differentiated between epistemic play and ludic play; the former refers to acquiring knowledge during playing with peers, and the latter involves an imaginative play, where symbolic representations form the basis of play (1989). One observes how far the notion of learning through epistemic play is from current mechanistic views of test-centred learning. Target-orientated learning can be traced back at the beginning of the 20th century, along with the rise of positivism and behaviourism to explain human development, where children's play and learning are shaped by stimulus – response contingencies and modelling.

At present, theories of play tend to fall into four main categories:

- play as a means of a physical development (burning excess energy, strengthening body muscles);
- play as a means of understanding the social world;
- play as a means of developing cognitive and language skills;
- play as a means of coming to terms with emotional and inner states. (Hyder, 2005: 14)

Play, according to these theories, is initiated by the children themselves, and is a free-flowing, pleasurable activity with no risk for failure, where the emphasis is on the process and not the product (Smidt, 2006). What needs to be highlighted is the notion of play as shaping and being shaped by children's culture and circumstances. Through play, children create meaning which, in turn, shapes their life, the ways in which they relate to others and their social position in a community. Children represent their daily reality through the symbolic use of the objects found in their families and communities, ranging from pieces of wood and stones to iPod devices. Through pretend play, they set rules and develop ways of negotiating and resolving conflict. To encounter conflict through playing is important for children to develop negotiation skills and the capacity to differentiate right from wrong. In contrast, during adult-structured and supervised activities, the opportunities for child-initiated negotiation and problem solving are reduced considerably.

Cultures of play and play within cultures

Children learn about their culture through play, but also, through play, they shape their culture. Play is both a 'cause and effect of culture' (Hyder, 2005: 21). It is a universal activity, with culture-specific aspects, manifested in the objects used and the nature, type and content of children's games, as well as their interactional styles and adults' understandings of the purpose of children's play. In some cultures, children do not initiate play with adults, whereas in others children expect adults to take part in their games. In many European and North American families, for example, parents ascribe a cognitive purpose in play, whereas in other cultures, e.g., Chinese, the focus is on the social and communal attributes of play (Concu and Gaskins, 2006).

Children develop their own culture of play, shaped by developmental needs, social/political circumstances and culture-specific expectations.

The cultural, social and political context in which children grow up has a powerful influence on their play. Children's play themes tend to involve roles and scripts that emanate from their family and cultural practices, reflecting the reality of their lives. Play is imbued with emotion, from exploring taboo issues to dealing with emotionally charged situations (e.g., death, isolation). Symbols, music, art, food and artefacts differ from one culture to another, and so are children's symbolic representations and play.

Play is a representation of events, experiences, objects and situations they encountered within their family and the community. In war and conflict-ridden zones, for example, children play 'martyrs', representing and re-enacting the only reality they know. Likewise, in the Western world, children's play reflect a consumerist culture, the changing face of families, the limited availability of physical, outdoor space and the perceived risks from the outside world (Concu and Gaskins, 2006).

Traditionally, research on play has had a strong developmental psychology focus where the function of play was examined along its impact on the development of certain capacities in children. Developmental psychology theories have contributed to drawing universal patterns in children's play (e.g., engaging in pretend games) considerably; however, the complexity and diversity of play contexts have not been thoroughly examined. Children's play is not a function in isolation that occurs at certain stages of children's development to facilitate learning; it is not a means to an end but a significant aspect of the human nature. Culture-specific considerations of children's play entail notions of the age that children are expected to stop playing, gender differences, artefacts and the symbolic significance given to objects and rituals and the degrees of adult involvement/supervision. Children's play has a universal and diachronic quality in that, across human cultures, children display a strong desire to play. At the same time, play is relational and contextual and central to human development and community cohesion.

Children's play or adults' play?

Increasingly, the movement of children in public spaces is becoming organized and controlled by adults. There is a tendency in our society for children to engage in structured, often adult-determined and adult-controlled activities that fulfil a specific purpose. In the past, children had been allowed out to construct their own spaces; however, fears about real or perceived dangers have resulted in mapping out children's days in a series of adult-organized and supervised activities. The breaking down of the neighbourhood relations has also restricted children's playing in a close proximity to their houses, in that their presence around a neighbourhood is perceived as public nuisance. Children rely on adults to transport them to clubs, sports centres, scouts or other places of organized activity that are not located within their neighbourhood.

An adult-structured and initiated play limits children's possibilities for self-expression and agency, e.g., self-determination and control. It also 'forces' children to imitate adult thought processes, by not allowing them space and time for fantasy play and supposition (Hyder, 2005). Likewise, it can be argued that a highly structured curriculum, especially in early years, may result in pushing children to approximate adult-type of thinking and problem solving which may be counterproductive to their development. Adult supervision and organization of children's time and space are particularly evident in children with disabilities. Although in certain cases, depending on the magnitude and implications of disability, constant adult support is necessary, there has been limited research on whether adult involvement contributes to children's disablement. The views of children with disability about the ways in which they negotiate space with adults and their experience of fear in public spaces are rarely acknowledged.

Children's opportunities for play, friendship development and exploration of the physical environment are denied in the name of safety and protection (Lansdown, 2001). The increase in the adult control of children's mobility has undermined the value of a free-flow play where children negotiate ways of constructing and responding to their surroundings, and reduced opportunities towards ownership of play (Bruce, 1997). Results from the Good Childhood Inquiry corroborate these views by stating that children engage in limited unstructured, self-initiated play, impacting on their development of social problem solving skills and a capacity to negotiate and resolve conflict (Children's Society, 2007). Moreover, in the YPSA survey, nearly a quarter of young people reported that they were not given enough freedom by their parents, stressing that some parents place constraints on children to keep them safe.

UK governmental guidelines, such as the Child Safety Week, reinforce adult involvement by perpetuating parental anxiety and fears with regard to children's safety. These guidelines also exacerbate children's vulnerability, losing sight of their resilience and the strengths that families bring into protecting children. Children need to be given responsibility about risk taking, and the chance to make mistakes and learn from them (Gill, 1999), and for society to become more tolerant of children's mistakes instead of criminalizing them.

The culture of supervision and entertainment that has been set up by adults leaves little psychological and critical space for children to entertain themselves, to find ways out of boredom and construct their own fantasy worlds. Not spending their after-school time with friends makes children more dependent on adults to organize their activities. Moreover, children who grow up with the view that adults are there to either entertain them or set up the activities for them are less likely to develop initiative and self-regulation as adults (Alanen, 1992; Kiili, 1998: 30–31; Pennanen, 2000).

There is a fine balance between safety/support and social control of children's lives. Research has shown that being alone at home after school was seen by seven-year-olds as a positive rather than a negative experience; they had opportunities to do things that their parents would have otherwise forbidden them to do (Kiili, 1998). The 'home alone' discourse equates being alone with being lonely and vulnerable. This argument needs to be revisited because constant adult supervision may hamper children's capacity for self-reflection and autonomy. Likewise, in his book *Solitude*, Storr acknowledged the benefits of solitude, arguing that the capacity to be alone is essential for children's creative development (1988). According to him, solitude not only fosters creativity, but also helps children to relate to their own and others' feelings. This view counteracts current schools' views that children should be kept constantly busy, with no time to be still, daydream, reflect or play (Ward, 2006).

Chapter 5

Children's Physical, Social/Critical and Virtual Spaces

Over the last decades, the physical space occupied by young people has started to shrink, and with it, their social interactions and peer conversations. Young people's limited movement in public spaces due to road traffic and regimented views about the design of children's outdoor spaces do not encourage children to transform space and create their own imaginary worlds (Aarnikko et al., 2002).

Children's spaces, be they physical, social or virtual, are not neutral; they reflect power structures and relationships. The meaning attached to social places that are used for different purposes is typically decided by adults in authority. Spaces influence children's identity formation and how they view themselves (Gupta and Ferguson, 1997; Christensen et al., 2000). Children do not always have ownership of spaces and thus they try to create their own subspaces by defining their limits and situating activities within certain spatial parameters. In so doing, they negotiate limits and define boundaries, exercising communication and problem solving skills. Even when they operate within highly organized spaces, children actively apply competent strategies to negotiate, resist, adapt and show 'strategic competence' (Eerola-Pennanen, 2002).

Physical Spaces

Recently, there seems to be an increasing intolerance of children in public areas (Lansdown, 2001). Children have a restricted access to public space; and when there, they are met with adults' distance, encountering suspicion and distrust. State regulation also promotes that children should be 'off the streets', in that being on streets is equated with anti-social behaviour. Spending time on the streets however helps children learn and test social skills, and develop a sense of ownership of their neighbourhood. Tim Gill, in his article Cotton Wool Revolution, advocates children's need to develop resilience and problem solving capacities through their engage-ment with the real world (2007). He stresses the importance of offering opportunities to children to learn from their mistakes, and develop capaci-ties for negotiation through interactions with both adults and peers, beyond their home and school settings.

A restricted physical space reduces opportunities for self-organization and experimentation in children. Shayer found that, compared with the 1990s, children's cognitive abilities have been declining as part of a down-ward trend from the 1970s, possibly, due to a limited experiential play (2006). He reported that, without time to play outside, children were being deprived of vital experiences with regard to role-playing and social interac-tion. Louv's views on re-engaging children with nature have also been timely (2005). He coined the term Nature Deficit Disorder, and offers an interest-ing, albeit pathologizing, perspective on the impact of a decreased physical space on children's development.

Guy Debord, a French philosopher and situationist in the 1950s, coined the term psycho-geography to study the effects of the geographical environ-ment on people's emotions and behaviour. Psychogeography is understood as an 'active search for, and celebration of, chance and coincidence, con-currently with the divination of patterns and repetitions thrown up by the [meeting/collision] of the chaos and structures of cities, personal histories and interpretations'.

One may ask what the psychogeography of childhood is, and to what extent the restrictions placed on community usage of public space, through privatization and gentrification, affect it. The physical space in neighbour-hoods is gradually transformed into commercial spaces, e.g., theme parks and shopping malls, where artificial constructions are made for children to experience them passively, as spectators, without being able to transform them and exercise their creativity. Moreover, activities that are organized by adults tend to occupy a specific area, governed by rules, allowing limited opportunities for children to explore, interact with peers and test models of acceptable behaviour. The 'fantasy worlds' have been constructed for children by adults, shaping their physical space in ways that are artificial, commercialized and controlled.

Research evidence stresses the importance for children to have access to good and free local spaces within their neighbourhoods, where they can play unsupervised. In the Needs Analysis study, many young people acknowl-edged that there are not any commercial or non-commercial places left in their neighbourhood to meet with their friends, resorting in bus shelters, each others' houses and parks as places for socialization. Young carers in this study expressed the desire to spend time in natural places within their neighbourhood, but felt that 'sometimes they do not feel welcome' when they gather in public places within their immediate neighbourhood, i.e., 'the park across the road'. Two young carers from the same neighbourhood, in particular, talked about how much they enjoy going to a river, close to where they live. They also stressed the need to have more places for sports activities located within their neighbourhoods.

Furthermore, children's physical space has been violated by imposing control and restrictions and reducing its spatial integrity through the destruction of the natural environment (e.g., excessive paving of gardens) and violence in streets. In the Needs Analysis study, half of the young people from the bullying group stated that they do not find the parks in their locality to be safe 'because there are gangs there and we cannot go, they ruin it'. They recommended the creation of parks that are 'guarded so we can go there' where a third child offered a suggestion to have 'a park for the gangs only and have cameras to watch them'. Children from the LDD group suggested that they would prefer to join activities in their locality and access to non-commercial areas such as parks, stating

> there's several parks near where I live, the council's cleared one near the crow's nest that's very bad it had glass smashed but the council's cleared it up . . . It makes you feel a lot better also there was a circle and three handles and it was very thin you had to aim yourself and let go at the right moment.

Restrictions in physical and social geographies are likely to result in limitations in children's critical exchanges, interaction and dialogue. Dialogue characterizes equal relationships; however with public space becoming increasingly privatized, power inequality is likely to transform interactions between children and adults from being dialectical and constructive to becoming regulated and contrived.

Social/Critical Spaces

The existence of physical spaces is likely to stimulate the formation of social/critical spaces where children are encouraged to engage in conversations, test assumptions and beliefs, accept difference and forge relationships. A social/critical space is dialogic and integrated, and functions as an important platform for socialization, especially for young people from diverse social–cultural, religious and economic backgrounds. Knowles extends the concept of children's spaces beyond their physical dimension, carrying the meaning of 'a domain of social practices and relationships' (1999: 241). Dahlberg and Moss describes cultural spaces as a platform where 'values, rights and cultures are created', children's voices are heard and dialogue and critical thinking is encouraged (2005: 29).

Young carers in the Needs Analysis study referred to a critical space that emerged as they negotiated with various professionals who entered their lives, and showed resistance when they felt that the professionals' input was not relevant to their circumstances.

Many young carers expressed uneasiness about 'people [professionals] visiting their house' and engaged in negotiation. They offered statements such as

> they [professionals] come and talk and talk and they do not do anything and then they leave or we make them leave, or I do not want them around because they pick on you and how you do things.

Friendships transform the physical and spatial parameters of children's spaces. Children, when interacting with friends, are more likely to explore physical spaces and maximize the opportunities it entails for testing social and conversational skills. Children's friendships also offer possibilities to counteract the increasing polarization of some communities.

Young people's friendships

The important role that friendships play in children's social, emotional and linguistic development has been documented in a plethora of research studies from within the developmental psychology and sociology. The influence of peer relationships extends from children's linguistic development (e.g., Donahue and Bryan, 1984), moral development (e.g., Damon, 1983) to social skills development (e.g., Grenot-Scheyer, 2004). The positioning of friends in young people's life has been recently reaffirmed (e.g., Children's Society, 2007; Hartas and Lindsay, 2007, UNICEF, 2007). In the Good Childhood Inquiry, 46 per cent young people said that they would talk to their friends, as a first port of call, followed by 35 per cent who would choose a parent (Children's Society, 2007). Four years ago, the results obtained from the YPSA survey indicated that 65 per cent of young people would turn to their mother when they feel down or upset, following by best friends as indicated by 42 per cent of young people (Park, Phillips and Johnson, 2004). This shift in the relative positioning of parents and friends further highlights the importance of friendships for young people.

This is an interesting trend, emerging at a time when the number of teen-agers without a close/best friend has increased, since 1986, from one in eight to one in five. Moreover, the number of peer-initiated assaults, e.g., bullying, have increased by 50 per cent over the last three decades (Children's Society, 2007). It appears that young people approach peer interaction and friendships as a refuge, a space that is separate from adults', where they construct a world with its own language, norms and culture.

In the Needs Analysis study, almost all young people stated that talking to friends, especially those who can be trusted, helps them to deal with stress. Specifically, they stated that, in moments of crisis, they would talk to friends first, followed by parents, teachers and pets. Young people from the bully-ing and young carers groups in particular valued having free time to socialize with friends, suggesting that time has become a precious commod-ity. Free time for social interaction and conversation was also seen as being crucial for resolving tension in schools. Children from the bullying group observed that

> what you can do is to give more opportunities to people to talk because if they have extra time they go and play sports and they do not talk to each other, this can solve many problems.

Young carers also stressed the importance of

> having time in our rooms and we can go there any time and be by yourself and write your thoughts and also talk with others in a relaxing place.

The young people's views about friends were found to differ as a function of their gender and social class. In the YPSA survey, girls from households of low income (e.g., less than 3,999 pounds per year) would rather spend time with family than friends. A diametrically opposite view was offered from boys from similar households who stated that they would rather spend time with friends than family. Also, among young people from house-holds with income at the 20,000 plus mark, girls, compared to boys, expressed a preference to spend time with friends rather than family.

These results suggest that social class influences young people's friend-ships differently for boys and girls. It appears that, for boys who experience socio-economic disadvantage, friends offer a refuge, possibly, the only plat-form for socialization. For girls, acceptance into peer groups is likely to require the social and cultural capital that is typically associated with middle-class practices. Better-off households are likely to offer social net-works that can support girls into forming relationships with their peers.

These results also suggest that girls are likely to experience multiple disadvantage, due to poverty, in terms of having a limited access to material resources and also social networks and friendships.

Young people's friendships were further examined by considering their ethnicity and gender. Across ethnic groups, girls reported a much smaller number of friends compared to that reported by boys. Specifically, girls of Black African and Black Caribbean origin have the smallest number of friends (approximately 3–4), compared to those who are of White European or Mixed origin (approximately 10). This is consistent with previous research suggesting that friendships among girls tend to be more exclusive and less extensive, whereas boys position themselves within larger groups and are likely to acquire a large number of friends (Pellegrini and Blatchford, 2000). Among boys, those of Black Caribbean origin have the largest number of friends (approximately 30), which is in stark difference to the small number of friends that Black boys of African origin have (approximately 1–2). White European boys appear to occupy the middle ground, having around 15 friends, with Asian boys having approximately 10 friends.

These results show that the number of boys' close friends varies hugely depending on their ethnic background, reflecting different cultural and socialization practices. Certain ethnic groups place more emphasis on interactions between family members and the formation of close-knit communities that offer the space within which friendships are likely to flourish. Other ethnic groups may place an emphasis on developing 'horizontal' social networks that expand their family and immediate community to include individuals from other social groups and communities, diversifying their social interactions.

Friendships among the same: zones of exclusion

Children show a preference to socialize with other young people with whom they share similarities not only in terms of interests but also in culture and lifestyle (Children's Society, 2007, UNICEF, 2007). Similarity has been found to influence the formation and maintenance of interpersonal relationships at three inter-related levels, namely, attitude similarity, demographic similarity and similarity in personality (Rubin, 1973). Although Rubin's research took place more than three decades ago, the results are still pertinent. In the UNICEF study, young people were found to prefer interactions with peers with whom they share similar characteristics, mainly demographic characteristics such as ethnicity and socioeconomic status.

Young people felt that interacting with peers with whom they share simi-larities is easier due to common cultural references and norms, and thus communication and meaning construction were less complicated. The exis-tence of a common ground is likely to enable young people to forge strong relationships; however, it may create zones of exclusion. Peer interactions based on similarity in social attitudes and perspectives are characterized by consensus, often confirming the 'rightness' of young people's beliefs, which may reduce opportunities for critical engagement, reinforcing a 'clique' mentality.

The Good Childhood Inquiry found that young people become increas-ingly segregated; those from minority ethnic backgrounds are twice as likely to socialize exclusively with peers from their own communities. It is not easy to ascertain the nature of the link between certain socialization trends and social segregation. Are young people's socialization styles the symptom or the outcome of segregation? Living in segregated communities, young peo-ple are more likely to socialize with peers in close geographical and social proximity, which, in turn, results in further segregation by limiting contact with peers from diverse social groups who may maximize access to educa-tion/training and employment opportunities.

In the Needs Analysis study, the young carers commented that it is diffi-cult to relate to peers with whom they do not share similar life experiences. They felt confident to talk about family and personal issues with other car-ers they meet, functioning as an outlet to their feelings, and realizing that they are not alone. Others stressed that the issue is not (and should not be) whether they are perceived favourably by peers, but making the first steps towards social relatedness. This is reflected in statements such as 'I talk to other people although sometimes I know they do not understand my life'.

Young people with LDD stated that they form friendships with peers who also display difficulties at the special schools and after-school clubs they attend. They reported to enjoy going to community centres to meet other young people with similar experiences and learning needs,

> some of your friends you're quite close with you'll have like a joke a few
> things that are quite personal and other people you're friends with but
> not that close you're (not going to talk about) personal things.

In such settings, they feel confident to talk about 'personal things', depend-ing on 'how serious they [other children] are' (serious in terms of the degree of difficulty/disability they display). Young people with LDD described the attributes of a good friend along the lines of 'one who helps' and offers 'emotional support'. Supporting, in this case, was confined to helping with homework, and did not involve any outside-the-school activities. This is consistent with previous research done with Israeli adolescents with mild learning disabilities in two different settings, i.e., mainstream and special education (Heiman, 2000).

In the literature on friendships in children with disabilities, six frames of friendship between disabled and non-disabled peers have been observed, namely the 'ghosts and guests' (invisible social status); inclusion kid (different treatment either positive or negative); helping (offering assistance to peers with disabilities); just another kid (no difference in treatment); regular friends (as being part of a larger group); and friends for ever (best friend) (Grenot-Scheyer, 2004). Friendships do not feature prominently in children with LDD; achieving the 'best friend' status is rarely attainable. The children with LDD who attended special schools talked about having 'lots of friends', and nearly half of them remarked that they did not have any friends at their previous schools (i.e., mainstream schools). For some children with disabilities, the driving principle behind mainstreaming, i.e., benefiting from interacting with non-disabled peers in mainstream classrooms, has not as yet been materialized.

The existence of a social and critical space is particularly important for children and young people with disabilities who have limited opportunities for partaking in integrated activities with non-disabled children. Data from the Needs Analysis pointed to a growing concern of meeting the socialization needs of young people with disabilities in centres where 'mainstream' children do not partake in joint activities. Children with learning difficulties/disabilities rely on clubs and organized activities for socialization (e.g., 'I like mostly clubs because you know you've got friends there where it's harder to make friends in the park'). Almost all children with learning difficulties/disabilities in this study put parents as a first point of contact in moments of crisis, and around seven of them stated that they do not have any close friends. They also stated that they do not play in the neighbourhood, mainly because of the high incidence of bullying, and the limited independence they enjoy in terms of participating in outside-the-house activities. With this in mind, community centres and play schemes play an important role in offering children with disabilities opportunities for socialization and integration.

At present, an increasing emphasis is placed on young people offering their views on issues that concern them. However, they have limited opportunities to meet, talk and debate. To support the right to childhoods, a collective community action is required to ensure that children's physical, social and critical spaces remain intact. The need for these spaces is heightened when considering current changes in children's friendship culture, as manifested in their virtual interactions. Social spaces serve many socialization functions; they are places where children test skills and norms, understand cultural references and practices and get feedback from observing other people's reactions to what they say (Arendt, 1998). To this end, a unified children's space is required where physical, social, cultural and critical/dialectical dimensions are interwoven, and are constructed for both adults and children to interact with each other in a dynamic way. Early-care and after-care places have the potential to provide this unified space as long as they are transformed into Dahlberg's and Moss's notion of 'loci of ethical practices' where children's rights are based on care and responsibility (2005). Moreover, virtual spaces have the potential to bring together the social, cultural and critical/dialectical dimensions in young people's interactions.

Virtual Spaces

From its initial conception, the internet has been viewed as a tool that brings people together, creating virtual communities that transcend geographical boundaries and societal structures. The proliferation of 'social networking' websites such as MySpace, YouTube and Facebook was initially greeted with widespread enthusiasm, but also fears about their impact on children's socialization and friendship development. The use of the internet and mobile phones offers a virtual space that is less adult controlled, a 'virtual plaza', where people can meet without restrictions (Mäenpää, 2000: 135–136; Kopomaa, 2000: 20, 49).

The internet-based social networks are described as 'mediated publics', internet-mediated spaces where people interact. An important question is in what ways internet-mediated publics are different from other public spaces, both commercial, e.g., shopping malls, cafes; and non-commercial, e.g., parks. At first glance, access, regulation and ownership differentiate virtual from physical spaces. A virtual space is not owned by adults as much as a physical space is, minimizing hierarchies and the presence of authority, with the activities and choices being child-initiated and organized (Matthews et al., 2000).

A virtual space is flexible and can be made by children to accommodate their requirements and interests, rather than children fitting into the structures of the physical spaces mediated by adults. In a virtual space, socialization and learning become decentred in terms of location, authority structures, rules and norms. Although this new mode of communication has come to fill a vacuum felt by children's shrinking physical space, it is debatable whether the social and psychological distance between young people is diminished, or it has become of a different nature.

In the cyberspace, intimacy and disclosure during friendships have taken a new form, and leisure time has become privatized. The scale of the interaction and the heterogeneity and diversity of participants, especially as messages can reach large audiences, alter the meaning of self-disclosure and friendship. In the virtual space, friendships are formed through a mutual assertion. A young person is asked by another if he/she likes to be friends and then their names are added to each others' lists. Becoming friends does not result from developing close ties over a period of time; rather, it is an instant decision based on similarities in features, characteristics and tastes. Friends appearing in network lists tend to be those with whom the young person shares similar views about music and lifestyle choices (Boyd, 2006).

In the Needs Analysis study, all young people stressed the importance of accessing communication technology, e.g., mobiles and internet. Almost all visit social networking sites in the internet, e.g., Bebo, and MSN for messaging. Although they like the idea of having many virtual friends (e.g., 'on bebo it tells you how many friends you have, and you realize you have more friends than you actually think, makes you feel good'), they stressed that having 'internet friends only would not have been enough'.

Interestingly, the linguistic and conversational patterns young people displayed during their virtual interactions were similar to those used in conventional physical places. When they talked about their virtual interactions, they described their activities in similar terms with those used to talk about their everyday life. For example, they talked about 'going around with friends and visiting each others' houses' in the cyberspace. Another child talked about internet-based interventions for bullies in one of the social networks sites he visits, describing it

> there is a room where they put all the bullies and talk to them about what they did and ask them why, felt angry and wanted to take out of my system.

The way language is used may suggest that young people perceive a small distance between their real and virtual encounters. To them, internet-mediated environments remove the barriers that exist in physical spaces, offering a sense of continuity in their life, especially for children with

transient lifestyles, e.g., those who have moved to different schools/locali-
ties a great deal

> it is good because if you move to a different school or place you can still
> have them and talk to them.

Another explanation may be that young people are at ease with virtual
interactions in the cyberspace because they resemble real life. If I take
Baudrillard's view that a real society is, in a sense, a simulated society
(1983) where simulations, e.g., symbols and signs, have replaced tangible
entities, then the distance between real and computer-mediated environments becomes not as wide as previously thought.

Internet-based interactions exceed conventional time for socializing with
friends (e.g., 'sometimes I just phone my friends on their mobile in the
middle of the night and they talk to me'). Moreover, they offer a sense of
emotional closeness for young people to feel confident to talk about personal issues, in that 'you can have private emails . . . and it is easier to talk to
them when it is not face to face'. However, they are aware of the possibility
of false identities, stating

> internet friends can be anyone and you do not know who they are; it is
> good if you know who they are. My mate has a girlfriend who is much
> older than he is.

Some interesting trends are emerging with regard to the nature and func-
tion/role of virtual friendships in young people. Among young people, the
use of the internet and mobile phones offers a sense of continuity, but also
promotes an element of temporary and provisional, in which agreements
can be made and altered quickly, spontaneously and flexibly (Kopomaa,
2000: 49–56). Disclosure is short lived, in that the information posted
changes very quickly and, although young people have a space to talk, the
influx of information and the limited time given to its posting may not allow
for emotional bonds to be built. Perhaps, we are moving towards a new way
of youth socialization where building bonds and differentiating between real
and public personas may not be important features for social connectedness.
Within internet-mediated social communities, a growing number of young
people represent themselves to others through a digital persona,[4] constructed via the use of video clips, text, pictures or music. This form of public
self-representation requires further examination to delineate the boundaries between the real, the perceived and the digitally constructed self.

During virtual interactions, friendships develop provisionally and intimacy becomes diffused. In conventional friendships, adolescents tend to gravitate towards an emotional rather than a physical proximity with others, with language and communication skills becoming particularly important for disclosure and exploration of feelings and meanings (e.g., Donahue, Hartas and Cole, 1999). Livingston observed that in virtual encounters, young people have seventy-five and not five friends, as in more conventional face-to-face interactions (Livingstone and Bober, 2004). In this context, intimacy means connected to a community of peers and 'feelings can be intense but distributed and not individual' with privacy not relating to a physical space. Young people may find themselves in a position to disclose personal information and views to a large number of people. One may ask whether these relational patterns can actually lead to a more tolerant society, a culture of openness. What is then the nature of disclosure, and is there a difference between young people's public and private/real persona? Possibly, in virtual encounters, who young people 'really are' is not a marker of individualism and identity.

Internet-mediated interactions display features that are not typically present in 'real' social interactions. In these networks, conversations leave a trace, a record that can be transferred or copied into other places. Electronic transference entails the danger of doctoring, which raises the issue of authenticity of sources. In internet-mediated social interactions, one may ask whether establishing authenticity actually matters. Moreover, an internet audience is hard to define, and this has implications regarding the nature of self-disclosure, visibility/invisibility of voices and legitimacy in knowing with certainty whose voice is. In face-to-face interactions, we rely on a multitude of contextual signs available through body language and cultural artefacts, assisting us with the interpretation and deciphering of meanings. Young people are deprived of semiotics during internet-mediated interactions, and this is likely to impact on their capacity to engage critically with the information they receive.

The use of the internet has been blamed for the limited civic engagement in young people. Many argue that the downward trend in people's face-to-face interactions can be attributed to virtual social networking, although it is not clear whether it a cause or an effect. Children's experiences are mediated by the media, which give them a platform to observe others, offering the illusion of participation without the need for reciprocity and commitment, reinforcing a voyeuristic experience. On a positive note, the virtual space can offer an arena for political participation and activism and a medium for political expression. In American university campuses, students vote or protest via these social sites. An example of this occurred when thousands of American teens used MySpace to organize protests against US immigration policies (Melber 2006). Cross-border activism and the creation of a cosmopolitan identity may be facilitated through technology-mediated interactions.

Understanding the complex virtual topography of children's lives requires us to reconsider current views about the impact of technology on socialization and reappraise the nature of the social interactions and relationships that are formed in the cyberspace. This would require a closer examination of the virtual, imagined or real relationships, as well as the nature of the public and private personas assumed by internet users. Through virtual encounters, young people may develop empathy and emotional intelligence, and a capacity for civic participation. The question remains how.

Chapter 6

Children's Happiness and Well-being

Exploring the literature on happiness within the field of education, it becomes apparent that there is limited research on children's and young people's happiness. The lack of research on children's happiness and its impact on human development, especially within education, is startling. There seems to be an assumption that happiness is a by-product or outcome (but not its precursor) of inclusive educational practices. In contrast, within the fields of psychology and economics, there are many studies exploring subjective indicators of happiness and their relation to measures such as individuals' health and well-being, employment and social capital. Some psychological studies offer evidence that children's happiness sets the stage for learning, creativity and good inter-personal relationships, functioning as a 'buffer' that protects individuals from adversity and negative life events (e.g., Argyle and Martin, 1991).

The landscape of children's happiness in the United Kingdom is troubling. Current research findings indicate that depression is more widespread than previously thought; it has been estimated that at least 25 per cent of the general population becomes clinically depressed at some point in their lives (Lewinsohn et al., 1991). By 2020, childhood depression is predicted to be the second most important cause of disability in children (WHO, 2001). Moreover, there has been a substantial increase in suicide rates between the 1970s and the 1990s for boys aged 15–19 years. This increase was associated with a rise in self-poisoning with vehicle exhaust gas in the 1980s and an increase in hanging which has continued into the 1990s. Although there was a slight decrease in the official suicide rates for females aged 15–19 years, the 'undetermined' deaths have increased. There is no indication of a major change in suicide rate in 10–14-year-olds' (McClure, 2001).

More than 4,000 children under 14 have attempted to take their own life in the past year, according to a report by the Information Centre for Health and Social Care that includes NHS data in the United Kingdom (2007). The figures reveal that 69 children attempted to hang or suffocate themselves and 2 tried to drown themselves. Many took overdoses of medicines, drugs or solvents in an effort to end their lives, but some resorted to more extreme measures. Thirteen children leapt from a great height, while four lay or jumped in front of a moving vehicle. One child attempted suicide by deliberately crashing a car. These statistical figures on suicide suggest an alarming trend with regard to children's mental health status. The deterioration in children's mental health and subjective well-being requires a profound cultural shift, and parents, educators and policy makers should engage with it.

The Role of Education in Children's Happiness

Traditionally, caring and the attainment of happiness in children have been the responsibility of the parents, the extended family and immediate community. However, for many children, the notion of a 'village', or a community of carers, is no longer applicable; many children experience a void of care, partly perpetuated by adults' anxiety and fears about actual or perceived dangers in the community. Most crucially, in this climate of paranoia and anxiety, some children may perceive others as a danger and, possibly, grow up with a limited capacity to care and empathize with others.

Increasingly, schools are expected to prepare children for both public and personal life. This view emerges at a time when children spend a great deal of time in educational institutions (e.g., early care and after-school care places). The assumption that underlies the discussion on the role of education in supporting young people attain happiness is that happiness can be learned. Research studies have shown that happy people display certain characteristics such as 'identity integrity', 'ego-strength', 'mental maturity', 'inner control', 'social ability', 'activity' and 'perceptual openness' (Veenhoven, 1991: 28). Extroversion, as a personality characteristic, has also been repeatedly found to relate to happiness. Extrovert people appear to have a more positive outlook to life and tend to smile more, initiate conversation more, and display certain verbal behaviours such as laughing or joking during social interactions (Argyle and Martin, 1991). One may argue that a civic education that acknowledges and respects difference, and places children's rights and citizenship at its centre, is likely to support young people to develop characteristics that are conducive to happiness.

Noddings asks to what extent schools within liberal democracies should prepare children for personal life, through the development of emotional intelligence, empathy, bonding, and, most crucially, contribute to the attainment of happiness (2003). She argues that responsive educational systems can contribute to the happiness of all, as long as schools take on roles that, traditionally, were assigned to family in preparing children for adult life by teaching them parenting and other everyday skills.

Noddings' account of happiness is based on the ethics of care which involve a relational understanding of how children relate to others, self, objects, bodies, ideas, conditions and reflective moments (Vanhuysse and Sabbagh, 2005). She offers a critique on Aristotle's emphasis on reason and intellectual powers as a means of attaining happiness, and also on the utilitarian views of happiness as the absence of pain as articulated by Hume and Mill.[5] Noddings argues against inflicting pain and suffering on others, especially in the context of education, through punishment and humiliation, and expose children to a 'justified' suffering, which robs them from the capacity to empathize and care for others (2003). Education should be able to accentuate the natural capacity that children already possess to infer others' emotional and mental states and respond to actual or perceived distress.

There is a growing realization that the space in education allocated for spiritual life, self-realization and happiness is limited. Even when an emphasis is placed on young people's personal well-being, it is often misguided in that it reinforces a climate of individualization and egotism that emanates from a view of happiness as meeting personal needs. Schools are governed by a restrictive logic, seeing their role as preparing individuals to contribute to future economies (Vanhuysse and Sabbagh, 2005). Happiness has become an artificial construction pursued within an individualization of children's life. In our feel-good society, a Disney-type happiness is based on the satisfaction of personal needs, whereas suffering tends to be seen as a punishment and not as an opportunity for reflection and re-evaluation. Happiness is understood through the lens of consumption, which, through the acquisition of goods, children feel better. Feeling good, however, is separate from being or doing good, pointing to an ephemeral and artificial sense of happiness without any moral purpose to which children are exposed daily. Research reviewed by Veenhoven suggests that, in order to go beyond the satisfaction of needs, schools should promote in children a contemplative attitude to life (1991).

Another way of maximizing happiness is by adjusting the gap between aspirations and achievement (Michalos, 1985), and approaching stoicism as a practice for moderating aspirations. However, one may argue that aspirations in young people may be constructed in a top-down manner, with the market economies creating more and more aspirations that cannot be met, considering some individuals' limited access to resources and social capital.

High aspirations are not necessarily a threat to happiness, especially for those who experience multiple disadvantage, as long as young people are supported sufficiently to meet the demands placed on them by complex, target-driven societies.

Although it is important for schools to develop a less technicist agenda and prepare children for personal life, the debate should not be centred on replacing certain curriculum areas with others. Offering a good quality of teaching and learning, as well as organizational support can shift the current target-orientated culture in schools. A large number of young people display difficulties clustered as low motivation to learn, behavioural difficulties, emotional distress, limited emotional intelligence and empathy, difficulties with language use for communication and disaffection. To enhance young people's well-being within the schools requires educators and parents to debate the nature of knowledge and morality (see Chapter 11, for a detailed discussion on civic education and its associated pedagogies) to support children develop a contemplative attitude towards life and society.

Many young people stated that areas such as youth socialization, bullying and conflict resolution in particular, should be incorporated into the school curriculum and approached at a whole-school level. However, a danger with this approach is to treat bullying, for example, as another curricular area. Schools should implement strategies that reflect their ethos, rather than, through over-regulation, to dictate how children should form friendships with whom and under what circumstances. Tackling bullying requires a maximization of children's physical, social and critical spaces to develop and test social knowledge. Lessons and open discussions about bullying, as well as young people's active participation in decision making at a whole-school level are likely to raise awareness about bullying and its wider implications. These may offer opportunities for students to decide on strategies that they deem effective in dealing with bullying (see Part IV for a discussion on young people as researchers towards tackling bullying).

Moreover, a reflective and self-evaluative attitude is required to offer the interpretive framework for young people to assign positive values to their life or a social situation (Csikszentmihalyi and Mei-Ha Wong, 1991). Within social and peer interactions, children engage in relationships that are mediated by their view of themselves as competent social beings. The happiness that young people may derive from peer interactions and friendships depends on their sense of control, the efficacy of their social skills and their capacity for empathy and commitment.

Friends and Happiness

Happiness is the cornerstone of children's well-being, and is closely related to the presence of friends. A large number of studies stress the importance of inter-personal relationships in the attainment of happiness and the formation of caring communities (Argyle, 1987; Csikszentmihalyi and Larson, 1984; Lewinsohn et al., 1991). The factors that have been found to contribute to depression and unhappiness in young people include lack of social support from friends; low satisfaction with peer relationships; little potential availability of help from others; limited social intimacy and low self-perceived social skills (Lewinsohn et al., 1991: 164).

More recently, a submission in the Good Childhood Inquiry reported results from a survey of 2,527 primary and secondary school children in the north west of England stating that 63 per cent of children reported that friends is what makes them happy at school (Children's Society, 2007). Given the important role that friendships play in young people's mental health, happiness and social adjustment, raising awareness about bullying and its impact on children's social interactions is crucial.

Bullying

Over the last decade, there has been a growing recognition of bullying and its consequences (Mishna, 2003; Rigby, 2000; Roland, 2000). The effects of bullying are wide ranging from academic difficulties, to psychosocial functioning to physical health (Rigby, 2003). Bullying involves direct (e.g., physical aggression, name calling) and indirect (e.g., gossiping, social exclusion) behaviours. It is often triggered by a perceived imbalance of power, mainly based on perceptions of difference that constitute the bully superior and the victim inferior, and thus 'worthy' of being victimized.

Bullying is an everyday reality for many children occurring within school and community settings. Both bullies and their victims are at risk for psychological and social problems that persist into adulthood, with bullies often displaying delinquency and alcohol abuse (e.g.., Prinstein et al., 2001), whereas victims of bullying are at risk for depression, and are more likely to feel insecure, anxious and socially withdrawn (e.g., Pellegrini, 2003; Hodges and Perry, 1999). The Mental Health Foundation has delineated the implications of being a bully and experiencing bullying in terms of 'a high social and economic cost: criminal behaviour and alcohol abuse in bullies and depression and suicidal behaviour in their victims' (Children's Society, 2007).

LIVERPOOL JOHN MOORES UNIVERSITY
LEARNING SERVICES

Recent research by the UNICEF into children's well-being pointed out that children in the United Kingdom have the worst peer relationships in the European Union. In many studies, perceived as being 'different' is cited as the major factor in bullying. Bullying among children with disability is high, with 9 out of 10 people with learning disabilities have been bullied frequently (UNICEF, 2007). Especially at risk for bullying and social exclusion are young people with learning difficulties and disabilities (Kavale and Forness, 1996; Mishna, 2003). There is limited research on the characteristics that are likely to constitute young people with learning difficulties vulnerable to peer victimization.

Compared to their non-disabled peers, research involving children with learning difficulties point to an array of social difficulties due to lack of adequate social and conversational skills to express emotions and show empathy (e.g., Kavale and Forness, 1996; Pearl and Bay, 1999). Specifically, children with learning difficulties have been reported to engage in 'fewer peer interactions . . . and be less tactful and cooperative than normally-achieving peers' (Greenham, 1999; 174). Approximately, 25 per cent to 30 per cent of young people with learning difficulties are socially rejected compared to 8 per cent to 16 per cent of their peers without learning difficulties (ibid., 1999). Limited social interactions further contribute to becoming vulnerable to peer victimization (Pettit et al., 1999). Victims of bullying lack friends and are likely to become further isolated by peers which, in turn, makes them vulnerable to bullying.

Moreover, peer victimization of children with learning difficulties may be explained by the social stigma that is typically associated with difficulties and disabilities. Children's attitudes towards peers with disabilities are generally more negative than their attitudes towards children without disabilities (Roberts and Smith, 1999). This suggests that some typically developing children attribute disability to deficits within the individual rather than in social structures. Young people in the Needs Analysis study showed awareness of the social stigma attached to those caring for persons with disability, acknowledging its negative impact on their peer relationships. The young carers, in particular, did not disclose personal and family circumstances to friends; disclosure happens only within the context of established friendships. This view is reflected in the statement

> when I am with other people I am nervous talking about my family and I am too scared they gonna know about my stuff, it would be horrible if they find out about our details; it is a bit annoying when they find out that I am going to Carers group and that I went to Alton Towers and when I show them pictures they are like uhh.

The different shades of bullying

Some young people in the Needs Analysis study expressed the view that bullying has become a 'blanket' phrase that describes a wide range of behaviours, from minor disagreements between children that are 'part of growing up' to serious incidents of intimidation, psychological trauma and physical abuse. Some young people observed that the term 'bullying' has been used loosely, commenting that

> the word bullying is used too much, if you hit somebody only once then it is not bullying but if you hit them repeatedly then it is bullying, and warned that if you use the word freely everybody may say well it is not such a bad thing, everybody does it, I will do it too.

Others objected to this view, stating that references to bullying have not been used lightly because bullying is indeed part of their everyday reality. Some young people expressed concerns about differentiating between the intention to cause harm and ill-conceived joking that escalates into bullying. For younger children, the distinction between joking and bullying was rather simplistic, observing 'it is easy to differentiate because if it is an accident they say sorry, if it is not they say whatever'.

Older children commented that the degree of force or harshness displayed should differentiate bullying from mere accidents (e.g., 'if they are not harsh, they just joke but if they start picking on you then it is bullying'). Also, responsiveness to the victims' requests to stop was seen as an important factor (e.g., 'if it is just started, ask them to stop and if they stop it is ok'). A couple of children talked about the frequency of the occurrence of bullying incidents as a differentiating factor (e.g., 'if they pick on you and do it a lot I tell the teacher to sort it out because they are bullies').

The young people commented that the severity of bullying should not be judged in terms of 'how long and how harsh it is because they need to know that the other person may get hurt easily'. They presented pre-mediated bullying with the intent to cause harm as being an extreme case of bullying, requiring severe punishment. Teenagers from the bullying group also discussed the difficulties of recognizing subtle bullying, 'the problem with this is that sometimes it is hard to identify the bully, if they do things not very obvious'.

The young people recommended that bullying should be dealt with at a whole-school level at the start of the school year, e.g., 'at the start of the year teachers in every class should have a talk about expectations and what you can do in case of bullying'. Moreover, they recommended that they should also be involved in drawing the distinction between bullying and mere accidents, stressing

> we are young teens and we should be given a bit of a freedom to do things and make decisions about what joking and what bullying is.

They all agreed about the importance of delineating the differences between bullying and other incidents in order to address its implications properly. As is encapsulated in the following statement, the boundaries between bullying and certain socialization practices are not clear cut.

> some people think, oh I hit someone, and thus I am a bully, or the other way around, I hit and I insult them once and then maybe I'll do it again, it is a little bit of fun without realising that this may be really hurtful.

There is also a view that the discourse on bullying offers an over-inflated view of children's social interactions, and their capacity to exercise responsibility and resolve conflict (e.g., Gill, 1999, 2007; Pellegrini and Blatchford, 2000). Everyday childhood activities such as name calling or exclusion from the peer group are being grouped under the umbrella of bullying, stressing the importance to differentiate among degrees of bullying, as well as between innocent joking and bullying. Pellegrini and Blatchford argue that systems to combat bullying may be more damaging than are the bullying incidents themselves. They pointed out that teasing may perform a social purpose in that it helps to 'denote limits . . . define and consolidate friendships, [suggest] sharpness in social discourse and [negotiate] for status' (2000).

The impact of bullying

Consistently, research on the effects of bullying indicates poor social adjustment in terms of children displaying an aversion to school; loneliness in adulthood; difficulties maintaining interpersonal relationships; psychological distress manifested in terms of chronic anxiety, fear and depression; and physical ill-health symptoms such as psychosomatic complaints (tummy aches) (e.g., Rigby, 2003).

There is some evidence that bullying is widespread in families and communities. In the Needs Analysis study, young people observed that bullying is not constrained within the school setting but also extends to families, communities and the cyberspace. One young person said

> well someone in my family was bullied . . . difficult environment . . . bullies like . . . used to hit my mother and stuff . . . we talk a lot about it.

Another person reported an incident of bullying involving step siblings, whereas many young people talked about bullying incidents in the neighbourhood, i.e., streets and parks, reflected in statements such as

> I was in a park and a boy with his mates from school and they started taking the phone from me and kicking their ball on me;
>
> when I go to the playground, kids whisper about my face and I do not play there, I leave;
>
> I was bullied at a birthday party, they hit me, and it was terrible.

The fear and threat, actual or perceived, of bullying in the neighbourhood limits young people's movement. They expressed comments such as 'If you go outside you may be too scared to do anything, you walk to home quick' or 'there is a man that was scary and followed me home and I was scared'. These views may also reflect parental anxiety about dangers in the community that is communicated to their children. The fact that bullying happens in families and communities is a huge challenge, but also presents an opportunity to engage parents to play an active role in tackling bullying.

Regarding cyber-bullying, divided views were offered regarding its impact. Around half of the children stated that cyber bullying can be controlled in that users of certain social sites can report the bully to the moderator of the social network (e.g., 'you can control it because you can block them and delete them'). Others described cyber bullying as not real ('made up') because it does not involve physical confrontation (e.g., they can't touch you on the internet), whereas a couple of children thought of it as offering a good piece of evidence against the bully (e.g., 'if you receive a written message then it is good evidence you go and show it to teachers').

Older children stressed the negative impact of bullying, observing that whether real or virtual, it hurts (e.g., 'It can get into your head and affect you'). A couple of secondary school pupils stated that the ramifications of bullying can be long lasting, and the 'trauma caused takes time to heal'. They also talked about the difficulty with non-continuous communication in their internet-mediated interactions which does not allow them to respond to the bully immediately (e.g., 'they come off the chat line and you cannot get back to them'). Finally, some children were concerned about bullies' concealed identity in that 'you do not know who they are, they may use another name'.

Overall, young people stressed that bullying poses obstacles to their learning and achieving academically. Specifically, they delineated the impact of bullying on learning in terms of

- frustration/crying (e.g., 'it affected my maths work I always had problems because one of my eyes has a muscular problem and I was crying all the time and it was fuzzy');
- unhappiness (e.g., 'bullying can make you unhappy and then you do not learn, because it messes up your head');
- loss of concentration (e.g., 'it disturbs their concentration, always thinking: what shall I do, shall I raise my hand and they will think that I am being nerdy but if I keep my hand down they will bully me for not answering the question);
- loss of confidence (e.g., 'when I was bullied it knocked my confidence and I got a bit shy for a year, and a bit scared. I was ok after that');
- shyness (e.g., 'it takes more time to talk to other people and work with them in the class');
- classroom participation (e.g., 'I did not raise my hand in the class so I do not get bullied for that');
- school attendance (e.g., 'you are scared to come to school because you do not know what is going to happen'); and
- school change (e.g., 'I was moved from my previous school for being accused for bullying').

These findings are consistent with research on the impact of bullying on children's academic achievement, social participation, positive peer interactions and well-being (see Mishna, 2003 for a review).

Resilience

Some of the young people in the Needs Analysis study showed assertiveness and self-confidence in the face of bullying by taking the initiative to confront the bully to protect either a friend or a family member from peer victimization. Assertiveness is particularly important in breaking the 'culture of silence' (Smith and Shu, 2000: 210), altering the role of a bystander from that of showing apathy to becoming active in tackling bullying. Young carers who look after siblings with disabilities felt confident to ascertain the rights of their brothers/sisters.

I do take some risks sometimes, if somebody tries to get to my brother I tell them you need to get me first and I make sure they are not near to my brother and I don't care if I get into trouble for that. If people try to get him I say back off . . . I feel that I can do it again, fight for my brother, it makes me stronger because when it started I thought I am not going to pull through it and since I've got older I get through and I help him.

The young people stated that their experiences with bullying have made them more assertive and capable of exercising agency in the form of control over their life. Many agreed with the statement 'I will not take it and I will stand up for my friends as well'. The experience of bullying has also helped them in moderating their feelings and reactions, and has stimulated thinking about ways of dealing with it.

you realize that there is nothing to worry about because you have not done anything yourself, and you can always go and talk to somebody, and they [are] always very good to sort things out. I feel more confident and snap out of it and stand up for myself and everything, and I feel now I can do it. It happened many times and I know what to do now.

Some young people said that they are more confident because they can see that the bully is not

that strong after all . . . They do not know how to make friends, they try to show they are strong but they are not and they have been bullied before.

Overall, the young people in the Needs Analysis study who have been bullied or have witnessed bullying, talked about gaining from the experience of bullying in terms of

- developing empathy (e.g., 'I try to advise the person who is bullied, encourage them to go and talk to somebody');
- encouraging the victims to talk (e.g., 'sometimes they will not talk and you have to encourage them otherwise the bully is going to keep doing it');
- being cautious in their peer interactions (e.g., 'I am very cautious. I think what if the same thing happens again. I have to know people a long time before I talk about myself or my family');
- coming closer to others with similar experiences (e.g., 'the relationships are closer and you know more stuff about each other');
- gaining in social maturity (e.g., 'I'm not going to judge someone by the way he looks, I judge people like who they really are');

- becoming wiser (e.g., 'it makes you wiser, you reflect on things. You know what to do if it happens another time. Mainly trying to learn afterwards, because some bullies have been bullied themselves');
- learning not to underestimate people (e.g., 'what surprises me is that people underestimate people. But people who are short then let's pick on them, those who look weak');
- becoming more determined (e.g., 'I have never stopped answering questions in the class for this because once you establish yourself as being clever it is not a good idea not to contribute because you may be bullied');
- understanding the other side of the story (e.g., 'Bullies have problems themselves, they have problems with their families, and maybe they have no friends and they are really lonely and that's why they do this').

Although many young people stressed the negative impact that bullying has had on their well-being, they also displayed resilience and assertiveness in breaking the cycle of silence that is inherent in bullying. They participated actively to offer solutions to tackle bullying at a systemic level (see Chapter 12 for a discussion on tackling bullying through researching difference).

Enjoyment and Free Time

Research studies have explored the relationship between leisure time and enjoyment in adults. Leisure time, defined as time away from employment, is seen as a source of enjoyment and an opportunity to develop new skills (dancing, sports); a sense of individuality and identity outside the work setting (being the organizer of charity events, playing an important role in a community, making new friends); and stimulation of interests/hobbies (writing, gardening, reading) (Argyle and Martin, 1991). However, there is a limited research on children's views about leisure time. For young people, spending time with friends is seen as an important element towards happiness, and a large number of young people have stated that they do not have enough free time (Children's Society, 2007).

In the Needs Analysis study, the majority of young people stressed the importance of having free time to engage in unstructured activities with their peers. Although they accepted that boundaries should be applied, they stressed that they need to be carefully drawn to allow for more unstructured spaces where, through conversation, children can understand each other and form friendships. Free time was seen by all young people as an important aspect of their enjoyment. Many expressed concerns about the lack of free time after school. One said 'my dad makes the decision to go to piano lessons – I would rather go to do things with other people; my mum is busy and I do things all the time at home'. Some young carers stressed the need to have free time by using school time to do the household chores, stating

> what I prefer is to help mum during the school hours and then be lazy after school hours do the things that I want. I do not mind help mum during school hours but I find it difficult after that. When I come back home this is pretty much my own time.

The majority of children in the bullying group complained that they do not have enough free time, referring to time that is not structured, nor supervised by adults. This concern is reflected in the following statement,

> I would like to go to local places like shops because nothing can happen in these places; I do not like structured activities all the time, I would like to be free and go to shops and get chocolate and then walk home or go to my friends house; I like to have time to go to places and see new things like clubs where interesting things happen.

Although many young people enjoy after-school clubs, they stressed that the existence of free time to be spent on self-initiated activities is important. Children with LDD in particular felt that 'teachers give you too much homework' and that was seen as compromising their free time. They affirmed that 'school is school and home is home, so we can do the stuff we like'. This may be explained by the fact that parents of children of LDD are more likely to structure and supervise the after-school time at home than are parents of children who are more independent. For the LDD group, time for fun activities, less homework and more trips and after-school clubs was important for their enjoyment.

The attainment of happiness for young people heavily relies on inter-personal relationships and friendships, their capacity to differentiate among shades of bullying and show assertiveness and resilience in dealing with it. Free time for enjoyment also plays an important role in children's socialization and identity formation.

Notes

[1] Spatial integrity: Suburban sprawl has fractured the spatial integrity of people. They travel much further to work, shop and enjoy leisure opportunities. As a

result, there is less time available (and less inclination) to become involved in groups (Putnam, 1995).

2 A civic community involves four themes:

Civic engagement: Citizenship in a civic community is characterized by active participation in public affairs. Being interested in public issues and prepared to be involved in debates and common activities contribute to community cohesion (Putnam, 1993: 87–91).

Political equality: Communities that are bound together by horizontal relations of reciprocity and cooperation, not by vertical relations of authority and dependency. Citizens interact as equals, not as patrons and clients nor as governors and petitioners . . . The more that politics approximates to the ideal of political equality among citizens following norms of reciprocity and engaged in self-government, the more civic that community may be said to be (Skinner, 1984 as cited by Putnam, 1993: 88).

Solidarity, trust and tolerance: Citizens should be 'helpful, and trustful to one another, even when they differ on matters of substance' (Putnam, 1993: 88–89). A civic community is not necessarily conflict-free, but is characterized by dialogue, respect for the other and a recognition of mutual dependency.

Associations: These refer to social structures of cooperation, the norms and values of a civic community which are 'are embodied in, and reinforced by, distinctive social structures and practices'. Participation in civic associations develops skills of cooperation, a sense of shared responsibility for collective endeavours and a means of engaging with broader political systems (Putnam, 1993: 89).

3 Civic disengagement refers to lack of active participation in public affairs. Being interested in public issues and prepared to be involved in debates and common activities are important signs of civic virtue (Putnam, 1993: 87–91).

4 During computer mediated interactions, young people develop a digital persona that is likely to be based on an ascribed rather than assumed identity. McLaughlin distinguishes between an assumed identity as 'social traits or group memberships we ascribe to ourselves', and ascribed identity as 'that which is attributed to individuals by others' (2007: 72). Bourdieu (1988) refers to 'habitus' which is an accumulation of personal attributes, dispositions and characteristics which constitute an identity, which seems to combine elements of both ascribed and assumed identities, acknowledging that they are bounded by societal structures.

5 In his work, Utilitarianism, John Stuart Mill argued that the cultural, intellectual, and spiritual pleasures are of greater value than mere physical pleasures. Within this mindset, happiness is achieved through intellectual and cultural pleasures (see Mill, J. S. (1993–1859;1861) *Utilitarianism, on Liberty, Considerations on Representative Government.* London: Everyman).

Part III

The Right to Childhoods

The best reparation for the suffering of victims and communities – and the highest recognition of their efforts – is the transformation of our society into one that makes a living reality of the human rights for which they struggled.

Mandela, 1999

In the previous two parts, several competing discourses have been presented to highlight the multiplicity and plurality inherent in childhood, and delineate the ecologies and images of children in the 21st century. Childhood occupies an ambivalent reality (Jans, 2004). On the one hand, childhood is constructed as a 'protected space' with children requiring care and protection and, on the other hand, as a distinct social group with rights and responsibilities. Childhood as a place and time of innocence and joy is a myth especially for a large number of children who live in the margins of society, experiencing 'unequal' childhoods and reduced rights (Penn, 2002). Across the developed and developing world, children occupy social and cultural borderlands, where the legitimacy of their rights is not always accepted. Children constitute a minority group with limited political and social participation, and a reduced moral status (Mayall, 2002). For many children, disability, the experience of becoming the 'other', social disadvantage and poverty, institutionalization and the rise of fractured communities pose serious obstacles in their capacity to exercise their rights and attain a citizenship status.

Constructions of children as being vulnerable, a minority or the 'other' marginalize them and deny their rights and humanity. To counteract the image of the dependent, vulnerable child, Malaguzzi constructs the rich child who is 'strong, powerful, competent and most of all, connected to adults and other children' (1993: 10). In this part, I argue towards a framework of children's rights, i.e., the right to childhoods, which places the 'rich' child at its centre. The right to childhoods takes a dialectical approach towards rights, care and responsibility. Its main premise is that ascertaining rights is a 'necessary precondition to the constitution of humanity, of integrity, of individuality, of personality' (Mayall, 1994: 57), to ensure that rights do not become a void discourse of entitlement. A key question raised in this part is whether current frameworks of children's rights recognize 'who the child is' over time, acknowledging the many childhoods and children's right to voice and participation.

Young people's participation in civic life and democratic processes are fundamental to the right to childhoods. Children's participation is a contentious area that sits on the intersection between ideology and policy, and is typically shaped by views of children from adults in power. The right to participation is the least realized right, especially for children with disability. There is a growing gap between the protection/provision rights that are granted for some children, and their participation rights that are nearly absent across societies. Even when children's rights for protection and provision are met, they are denied other fundamental rights, such as the right to a citizenship and the right to be considered equal citizens.

Children's rights suffer from a crisis of legitimacy regarding their nature and ideological and conceptual basis, i.e., being a universal code of conduct which relies on what Dahlberg and Moss call 'universalist ethics' (2005). Children's right to childhoods involves questions of politics and ethics, rather than the outcome of the application of a universal code of conduct. The right to childhood is often understood as the right to a protected or 'sacred' space where adults make decisions for children who have free time to explore and develop, untouched by the evils of the adult world. This view of rights is limited and limiting in that, even under the best circumstances where children are protected and provided for, their social and moral standing is likely to be compromised. The right to childhoods, as it is discussed here, focuses on provision, protection and participation and, most crucially, it acknowledges that the experience of growing up is diverse, shaped by the particularities of children's life. Moreover, the right to childhoods expands current children's rights to encourage an ethical praxis that is particular and contextual, relational in terms of being embedded in human experience and responsive to difference, care and responsibility.

Chapter 7

Current Frameworks of Children's Rights

The United Nations Convention on the Rights of the Child (UNCRC) was adopted by the United Nations in 1989 and ratified by the UK government in 1991. It sets out the framework for governments to recognize and actively pursue, through policy and legislation, the rights of all children (Hyder, 2005). The UNCRC requires all children to be respected as persons in their own right, including very young children, by establishing a new kind of universal standard. The fundamental principles of the UNCRC are

- non-discrimination (rights are applied to all children);
- best interest of children (in that the decisions, actions and policies should take into account their impact on children);
- participation (children have the right to express opinions on matters that affect them);
- survival and development (Hyder, 2005: 4).

These principles underpin five legal frameworks, namely, child protection, child emancipation/participation, child as a potential adult, child in need for traditional authority and social resource distribution (Minow, 1995). A number of competing discourses emerge from these frameworks, namely, universalist and particularist[1] ethics; child as a concern and child as a moral and social agent; rights and needs; rights and obligations; and last but not least, equality and difference. These discourses do not present artificial dualisms; rather, they offer comparing and contrasting views regarding children's rights, including notions of ethics, responsibility and citizenship.

Universalist and Particularist Ethics

Children's rights are situated within the conceptual framework of modernity, whereas the emphasis is on universal and abstract discourses and objective knowledge. These discourses acknowledge the existence of a nomological universe where law defines relationships and knowledge is legitimized through power structures. Children's rights rely on the assumption that individuals are atomistic units in the need for a moral authority to set objective rules for them to follow. Rights, as they currently stand, are abstract codes based on reason, offering ahistorical and apolitical views about children's experiences (Dahlberg and Moss, 2005).

Children's rights, as a universal code, have received extensive criticism for their reliance on deterministic understandings of who the child is (e.g., Gould, 2004; Santos, 2001). Determinism, be it biological or social, has played a central role in constructions of childhood. Children have been described as essentialist beings with universal patterns of development, or as a tabula rasa, empty vessels, who through socialization and normalization, develop into beings whose identity is shaped entirely by their environment. Both approaches have reduced the complexity of children's human nature.

In her book, *Globalizing Democracy and Human Rights*, Gould argues for a human rights framework that is less universal and more concrete (2004). To this end, she distinguishes between abstract and concrete universalism, commenting that the former encapsulates Western views of liberal autonomy. Her main argument is that abstract universalism is essentialist in nature, relying on a list of characteristics that are thought to be shared by all human beings. Gould warns us against an abstracted view of what is common to all humans because it may not account for cultural and historical differences and power structures and, thus, leave out important differences that contribute to understanding humanity.

Traditionally, human rights have relied on Western concepts of liberal autonomy, and this has reduced their applicability across geographies and cultures. Gould is uneasy about universal truths that turn particular claims into diachronic and universal principles, arguing that 'it would follow that . . . all historical and social differentiation drops out and only those abstracted properties that remain invariant for all humans and all societies count as essential. These characteristics are seen as fixed instead as of historically changing' (2004: 567). Against this background, she approaches democracy and rights as situated within 'reciprocal and empathic personal relations' that extend through 'plural and cultural contexts to a transnational and indeed global level' (2004: 2). This transformation is articulated by the concepts of cosmopolitan association and intersociation which emphasize the importance of networks of relationships (both real and virtual) in a globalized society. Cosmopolitan association involves extending relationships and interactions from 'local interpretations towards global ones', whereas intersociation involves 'reciprocal and empathic relations as being the organizing principle of society' (2004: 62).

Historically, cosmopolitanism[2] has been equated with universalism and essentialism, and has been critiqued for contributing to erasing difference. To counteract this view, Santos offers a different type of cosmopolitanism, namely a subaltern cosmopolitanism, which is free from notions of globalization (2001). Furthermore, Gould constructs cosmopolitanism along the lines of a 'cosmopolitical democracy', which refers to a world community, a world citizenship that entails both transnational/global characteristics and local contexts, offering a communitarian view to rights and diversity (2004: 182).

A cosmopolitical framework for children's rights has the potential to bridge universalist and particularist ethics by emphasizing mutual dependency and relational approaches to understand the ways in which context and power structures influence children's rights. Rights framed by a cosmopolitan association and intersociation account for the particular and contextual elements of children's life and respect difference where, at the same time, support the process whereby the local interpretations and stories are transformed into global ones.

Within a cosmopolitical framework, the dilemmas about retaining a cultural and social differentiation at a local community level and ensuring that children's rights are not violated in the name of diversity become central. Cultural practices that are embedded within certain cultural structures and systems of belief, such as bride children, female genital mutilation, violate children's right. Challenging these practices requires new conceptualizations of rights and a form of criticality that enables thinking in 'new cosmopolitan ways' about these issues, and feeling 'empathy and solidarity with those at a distance' (Gould, 2004: 2).

The Child as a Concern and as an Agent

Current frameworks on child protection construe children as being dependent and vulnerable, objects of concern and in the need for traditional authority (Lansdown, 2001). This resonates views of childhood as a 'protected space', and has influenced the UN convention that rests on the assumption that children are vulnerable, as reflected in the content of the following Articles:

- Article 3 – the best interests of the child should be a primary consideration when action is taken concerning children;

- Article 23 – a mentally or physically disabled child should enjoy a full and decent life, in conditions which ensure dignity, promote self-reliance and facilitate the child's active participation in the community;
- Article 24 – the right of any child to the enjoyment of the highest attainable standard of health and to facilities for the treatment of illness and rehabilitation of health;
- Article 25 – the right of a child placed by competent authorities for the purposes of care, protection or treatment of his or her physical or mental health, to a periodic review of the treatment provided to the child and all other circumstances relevant to his or her placement;
- Article 39 – all appropriate measures to be taken to promote the physical and psychological recovery and social reintegration of a child victim of any form of abuse and neglect.

Several policies and services emanating from children's rights focus on protection and provision, and have regulatory aims, e.g., surveillance, social control, management of children's time and movement. Social regulation and engineering of children's life appear to be at the heart of current children's policies, filling the vacuum left by economic and market deregulation (Moss, 1999), and the melting down of a social contract (Santos, 1995).

Freeman differentiates between certain rights such as freedom of religion, racial equality, freedom of expression and a right to privacy as adult-type rights, and the right to education as being unique to children (1992). A danger with separating adults' and children's rights is that children are likely to be perceived as potential adults, as 'not yet being', a 'project in the making' (Verhellen, 1997), 'human becomings' rather than 'human beings' (Qvortrup 1994) and 'noble causes' rather than 'worthy citizens' Knuttson (1997).

Mayall argues that children have a low moral status in society, evident in their limited presence in the public arena. Children's moral status is normally enacted in the context of their family and peer interactions, places that are not 'visible to people whose opinions shape ideologies of childhood' (2002: 87). Operating within these micro contexts, children's and their parents' views become less visible to those in position of power. Increasingly, the shrinking of children's social and physical spaces reduces their critical space that is required for developing and testing the capacity to formulate moral judgements.

The moral positioning of children in our society is paradoxical. On the one hand, the 'under age' are perceived as being less than equal citizens, and, on the other hand, children are expected to exercise moral

responsibility (Mayall, 2002). Historically, the politics of children's participation share the same trajectories with those of parent participation in
terms of their views being secondary or in the need for compensation/
remediation (Liwski, 2006). Deficit assumptions about children's social and
moral competency constitute children a concern, a problem that requires
intervention.

Although, there has been a growing emphasis to educate children to
function as active and responsible citizens, their rights to participation and
decision making have not been acknowledged fully. Not having a voice
compromises the sense of being part of the decision making on issues that
affect children's life, ultimately compromising their citizenship. A contrasting view is offered by Reggio Emilia that places parental and child
participation at the centre of educational policy and practice (Hugh and
MacNaughton, 2002). Re-examining children's rights requires us to view
children as individuals in their own right, rather than objects of concern,
who are capable of articulating views and participating in decision making.
To shift children's current social and moral positioning and overcome the
barriers towards genuine participation and citizenship, require a transformation of children's rights from an abstract code into a living reality.

Rights and Needs

The interplay between 'rights' and 'needs' is articulated by placing rights
and needs on two continua. The first continuum involves rights as based
on universalist ethics, and needs as defined within power structures. The
second continuum approaches rights as being based on 'particularist
ethics', and needs as responsiveness, responsibility and mutual dependency
(Dahlberg and Moss, 2005).

On the first continuum, rights as a universal code are articulated along
the 'legal imperatives that governments and institutions have a duty in law
to uphold' (Hyder, 2005: 3). Current human rights frameworks have been
influenced by the principles of the Enlightenment era, where ethics are set
on reason, and moral judgement is abstracted, impartial, objectified and
based on universal principles and understandings of right and wrong. Universal ethics have been criticized for not being bounded by culture, history
or political circumstances, and not being situated within human relational
experiences (Gould, 2004). Rights as a 'legal imperative' are also problematic because they imply that judgement over right and wrong should be left
to legislators. This mindset reduces rights into a set of rules to be followed,

and removes responsibility from individuals to make moral judgements through reflection on their everyday actions. In this context 'responsibility is exchanged for legislation, the need to choose for rule-following, ambivalence for certainty' (Dahlberg and Moss, 2005: 68).

The concept of need reflects power inequality, with the needs of individuals or groups being defined by those in power, involving an element of charity and not entitlement. Recognizing needs in others also involves assumptions that their needs are similar to ours, ultimately reducing difference by imposing sameness on the Other (Tronto, 1993). Moreover, the concept of need is contested in that it signals adults' views of children as being a problem (Woodhead, 2006). Liwski argues that 'a needs-based focus produces a vision aimed at solving specific problems . . . it concentrates on specifics and converts the citizen into a passive subject who must be considered from the standpoint of the problem' (2006: 9).

On the second continuum, rights are shaped by what Levinas called the ethics of an encounter, involving care and intersubjectivity, and the capacity to 'foster a vision of citizenship whereby the citizen is a holder of rights' (Liwski, 2006: 9). An implicit understanding of the ethics of an encounter is that individuals are capable of engaging with ethical dilemmas and accept that uncertainty is inherent in making moral judgements. The ethics of an encounter counteract Kant's thesis, that through reason, individuals will form moral judgements that are impartial and dispassionate, based on an objective understanding of truth. What is suggested instead is a relational approach to rights, embedded in human experiences, being non-rational by not following rules and calculating events (Dahlberg and Moss, 2005). As Beilharz comments 'moral behaviour is more like intuition than reason: we are not ignorant of what is right and what is wrong, but we cannot always fully justify or explain a particular course of action or inaction' (ibid.: 35).

On the second continuum, the concept of need is understood as mutual dependency, care and responsiveness to the 'other', engaging with dilemmas when dealing with uncertainty. Rather than defining needs as vulnerability and weakness, they are approached as another side of the human experience, interwoven with empathy, compassion and responsibility or what Sevenhuijsen calls the 'feminist ethics of care' (1998).

Rights and Obligations

Distinguishing between rights and obligation poses many challenges in that it juxtaposes political agendas with moral and social contracts. O'Neill considers rights to have a political advantage, whereas obligations have a moral advantage, implying a sense of moral responsibility towards children's well-being (1988). She claims that children's rights should be embedded in obligation in terms of placing expectations and duties on those who exercise rights. This view suggests that rights and obligations should be inter-connected, offering a social contract on how people relate to each other in terms of having rights and fulfilling obligations. It also implies that obligation and responsibility are restricted to those who are capable of being impartial and objective followers of rules and prescriptions of ethical codes. Nussbaum considers the social contract tradition to be fundamentally flawed because the reciprocity it implies assumes equality among those who enter the contract, and constitutes those who cannot enter as being less of citizens (2004).

Santos also challenges the view that rights should be granted to those who can fulfil responsibilities through some sort of 'restricted reciprocity' (1995: 51). The notion of restricted reciprocity suggests that rights and their corresponding duties have an instrumental value rather than 'an open-ended responsibility and sense of obligation' (Dahlberg and Moss, 2005: 83). Within this mindset, obligation and responsibility become not a deliberative human act but a rule to follow irrespective of human differences. This has implications for social exclusion with often devastating consequences, especially for families and children at the margins of a society. Abiding by a moral authority, be it religious or political, removes responsibility for everyday actions, constituting ethics irrelevant to people's lived experiences.

The tensions between obligations and the rights of the child are highlighted in contrasting UNCRC with the 'rights and duties' within the African Charter on the Rights and Welfare of the Child (OAU, 1990, discussed in Burr and Montgomery, 2003). The Article 31 of the African Charter states that 'Every child shall have responsibilities towards his family and society . . . The child, subject to his age and ability, . . . shall have the duty: to work for the cohesion of the family, to respect his parents, superiors and elders at all times and to assist them in case of need . . . etc.'.

The relationship between rights and obligations has immense implications for children's rights. Dahlberg and Moss consider current conceptualizations of rights to be problematic because they marginalize obligation because 'rights entail a contractual and finite exchange between calculating and independent individuals; care and encounter foreground inter-dependence, infinite responsibility and the impossibility of being free of obligation' (2005: 30). Elements of obligation and responsibility should be introduced into the children's rights framework. However, it is important to note that obligation may be interpreted in relativistic terms that reflect the political and moral agendas of those in power, rather than individuals' relational understanding of right and wrong.

Equality and Difference

The right to be the same . . . and the right to be different . . . were not opposed to each other. On the contrary, the right to be the same in terms of fundamental civil, political, legal, economic and social rights provided the foundation for the expression of difference through choice in the sphere of culture, lifestyle and personal priorities. In other words, provided that difference is not used to maintain inequality, subordination, injustice and marginalisation.

Sachs, 1997: 15

Equality and difference are competing entities that have influenced the current frameworks of children's rights. Rights, as a universal code, rely on the principle of sameness which constitutes difference as inferiority because 'differences, whether speculative in nature or accompanied by convincing evidence, are always considered deviant and negative in relation to a universal norm' (Sevenhuijsen, 1998: 45). Children's rights have been influenced by views of biological and social determinism, which has consistently undermined difference. These views reflect partly a drive towards biological and social engineering to erase difference and create a well-ordered world from which the other is excluded (Dahlberg and Moss, 2005).

The current politics of rights do not account for difference and the ways in which it shapes human dignity (Santos, 2001). The universality of human rights should be reconsidered to account for the cultural contexts and the different languages that surround and influence children's lives. Santos argues for a collage or a 'hybridization of the most comprehensive and emancipatory conceptions of human dignity, based on many different cultural conceptions of children's rights' (2001: 190). The friction between equality and difference is evident in rights movements that focus on equality (e.g., child labour, access to education), and those that acknowledge and respect difference (e.g., demonstrations against xenophobia, anti-Semitism). The ambivalence between equality and difference calls for a contextual approach to exercising children's rights.

To bridge difference and equality, Santos introduces the notion of meta-right, 'the right to have rights, that is the right to be different and the right to be equal'. This view offers a 'dynamic equilibrium between difference and equality', stressing that if equality is 'understood as equivalence among the same' then it excludes what is different (2001: 192). The coexistence of the right to be the same and the right to be different accounts for the circumstances that surround children's place and time. Santos stresses the importance of fluidity and 'fit for purpose' in children's rights, stating that 'we have the right to be equal whenever difference diminishes us; we have the right to be different whenever equality decharacterises us' (2001: 193). With this in mind, the shift from universal rights to the cultural embeddedness of children's circumstances is crucial to sustain the right to survival, protection and participation in young people.

To sustain this new culture, we need to question the rigidity of current educational systems and social attitudes that equate difference with inferiority, resulting in a passive acceptance of people with disabilities. Clearly, difficulties in defining children's rights along diversity, care and obligation towards the other reflect, as a society, our preoccupation with homogeneity and ambivalence about diversity and difference.

Rights as a universal code that is separate from obligation and ethics cannot be translated into policies and practices that protect children from systematic abuse at a local level. There is a widespread assumption that adults know best and always act in the best interest of the children under their care. Sadly, there is evidence that this is not the case. A number of public inquiries (e.g., Victoria Climbie) have documented systematic abuse and violation of children's rights that have been done intentionally and unintentionally. Intentionally, through exploitation, children suffer abuse and neglect within the context of their families and institutions. Unintentionally, children can be harmed through rights-based policies and practices that were implemented to support them in the first place, such as poor quality of teaching and learning for children with disabilities, institutionalization of street children, court decisions that ban parental access to children or limited genuine participation.

Chapter 8

Young People's Voice and Participation

There has been an increasing interest in children's participation in recent years, occurring at a time when opportunities for the creation of public fora are diminished. Many societies around the world accept that children should have the right to protection and provision. Recognizing the value in children's perspectives and voices and taking them into consideration, however, have challenged dominant views of children as being objects of concern and not sufficiently competent to make decisions. The introduction of the right to be listened to and taken seriously and the right to participation is changing the status quo of childhood, blurring adult–child divides. The right to participation has given 'an additional dimension to the status of children by recognizing that children are subjects of rights, rather than merely recipients of adult protection' (Lansdown, 2001:1). This recognition is embedded, implicitly or explicitly, in a number of articles in the UNCRC. These are reflected in the content of the following Articles:

Article 5 – parental provision of direction and guidance in accordance with respect for children's evolving capacity;

Article 9 – non-separation of children from families without the right to make their views known;

Article 12 – the right to be listened to and taken seriously;

Article 13 – the right to freedom of expression;

Article 14 – the right to freedom of conscience, thought and religion;

Article 15 – the right to freedom of association;

Article 16 – the right to privacy;

Article 17 – the right to information;

Article 29 – the right to education that promotes respect for human rights and democracy. (Lansdown, 2001: 1)

In the United Kingdom, under a consultation on children's voice (DfES, 2003–2004), Charles Clarke, the then Secretary of State stated that 'giving children and young people a say in decisions that affect them will impact positively on standards, behaviour and inclusion (2003: ii). Although one may argue against an instrumental value of participation, implicit in the above statement, there is a growing acknowledgement of the importance of encouraging young people to

- become more active participants in their education, including evaluation of their own learning;
- participate in creating, building and improving services to make them more responsive to their needs and those of the wider community;
- make a difference in their schools, neighbourhoods and communities;
- contribute to a cohesive community;
- learn from an early age to balance their rights as individuals with their responsibilities as citizens; and
- develop, through the way they are involved, the knowledge, understanding and skills that they will need in adult life. (ibid.: 3).

The legislative framework of children's rights, especially that of participation, has not been transferred into schools and other school-related organizations where young people spend a considerable amount of time. The reasons are complex, mainly involving somewhat, conflicting interpretations regarding young people's participation. The plurality in discourses on young people participation becomes evident when considering the many perspectives that have been offered to understand its nature.

Perspectives on Young People's Participation

Children's participation in education and civic life has been approached from several perspectives, namely a citizenship perspective (Roche, 1999); an educational benefits perspective offering a critique on how young people are viewed during consultation processes (Flutter and Ruddock, 2004); a human rights perspective (Alderson, 2000); a personal development perspective (e.g., Kirby and Bryson, 2002); an empowerment perspective with young people being seen as resources (Chawla, 2001; Hart, 1992); a power shifting perspective (e.g., Bragg, 2007; Fielding, 2001); a societal benefit perspective (Van der Veen, 2001); and a legal perspective (Lundy, 2007).

Young people's participation has been central in numerous discourses. The personal development discourse addresses the best interest of children, implying that participation contributes to young people's sense of personal responsibility and community belonging (Franklin, 1994; Hart, 1992; Kirby and Bryson, 2002; Miljeteig, 1994). Commonly listed benefits of participation include self-respect, competence, confidence, trust in adults and themselves, self-esteem, social inclusion, increased responsibility for taking control over aspects of their lives, an understanding of decision-making processes and becoming self-reflective learners (Fielding and Bragg, 2003).

The children-as-a-resource perspective views children's participation as having positive implications for a society as a whole, especially with regard to the environment, social justice and sustainability of local communities (Chawla, 2001; Hart, 1992; Verhellen, 1994). This discourse perceives children as being capable of developing participatory patterns that are conducive to sustaining local communities and the environment. Along these lines, Van der Veen's system-based young people's participation is seen as fulfilling the requirements for a society to function (2001). The nature and scope of a system-based participation are instrumental, with young people, through their participation in civic fora, offering solutions to social, economic and environmental problems, and contributing to a collective good as defined by adults.

The system-based participation raises important ethical concerns with regard to adults influencing children's perspectives and views and highlights the importance for supporting children develop a capacity for critical thinking and moral judgement to avoid following adult-centric agendas. Issues in children participation as a means to promote adults' agendas should be transparent, especially when the subsequent decisions have implications for children, their families and communities. As Stephens states

> There are important critical questions to be asked about hidden forms of cultural imperialism underlying some children's participation models, for example those that would use children's participation projects as points of entry into and catalyst for change within families and local communities, without sufficient regard for the meanings and textures of local worlds. (1994: 12)

Similarly, Lansdown stresses that 'bringing children in to promote an adult agenda is at best tokenistic and at worst exploitative' (2001: 17). She argues that it is against the principles of participation for children to become involved in something without understanding the agenda and without having been part in formulating it. Hart also warns us against viewing children's participation as a means to an end by imposing adult-centric agendas (1992). Rather, children should be encouraged to participate and offer views about issues that are of direct interest and significance to them.

The personal development and community functioning perspectives are not in conflict as long as children enjoy and develop personally while they participate to ensure that aspects of their local communities function properly. However, there is a danger that the instrumentality of system participation may become a tool for social control. Jans argues that, within an 'active welfare state', participation is likely to be reduced to an 'active input in society', mainly in paid labour, and a response to the 'insecurities and unpredictability of a risk society' (2004: 31).

A life-world perspective on participation, on the other hand, approaches children as active citizens with a capacity to enact decisions on collective issues at a global level (Van der Veen, 2001). An example of this participatory model is the growing use of computer-mediated social networking sites by young people to stimulate and support border-crossing activism on global matters such as the environment or terrorism. Computer-mediated participation also exemplifies the social democratization argument for participation, which regards children a social group with equal democratic rights (Chawla, 2001; Hart, 1992; Horelli and Vepsä, 1995; Miljeteig, 1994; Verhellen, 1994).

In much of the literature on young people's participation, it is accepted uncritically that involving children in participatory research or other activities is always a good thing. Some critics have questioned such emphasis on children's participation, arguing that silence may be a form of resistance, with privacy being an important right to ascertain (Bragg, 2007; Lansdown, 2001; Lewis and Porter, 2007). Lewis and Porter argue against the increasing over-formalization of the processes that underpin children's participation. Making participation over-regulated and over-formalized may put pressure on children instead of supporting them to articulate their concerns. We shall not underestimate children's right to be silent and retain privacy, if they wish to, by placing high expectations on them to participate or offer a view. Most crucially, adults should not intrude children's social and critical spaces, especially given that children can be susceptible to adults' views. With this in mind, we should operate within a participatory continuum to delineate various degrees of participation, and an emancipatory continuum to illuminate whether children feel emancipated from being involved in decision making (Lansdown, 2001).

The current debates on young people's participation have barely engaged with shifts in power and the tensions between authenticity and empowerment, accepting uncritically that young people's participation will trigger the sharing of power between children and adults and blur the exiting boundaries and hierarchies (Bragg, 2007; Fielding, 2001). Within the school improvement discourse, a growing acceptance of student participation has raised scepticism with regard to what and whose purposes participation serves and what the real interests for those in power are. Against this criticism, children's participation and visibility have an instrumental value. Fielding questions its foundation and purposes

> are we witnessing the emergence of something genuinely new, exciting and emancipatory that builds on rich traditions of democratic renewal and transformation? . . .Or are we presiding over the further entrenchment of existing assumptions and intentions using student or pupil voice as an additional mechanism of social control?(2001: 100)

Fielding debates the origins of young people's voice, questioning whether it is something genuine, a 'narrative of democracy', an extension of Foucault's notion of governmentality or a 'neo-liberal project' (2004: 132). The school improvement rhetoric is being gradually replaced by an increasing emphasis on 'networking, collaboration and personalization' (ibid.: 132). This transformation may stimulate a reflection on organizations' and schools' insistence on choice and voice by questioning whose voice and whose choice is, and engaging with the dilemmas of the extent to which young people benefit from participation and joint decision making.

The ethics and politics of young people's participation reflect ambivalence in the ways participation is negotiated through dialogue to avoid marginalizing children or through tokenistic gestures towards inclusion. The issue is not participation or no participation, but whether adults are genuinely attentive and responsive to young people's perspectives, and aware of the plurality and polyphony in their voices.

UNCRC in Action:
From Interpretation to Policy and Practice

Increasingly, organizations are required to involve young people in an attempt to interpret and transfer UNCRC Articles, such as Articles 12,13 and 3, into practice. Article 12 of the UNCRC has caused a great deal of controversy because, implicitly, it approaches children as full human beings with a capacity to exercise judgement. This view of children as citizens now rather than becomings or future citizens has been the key reason the United States of America did not ratify the Convention (Kilbourne, 1998 as cited in Lundy, 2007). Moreover, inconsistencies in the semantic understanding of the terms and phrases used in Article 12 have accentuated this controversy. For example, phrases such as 'all matters affecting the child' or the 'right to participate' or 'the right to be consulted' are shaped by power structures and can be interpreted fairly loosely. Issues such as who decides what matters affect children, under what circumstances decisions are made for children and by who, and how decisions underpin policies, require, as the Article 12 stresses, 'consistent and on-going arrangements' to ensure that the Article 12 is implemented effectively. Moreover, the Article 42 requires States Parties to 'make the principles and provisions of the convention widely known, by appropriate and active means, to adults and children alike'. Thus, the procedures and the systems that support children's rights to voice and participation should be transparent and legally binding.

The implications for respecting children's voice are both pedagogic and legal in nature. Lundy reconceptualized Article 12 to incorporate four important factors that affect its implementation, namely, space, voice, audience and influence (2007: 933). Space refers to the opportunities to express views, and this requires an access to physical, social and critical spaces. These are spaces where young people meet and, through dialogue and critical engagement with peers and adults, create opportunities for participation (see Part II for a detailed discussion on children's spaces). Voice refers to children being genuinely supported to express their views or remain silent if they wish by taking into consideration their best interest, and avoiding coercion or tokenistic approaches to participation. Lundy's model places children's voices in the wider UNCRC framework by considering Article 2 (non-discrimination), Article 3 (best interest), Article 5 (right to guidance from adults), Article 13 (right to information) and Article 19 (right to be safe) to explicate the ways in which young people's participation is actualized. Specifically, children's spaces should be non-discriminatory and inclusive, where children feel safe, and guided by adults, as appropriate, to share views and participate in civic matters. This is particularly important for children with disability who are likely to experience a 'double denial' in exercising their rights when adults question their competence (Committee on the Rights of the Child, 1997: 334).

The Article 3 of the UNCRC, which states that children's best interest should be 'a primary consideration', does not clarify who decides about children's best interest, and whether children should delineate their interests or rely on adults to do this for them. The Article 3 is in conflict with Article 12 because an emphasis on expressing views may not always be in the best interest of a child. This is particularly true in situations where children are pressurized to participate without respecting their right to silence and privacy, or in cases where they feel demoralized when their views are not genuinely listened to. Children's autonomy with regard to the legitimate limits in exercising their rights has been debated extensively. Many arguments have been put forward to justify restrictions in children's voice and resulting actions, namely 'children's right to an open future' and the argument that rights should not interfere with children's developmental needs (Feinberg, 1980).

The Article 12 implies that there are degrees of participation and capacity building depending on the child's phase of development by introducing factors such as age, maturity and evolving capacities. The requirements posed regarding competence can be interpreted as 'readiness' or prerights behaviours that children need to acquire before they are in a position to exercise their rights. They can also be seen as enabling with children becoming increasingly more competent in expressing their views. The child's age and maturity should not constitute young children incompetent in actively offering their views (e.g., Lansdown, 2001; Lundy, 2007). Lundy argues for the need to interpret Article 12 in conjunction with the Article 5 of the UNCRC which states that adults should provide 'appropriate direction and guidance'. The Committee on the Rights of the Child[3] also stresses that

> Evolving capacities should be seen as a positive enabling principle. It should not be interpreted as an endorsement of authoritarian practices that restrict children's autonomy and self-expression and which have traditionally been justified by appealing to children's relative incompetence and their need for socialisation. (2005: para. 14)

Moreover, different views on young children's evolving capacities should not necessarily be in opposition as long as they balance the rights for participation and protection with the best interest of the child. Lansdown interprets the notion of evolving capacities as a 'developmental' concept – fulfilling children's rights to the development of their optimum capacities; an 'emancipatory' concept – recognizing and respecting the evolving capacities of children; and a 'protective' concept – protecting children from experiences beyond their capacities (2005).

Notions of evolving capacities and competence bear implications with regard to children's legal competence for decision making. Hillary Clinton, in her work on *Children Under the Law*, that was published at the Harvard Education Review, argued that courts should not assume that children are vulnerable and legally incompetent, and that decisions regarding competence should be judged on a case-by-case basis (1973). Young people with the capacity to exercise agency maybe in a position to challenge conventional power structures based around children's age, maturity and development, their gender, or any other social classification (John, 1996).

Challenging notions of incompetence and vulnerability in children may also be achieved by what Minow refers to as a 'second stage' in women's movements. The aim of such movements would be to advocate developmental rights such as rights to education, cultural activities, play and leisure, and freedom of thought, as well as family-friendly policies such as childcare and flexi-time for workers (1995). Moreover, the social resource distribution model, i.e., reallocating power and responsibility among child, family and the state, is relevant in challenging views about dependency and vulnerability in children. A resource distribution model offers an interesting perspective at a time when state over-regulation of both family and children are on the rise.

Often, children's views are not sought, and when they are, they are not acted upon, highlighting the need for moving consultation to participative decision making where young people's voice has an impact on influencing decision making (Alderson, 2000). The Article 12 requires that children's views should be given 'due weight'. Implicitly, this suggests that children's voices may be heard but not listened to, and thus, audience and influence become important dimensions in translating the Article 12 into practice (Lundy, 2007). The reasons for a limited authentic inclusion of young people in decision making are complex, ranging from lack of resources and appropriate staff training to dominant views about children's incompetence and invisibility. Adults' resistance to accept competence in children may be due to a lack of procedural systems that incorporate children's views (for example, having a system in place to disseminate the minutes from school councils to the governors' meeting – Hallgarten et al., 2004).

The UNCRC has debated participation and consultation for school-age children on issues such as school exclusion, homework or play time. The committee recommended that the UK government should 'take further steps to promote, facilitate and monitor systematic, meaningful and effective participation of all groups of children in society, including in schools, for example, through schools councils' (2002: 7). Moreover, legislative frameworks such as the Children Act 1989, Health and Social Care Act 2001, Education Act 2002, Learning to Listen Core Principles (CYPU, 2001) and the Children's National Service Framework reflect a growing shift in UK policy to involve children and young people in decisions. The Core Principles of Participation offer guidance to governmental departments about participation, providing a framework for an effective involvement of children and young people in the design and provision of policies and services (English Children and Young Persons Unit, 2001).

The Green Paper Every Child Matters emphasizes children's participation to express their views about developing policies and services (DfES, 2003). This has led local authorities and other public sector agencies to consult young people. For instance, the Children's Fund, aimed at children aged 5–13, at risk of social exclusion, sets participation as a requirement to ensure that children's views influence the shape, delivery and subsequent evaluation of services (Coad and Lewis, 2004). The Education Act 2002 places a duty on schools and Local Authorities to consult pupils about the decisions that affect them. The Early Years Development and Childcare Partnerships are required to seek children and young people's preferences for childcare and other support services (Clark, McQuail and Moss, 2003; Lansdown, 2001). Finally, the Office for Standards in Education (Ofsted) school inspection framework requires schools to seek the views of young people.

Although there is a surge in developing and implementing policies to support children's participation, some policies may compromise it, perpetuating social inequalities. For example, contradictory policies and practices around diversity, capability building, power inequality and empowerment, are likely to compromise children's right to participation. Also, under certain circumstances, young people's participation may be used as a tool of social control, a way of disguising conventional power relationships that are built around adult agendas.

The Reality of Young People's Participation

Research evidence shows that young people want to play an active role in the political decision making and become involved in civic matters. At the same time, there is a growing criticism in current political systems and practices regarding their capacity to support genuine participation (e.g., Bragg, 2007; Fielding, 2004, Lansdown, 2001). Lansdown highlights a contradiction in young people's interest in political issues; on the one hand, there is a perceived apathy in the ways in which young people approach civic life. On the other hand, young people are offered limited opportunities for genuine engagement with political structures and processes. What appears to be disaffection and lack of interest are deep-seated attitudes that young people's views do not matter, that 'they cannot influence outcomes and that democracy does not work for them' (ibid.: 11).

The young people's perceived apathy is not a form of self-induced civic disengagement; it is rather a realization that their political arena does not exist. The findings from a survey carried out in Austria in 1997 revealed a significant desire in young people for greater involvement in civic life. Ninety-three per cent of 800 young people, aged between 13 and 17 expressed the desire to be informed when new projects were planned in their municipality. Moreover, 65 per cent wanted youth consulting hours with politicians as a means of creating public fora for debate on issues that affect their lives (Lansdown, 2001: 11).

Research conducted on behalf of the Northern Ireland Commissioner for Children and Young People (NICCY) by Kilkelly and colleagues (2005) yielded interesting results with regard to young people's rights and involvement in public affairs. The research aimed at identifying areas in children's life where their rights were undermined, covering six main dimensions, namely implementation, family life and alternative care, education, play and leisure, health, welfare and material deprivation and criminal justice and policing. One of the main findings of the NICCY study was that 'not having a say on issues that affect their lives' was a prominent feature in children's life at school and the community.

Consistently with the NICCY study (Kilkelly et al., 2005), the Needs Analysis study (see Appendix) showed that children felt that their views are not listened to at school (Hartas and Lindsay, 2007). Specifically, although young people from the bullying group showed competency in offering solutions about tackling bullying, many felt that their views and experiences are less likely to be taken into account by their schools. Not giving a 'due weight' to young people's views was reflected in comments such as

> I say things, I come up with an idea but they do not listen. Teachers have an idea and do not listen to anybody else . . . If something happens at the playground and you go and tell them they tell you to come and tell them if it happens again, but they still do not do anything.

Another young person stated that

> in Y3 this new girl moved in and said bad things to me in front of teachers and dinner ladies but nothing seemed to happen. She stopped only when I talked to her.

This data show that children are willing to offer views about issues that affect their lives, and create opportunities to have their views being listened to. However, they realized that participation can easily become a meaning-less exercise when their views were not listened to and did not influence decision making. When the students were offered opportunities to express their views about bullying during discussions with the teachers, they were neither involved nor informed about the decisions made. The effects of this type of restricted participation can be counterproductive in that children may lose faith in democratic procedures and feel disempowered to participate in public matters. Schools should make the process of partici-pation and decision making transparent and accountable for the mechanisms they have put in place to support children's voice. Reflecting on Lundy's model regarding the implementation of Article 12, the existence of 'space', 'voice' and 'audience' is a necessary but not a sufficient condition to ensure that children's views actually shape policy and practice in schools. Influ-ence, manifested in acting upon children's views and supporting them, when appropriate, to transform their ideas into practice, is a crucial compo-nent of participation.

As Lundy's model suggests, participation is a multi-dimensional construct, and there are bound to be variations in young people's participatory behav-iours and the reasons that trigger and sustain them. Analyses of the YPSA data revealed a relationship between young people's civic and political interests and participation and their ethnic and social background. Specifi-cally, Black young people of African origin, as well as those in fee-paying schools, expressed more interest in politics than did their European peers and young people in state schools. These differences can be interpreted along Lundy's components of participation, i.e., space, voice, audience and influence. Those who expressed an interest in political participation were more likely to have the space and audience to express their views and believe that their contribution is likely to influence decision making. The existence of space, voice, audience and influence are shaped by the cultural and political circumstances that surround young people. Thus, across dif-ferent cultures and ethnic groups, there are variations in the ways in which these participatory components manifest themselves and define young peo-ple's experience of participation.

Participating as Service Users

Increasingly, children's views are sought, mainly as users of services and consumers of products. User-led consultations have created a new culture of participation that is fuelled by market forces. Although current policy shifts are a positive step towards young people's engagement and participation, some are embedded in market and institutional cultures, stimulating a corporate interest in participation. Participation as service users has an instrumental value, rationality and purpose, encouraging young people to take initiative to develop business solutions and meet institutional and policy prespecified targets.

Placing instrumental and market values on participation by situating it in a market culture is likely to create a 'hierarchy of rights' (Kobayashi and Ray, 2000: 402). This may result in some public institutions to perceive certain rights, such as expressing views or engaging in decision making, as not a priority. Considering certain rights, i.e., rights as a consumer, to be more important than other rights, i.e., rights as a citizen, may force children to exercise rights in a selective manner. Important questions are raised with regard to who decides on the hierarchy and significance of rights for young people's life, and what mechanisms support diverse cultures of participation.

Young people's participation as service users has multiple aims. It enables young people to access services and enhances service accountability by improving services instead of individuals' best interests. Children and young people, as users of services, are encouraged to participate to ensure that resources are allocated appropriately. At its best, participation as a service user involves a capacity building for individuals to align themselves with the culture of an organization, i.e., schools, by undergoing changes in their identity and dispositions. Du Gay notes that young people's participation in an organizational culture tends to have an instrumental value, a degree of pragmatism, in that the more involved individuals are, the more likely it is for the organization to work effectively (1997). On a less positive note, participating as service users may be underpinned by managerialist values regarding children's education and well-being. Corporate and managerialist ways of thinking towards participation are less likely to encourage and take on board children's views about developments in educational policy and practice.

Consultation has been the most commonly used mode for engaging children in service development and service evaluation. Consultation involves seeking users' views about the quality, structure and function of an existing programme or initiative, often, initiated by the stakeholders. Consultation is different from involvement in policy development in that the former aims to obtain people's views to inform decision making, whereas the latter actually involves young people in the decision making process itself. Nevertheless, voluntary and public sector organizations are keen in developing participatory consultation methods, and there is a precedence of such methods that include young people in the developing world (Ackerman et al., 2003).

Views about Needs-led Services

The Needs Analysis study yielded interesting results regarding the participation of young people as service users. One of the aims of this study was to obtain young people's views about availability and access to services, with their participation being seen by the local authority as being instrumental in developing needs-led services. The young people involved have encountered challenges, ranging from looking after family members with disabilities, to having experienced bullying and learning difficulties/disabilities.

The results yielded a preference for services of a practical nature. Specifically, young people requested access to physical spaces for outdoor activities and trips (e.g. flexible transportation; physical rearrangements of inside/outdoor space in community centres and schools); access to social places/clubs and activities and communication technologies; learning and homework support, especially in mainstream schools; practical support targeting household chores (young carers group); and a space to negotiate professionals' involvement in their life.

Young people with caring responsibilities preferred to receive practical support such as help with housework, transportation to medical appointments or tutoring with homework. Many expressed concerns about the lack of school-based services such as learning support for their brothers/sisters with disabilities. Their concerns were captured in comments such as 'school should support more children with disabilities, they do not do enough, help them one to one'. For another young carer, if he could change one thing that would have been 'school to help disabled people more not just for 10 minutes only '. These findings are consistent with previous research, where young people showed a preference for practical services such as improved leisure and sports facilities within their locality, social space to meet with their friends, and access to physical environment (e.g., parks) in their neighbourhood where they feel safe and welcome (Borland et al., 2001; Sinclair, 2004).

The majority of young people, across groups, showed limited awareness about the existence of services such as mentoring, respite care, a 'buddy' system and advocacy to facilitate future planning with regard to accessing services. Their capacity for agency and negotiation, manifested within their family and peers, was not extended to the wider socio-political macro contexts of their life.

The young people's views, as service users, are discussed by referring to the notion of children's services as 'children's spaces' because their input about services and access to resources were, in many ways, a discussion about spaces (Moss, 1999; Moss and Petrie, 2002). The young people raised the need for physical and social spaces to meet with friends and form relationships. They also spoke about the importance of having critical spaces for dialogue and critical engagement, where their decisions have the potential to transform policy and practice.

These findings suggest that the young people displayed agency in the context of their family and peer interactions (micro settings). They felt confident to negotiate and challenge the assumptions made by professionals, showing a preference to engage in joint decision making with their parents. Young carers in particular stated that they negotiate with their parents the degree of their involvement with household chores and other caring responsibilities. Du Bois-Raymond coined the phrase 'negotiation families' whereas the patterns of interaction between parents and children are subject to negotiation rather than authoritarian structures and relationships (2001). Furthermore, within their peer circle, another micro setting, young people negotiated and ascertained their right to be respected and not discriminated against, especially in relation to bullying, and the rights of their siblings with disability. Within their family and school, children showed the skills needed to act powerfully and competently. However, they appeared to lack formal powers to influence the decision makers at their schools. Outside the sphere of the family, school and peer culture, the young people appeared to be less aware of opportunities available to exercise choice and access resources and services.

It appears that taking negotiation and decision making to the next level in terms of influencing policy and service provision is challenging for some young people. Exercising power involves exercising choice; for some, choice for matters such as access to advocacy services or participatory structures and practices at school has been outside their sphere of influence. This suggests the existence of a continuum of influence; at one pole of the continuum (micro level) young people show resilience, whereas, at the other pole (macro level), they show vulnerability. The existence of the resilience – vulnerability continuum is interesting, especially when considering that young people, especially those with caring responsibilities, engage actively with social and cultural changes in their role as carers and economic producers, within a care-deficit context. Young people's display of resilience and vulnerability appear to have a contextual and structural basis that shapes the ways in which choice and power operate during the development of policy regarding service access.

The young people's limited awareness of and engagement with advocacy services and decision making at school, may also be explained by considering the effects of disadvantage and lack of opportunities to enable choices (Lansdown, 1995; Mitchell and Sloper, 2001). Lansdown commented that disadvantage and lack of formal power have a two-fold impact on young people: it makes them feel less confident in the validity of their views, and also their views are less likely to be taken into account. Vulnerability and disadvantage impact on people's opportunities for real choices, including awareness about these choices. They also affect structures and processes that are internal and external to them, such as self esteem, lack of verbal fluency, disaffection, discrimination and poverty, that may, in turn, pose further obstacles to achieving a genuine involvement.

The relationship between power/choice and participation is complex. Power shapes participation in many ways, and 'articulations of power in participation are very often less visible, being as they are embedded in social and cultural practices' (Cooke and Kothari, 2001: 14). This raises issues regarding the nature and role of cultural and social practices in empowering children to participate, as well as children's internalization of certain assumptions without being unchallenged (Foucault, 1977). Cultural practices and assumptions tend to be shaped by dominant views about the nature of knowledge and what we hold as 'truth', as well as our capacity to interrogate and challenge them.

The discrepancy between being involved in decision making within families and schools (micro level) and young people's lack of influence regarding the wider networks (macro level), can be explained by deploying social capital theories. In so doing, explaining the gap in participatory practices requires an understanding of the patterns of relations between individuals and networks or institutions (e.g., Putnam, 2000). Social capital underpins social relations and practices that occupy the spaces between micro and macro systems in young people's lives.

In the literature of social capital, bonding, bridging and linking capital is discussed (Putnam, 2000; Woolcock and Narayan, 2000). Bonding capital emanates from within-the-family social experiences and interactions and refers to emotional and practical support provided by members of nuclear and extended families, as well as small close-knit communities. Bridging capital refers to 'heterogeneous horizontal social networks' that support individuals to access information, advice and services from an array of professionals and organizations. Linking capital refers to links between communities 'upwards to powerful people, institutions and agencies' (Gewirtz et al., 2005: 668) (see Chapter 12, for a discussion on social capital).

Social and cultural capital influences young people's participatory practices. At a micro level, young people generated bonding social capital, through
family interactions and cultural practices and peer interactions. However, for
involvement at a macro level, the capacity to deploy bridging and linking
forms of social capital is required, in that a young person would need to negotiate within a context of unequal power relationships. Moreover, they would
need to develop skills to build links with networks/institutions/organizations
and access services such as respite care, coaching and advocacy support.

It appears that the young people in this study lacked the social capital,
and the choice and opportunity that come with it, to engage in political
processes beyond their immediate family setting. They were not voiceless,
nor did they lack in assertiveness and resilience. However, their capacity to
exert influence at a macro level was limited, perhaps because of a lack of
socialization and a limited access to social capital to enable young people to
participate actively at a political/civic level.

Children are expected to exercise democratic responsibilities as citizens;
however, they need to be nurtured to develop the intellectual, social and
emotional maturity to participate actively. Important ethical dilemmas arise
when considering the educational systems and processes that encourage
independent judgement, critical thinking, capacity for self-reflection and
problem solving in children. Many factors, such as the nature of child–adult
relationships, cultural notions of childhood, disability and adults' capacity
to exercise their rights affect the nature of children's participation.

Participation of Persons with Disability

The existing framework of human rights has not been sufficiently effective
in offering genuine protection and opportunities for participation to
persons with disabilities (Herr et al., 2003). As a result about 'ten percent
of the world's population is exposed to the most extreme forms of denial
and violation of the full range of human rights' (ibid.). In August 2006, The
United Nations High Commissioner for Human Rights welcomed considerations regarding the introduction of the International Convention on the
Rights of Persons with Disabilities. The Convention elaborated on the
human rights of persons with disabilities, in areas such as equality, non-
discrimination and equal recognition before the law; liberty and security of
the person; accessibility, personal mobility and independent living; right to
health, work and education; and participation in political and cultural life.

Increasingly, children with disabilities are offered opportunities to express
their views regarding service development (e.g., Cavet and Sloper, 2004;

Sloper and Lightfoot, 2003). In the United Kingdom, a number of governmental initiatives have been implemented to support participation of young
people with disabilities in decisions regarding their welfare and access to
services. A growing number of local health authorities and governmental
agencies consult young people with illness and disability, with the scope to
incorporate their views into service development, and also get feedback on
the quality of services (Sloper and Lightfoot, 2003; Mitchell and Sloper,
2001). The British Medical Association proposed that health professionals
should facilitate young people's participation and decision about issues
regarding their healthcare (2001). The Quality Protects Programme, the
Expert Patient Programme (Department of Health, 2001), and the SEN
Code of Practice (DfES, 2001) offer a legislative framework on disability
and participation. In all these frameworks, the notion of competence is
raised, stressing the need for the professionals to take all reasonable steps
to enhance children's capacity for participation.

The right to express views appears to be 'reserved' for children who are
capable of forming their own views. This raises ethical dilemmas for children with disabilities who may be less capable of forming and expressing
views. Although age and maturation play an important role in understanding and voicing issues, young children and those with disabilities are
often seen as being less capable of articulating their concerns and views.
Lansdown argues that various degrees of competence 'does not mean that
young children's views will automatically be given less weight' (2001: 2).
Adults have the responsibility to create opportunities for children to express
their rights by putting in place structures that are fluid and facilitative.

The UNCRC stresses that the notion of

> evolving capacities should be seen as a positive and enabling process, not
> an excuse for authoritarian practices that restrict children's autonomy
> and self-expression and which have traditionally been justified by point-
> ing to children's relative immaturity and their need for socialization.(UN
> Committee on the Rights of the Child, 2005).

Disability studies have provided many innovative ideas in terms of devis-
ing creative ways to include children with impairment and difficulties.
Strategies that have been found to facilitate participation of young people
with disabilities involve

- a multi-media approach (Morris, 1998a; Stone, 2001);
- access and suitability of communication aids following appropriate assessment of their communication needs (e.g., Morris, 1998b; Stone, 2001);

- maximizing the number of meetings, amount of contact to allow for rapport and understanding of their individual circumstances not only with regard to the impairment or disability but also considering other factors such as language, ethnicity (e.g., Morris, 1998b); and
- building up trust to ensure that children are not placed under any pressure from adults, especially when offering views about the quality of the services they receive.

However, these practices raise dilemmas, requiring us to think about the challenges and the methodological shifts that we encounter to make the participation of young children, especially those with disabilities, possible. Lewis and Porter argue that children with disability require a second-order representation, in that mechanisms that are likely to capture typically developing children's voice may not be appropriate for capturing the voice of disabled children (2007). In an evaluation study, concerns were raised with the limited consultation of young people with disabilities in residential schools (Department of Health, 2001). Moreover, limited availability of communication aids to children who require them has also been reported as an obstacle to self-expression and participation (Morris, 1998a; Stone, 2001).

Children should be treated with equal respect regardless of their age, situation, ethnicity, ability or disability. Children with disability require differentiated or diversified levels of support and can contribute in different ways. Ethical dilemmas are raised in that in certain cases of disability, where it becomes difficult to draw a line between children talking for themselves and adults talking for them. Children with disabilities, as well as those from minority ethnic and linguistic backgrounds are likely to face multiple disadvantages and become victims of exclusionary policies. They have to overcome invisibility and prejudice that already mitigate against their right to participation.

The Disability Discrimination Act 2005 signifies a broader move towards young people's inclusion in society, not just in schools. Current understandings of inclusion need to be challenged by redefining inclusion from being a moral imperative to becoming a space for nurturing children's participation in democratic processes, contextualizing rights within an ethical praxis and widening children's citizenship. This would require a shift in power structures, rules and regulations, as well as the development of advocacy systems. Current inclusive models do not take into account the concept of inclusive education (and inclusion in general) as defined by disabled people, the largest minority group excluded, worldwide, from schooling (Gabel and Peters, 2004). Participation, in young people with disabilities, appears to mean different things to different organizations and decision makers and, like inclusion, is translated into yet more varied concepts and practices by practitioners at school levels.

For persons with disability, inclusion is an important first step to participation. However, Santos argues that the mechanisms of inclusion tend to be similar to those that underpin exclusion (see discussion on Disability and the Entrepreneurial Self in Chapter 3). This view is exemplified in children with disabilities who are placed in mainstream settings without appropriate support and guidance (see Lindsay, 2007 for a review). Furthermore, for displaced children in refuge camps or children who experience poverty and disadvantage, the rhetoric of inclusion reflects exclusionary processes by not addressing diversity and marginalization (Santos, 2001). Inclusion is a social and cultural mechanism that should reflect in its process the make-up of society to ensure that society and education do not exclude pupils as a result of their diverse needs, be they emotional, cultural, linguistic, medical, neurological, physical or social (Ainscow et al., 2004).

Participation of Young People: A Way Forward

Sen advocates that 'since participation requires basic educational skills, denying the opportunity to schooling to any group, for example, female children is immediately contrary to the basic conditions to participatory freedom' (2000: 32). The development of child-centred organizations[4] or Rights Respecting Schools, for example, with an ethos where achievement is rewarded in the public sphere (via media, digital technology) are likely to offer young people the skills required for participation. The practices of learning for participation and citizenship can benefit children intellectually, socially and emotionally.

Children, through participation, develop new skills (e.g., clarity of communication, negotiation strategies, building arguments and engaging in debates); enhance their self-esteem and challenge vulnerability or lack of ability to deal with 'adult issues'; identify and recognize their strengths and articulate their rights; and developing a sense of responsibility. Young children may be less skilled, requiring a period of growth and maturation. However, cultural and societal interpretations of maturity should not result in inequality and violation of their rights. A lack of rights to voice and participation in decision making, eventually compromises the rights to protection, survival and provision, imposing a multi-fold discrimination against children and their families.

Taking all these dilemmas into consideration, young people's participation should rely on the principles of

- inclusion in terms of providing inclusive practices that draw in those often excluded (e.g., young children, carers, asylum seekers and disabled young people);
- empowerment by supporting the development of skills, knowledge and maturity (confidence, self-efficacy) to engage in decision making and become agents of change;
- citizenship and political education, including knowledge of children's rights, structures, services, etc.;
- independence expressed as responsibility for actions and ownership of services; and
- community in terms of a relational approach to exercise rights in the context of interactions with peers and adults.

These principles are based on the concept of minor politics or minor engagements, which are described as 'cautious, modest, pragmatic, experimental, stuttering, tentative. They are concerned with the here and now, not with some fantasized future, with small concerns, petty details, the everyday and not the transcendental' (Rose, 1999a: 280). Minor politics offer an important framework within which to place inclusion, empowerment and citizenship in ways that relate to young people's everyday life. It is only then that the right to participation becomes a lived experience.

The minor politics, practised in children's everyday life, ensure that the voice of the child is included and their participatory rights are ascertained (Clark and Moss, 2001). The minor politics are contextual and defined by the culture and social reality of children's worlds. The children's rights legislation can certainly gain from grassroots movements, advocacy networks, and family and community practices that offer possibilities for political participation at a local level with a global impact. Finally, the minor politics can stimulate what Beck calls emancipatory subpolitics that are thought to bring changes by raising issues and counter issues and challenging consensus, as well as the few who make decisions that affect the many (1999).

The scope for children's participation is huge, affecting all facets of their life, from school, to local community, to policy and service development. Young people should be supported to have a first-hand experience of the issues under consideration, rather than becoming involved in top-down, adult-centred participation agendas. The young people have identified a range of systems and processes to support meaningful engagement and participation, such as 'time to understand the important issues and thorough information about them; access to child-friendly information and documentation; capacity building with child-led organizations and training for adults to overcome their resistance to child involvement' (Lundy, 2007: 935).

The procedures to be implemented at schools and other children's institutions to support children's participation include

- providing children with information in formats that are accessible to them;
- negotiating with children the rules and boundaries from the beginning;
- ensuring that participation is voluntary, without any explicit or implicit form of coercion;
- ensuring that power relations and decision-making structures are transparent and accessible to children;
- ensuring that the language is used in ways that children understand. Moreover, employ other non-verbal modes of expression, such as drama, play, art;
- assisting children to identify the issues that they consider as being important;
- understanding children's priorities and that they may be different from adults;
- ensuring that is not an one-off approach but a sustainable one; and
- developing a sense of ownership by ensuring that children are involved from the early stages of the project; (Lansdown, 2001; paraphrased).

Another principle I would like to add is giving opportunities to adults to examine their ambivalence and biases about children's roles and responsibilities and visibility in public life. Children with disabilities, in particular, are absent from the public sphere as symbolic representations and as physical entities. Although, there is a proliferation of representations of children in poetry, paintings and novels over time, some images of children and young people with disabilities have entered the popular culture fairly recently (e.g., a couple of movies and documentaries on children with autism), raising mixed feelings about cultural representations of disability.

Chapter 9

The Right to Childhoods

The right to childhoods is more than an accumulation of the rights of the child as stated in the United Nations convention. It encapsulates the right to cohesive communities and civic engagement, to not be seen as a commodity. It also involves the right to diversity and difference, to form and manage complex cultural identities, to withstand the corporatization of childhood and to ameliorate social inequalities through public discourses and practices that acknowledge diversity. Most crucially, it involves the right to embrace the pluralism inherent in children's lives and acknowledge the many childhoods that children experience as they grow up in the 21st century. Finally, it is a democratic right for children to have a voice and participate with the purpose of engaging in decision making to transform the reality of their life and promote an active citizenship.

Above all, the right to childhoods encompasses the right to be considered a 'rich' child (Malaguzzi, 1993). The 'rich' child operates from a perspective whereby individual and collective rights are not in conflict and engages critically with the world by being an active participant in meaning making and reflexive and dialogic within communities of practice. The right to childhoods is shaped by Levinas' ethics of an encounter that advocate care and a relational approach by embedding rights in children's lived experience. In this context, needs are construed along the lines of mutual dependency, empathy and care. Within the right to childhoods framework, rights and obligation are interwoven, bringing together political and moral advantages towards children's well-being.

The right to childhoods does not approach equality as sameness but advocates difference and child-centric perspectives, avoiding rights neutral perspectives that often resonate the views of those in power. It accepts that the right to be equal and the right to be different are not in conflict; rather, they work in a complementary fashion. As Santos argues, we have the right to be different when equality reduces our individuality, and the right to be equal when difference imposes inferiority and disadvantage. Moreover, it asserts different cultural conceptions of children's rights without embracing moral particularism and moral relativism. Human agency and relational approaches to children's rights go at the heart of the right to childhoods. Gould referred to the concept of social ontology, a conception of individuals in relation rather than individuals as abstract entities, to articulate the social reality of children's lives and retain cultural differentiation (2004).

As a framework, the right to childhoods is underpinned by the following principles, namely

- multiplicity and plurality of childhood, in that there are many childhoods as experienced by children in different places and time;
- ethical praxis that construes rights along the lines of care and responsibility, as relational and responsive towards the 'other', instead of a calculating social contract;
- dialectical approach that encourages a new form of criticality;
- Gould's concrete universalism and cosmopolitical democracy (2004);
- children's well-being, defined as being more than a mere accumulation of the convention rights, i.e., provision, protection and participation, is fundamental to the right to childhoods;
- contextual approach to children's rights by accounting for the particularities of children's life;
- advocacy for the 'rich' child who is a moral and social agent, and a citizen now; and
- emancipation that is achieved through governance rather than over-regulation.

The Many Childhoods

As discussed in Chapter 1, childhood is not a unitary entity; there are many childhoods that are interpreted and constructed differently all over the world. Childhood is embedded in place and time, and is shaped by biology, society and culture. Children's similarities and differences are understood in relation to the value and meaning of children's communities. The experience of growing up is not solely defined by the cultural/social norms, practices and expectations; certain trajectories in children's development are common across cultural and ethnic groups, pointing to the importance of accepting both the universality and particularity of children's lives. The many childhoods should not be bounded by dichotomous views of nature vs. nurture to ensure that the complexity of children's nature is not compromised.

Childhood is heterogeneous and diverse, encapsulating the lived experiences of boys and girls from different ethnic backgrounds, who display various degrees of ability, disability and possibilities. The right to childhoods is the right to the multiplicity and plurality of childhood, the right to acknowledge that, although children around the world share many commonalties, childhood is shaped by the circumstances that surround children's life. I use the plural 'childhoods' instead of 'childhood' to stress the many childhoods that children experience, which are different, unequal and bounded by children's place and time.

A Dialectical Approach

A dialectical approach to knowledge emphasizes the social and interactive nature of knowledge as constructed in the spaces between the learner and the social/political context within which the learner is situated. The right to childhoods has an ethical basis, and its discourse is dialectical; it accepts a diversity of perspectives and places an emphasis on care, responsibility and empathy. A dialectical approach to children's rights stresses the importance of situating rights within children's lived experience as shaped by their surroundings.

Moreover, it is important to ensure that one narrative or perspective is not replaced with another, but stimulates critiques on how power structures transform certain narratives into grand narratives, which subsequently influence children's rights. To this end, the conceptual framework that underpins the right to childhoods should be informed by a diversified philosophical thought, including liberal[5] political views and feminist ethics. The right to childhoods should be located within the spaces of the personal and political and these spaces are dynamic in that they involve interchanges and movements back and forth between the poles. Being dialectical also involves exercising a criticality that would allow young people to show agency and distinguish between personal, social and moral crisis.

Agency is reflected in individuals' capacity to act with intent and awareness with regard to the construction of the self and social relationships (Robinson and Diaz, 2006). It is a process of self formation that involves the capacity to exercise choice, determination and being active in forming subjectivity and a sense of selfhood. Agency may be built through a genuine engagement with the world. It entails resilience, reflexivity, problem solving and a balance between personal and collective responsibility, stressing the role of individuals as active agents in dealing with crises in ways that distinguish them from personal deficits. By presenting a social crisis as an individual crisis, the important role that social, political structures play in children's lives is diminished.

Taking a dialectical approach to rights is likely to support young people in actively forming their own identities and negotiating crises in their life. Moreover, a dialectical approach is likely to bridge seemingly contradictory views about the validity of knowledge as reason and knowledge and as a cultural artefact towards what Santos (1995) describes as a 'new common sense' that encapsulates both logos (reason) and mythos (folklore).

Cosmopolitical Democracy and Concrete Universalism

Children's rights as an abstract code do not allow for an exploration of ethics, sites, sources and structures of power that shape the application of human rights across diverse cultural and political contexts. The right to childhoods relies on a cosmopolitical democracy that aspires to bring together diverse cultural contexts and communities at a local and global level. The right to childhoods engages with the dilemmas of how to 'combine a commitment to the universal recognition of others – whether it be a matter of ethical, cultural or legal recognition – with a respect of a concrete particularism, difference or asymmetry of others' (Hanssen, 2000: 130, 166).

These dilemmas have been articulated along the lines of Gould's concrete universalism, which accommodates cosmopolitan perspectives and communitarian approaches towards the ethics of care and respect for difference and diversity (2004). The notion of a concrete universalism stresses plurality and diverse cultural perspectives, and includes social interactions and the conversations and narratives that young people construct as part of a lived experience. Santos has conceptualized rights legislation and practices within a 'cosmopolitan legality' at three levels, namely, international, state and community, in an attempt to combine global and local rights frameworks. Specifically, he argues for a political mobilization of international human rights, state-defined human rights conceptualized along citizenship and inclusion, and rights, at a local level, as established by local communities.

The absence of a universal framework of children's rights does not result in a moral relativism. On the contrary, individuals are expected to 'be more active in ethical practices . . . by making choices and taking responsibility for those choices' (Dahlberg and Moss, 2005: 71). Acting socially responsibly can be challenging, especially in a fast-changing, increasingly diverse world where there are no certainties, and personal interpretations of right and wrong may bring further conflict and disengagement. Bauman advocates a 'personalisation of ethics and personal responsibility' (1993: 35). Exercising personal responsibility does not mean that individuals cannot and should not try to reach a consensus on agreed-upon positions and make collective decisions.

Santos argues for a transformative framework of rights that incorporates local, community-based social principles to represent all children, especially those who have been in the periphery of grand narratives, exclusive of the 'other' (Dahlberg and Moss, 2005: 65). These principles include 'solidarity', 'co-responsibility', 'participation' and 'new aesthetics' to encourage multiple voices, capable of generating a new common sense (Santos, 1995: 53). In this context, children's rights are built in a bottom-up manner (Dahlberg and Moss, 2005) while, at the same time, they are bounded by a 'cosmopolitical' citizenship.

Children as Moral and Social Agents and as Citizens

The right to childhoods encapsulates the right for children to exist as a recognized social group, as citizens who have rights and responsibilities. Children are not future citizens or citizen becomings; they are citizens from the moment they entered the world. With this in mind, notions of participation and children's rights require rethinking. Children should be empowered to remove an externally imposed 'protective space' and become active members of a society. The right to childhoods incorporates legislation and advocacy to ensure children's protection, participation and citizenship and, most crucially, children's well-being. Well-being is an all-encompassing term that involves survival, protection and participation, as well as the attainment of happiness and a rewarding and fulfilling life.

The adults' moral panic may be channelled in supporting children face the challenges of complex societies by building their strengths for participation and agency. Participation is critical for democratic processes and citizenship rights, especially in the light of the increasing number of young people who live in urban inner cities and who are kept out of any social contract (Santos, 1998). Children who have access to resources and are in a position to exercise choice are more likely to participate in decision making, compared to those with a limited social and cultural capital. The right to participation should not be an economic but a political one, capable of encouraging and sustaining the multiplicity of children's voices.

Participation in a civic and political life is the cornerstone of being a citizen. Shier places participation on a continuum of five points, namely, children are encouraged and supported to express their views; children are listened to; children's views are taken into account; children are involved in the decision making; and children share power and exercise responsibility with regard to the decisions made (2001). This continuum is likely to raise young people's moral and social status, a necessary precondition for the right to childhoods.

Express views

Children, regardless of their age and maturity, are in a position to express their views on matters that affect their everyday life. They offer views about the interactions and negotiation they make with other children, what they like and dislike at school, about ways that learning can be more enjoyable, their views about fairness and aspirations regarding their future.

Young people have not been adequately supported to exercise the right to freedom of expression as stated in Article 13, 'the child shall have the right to freedom of expression; this right shall include freedom to seek, receive and impart information and ideas of all kinds, regardless of frontiers, either orally, in writing or in print, in the form of art, or through any other media of the child's choice'. Adults should experiment with different modes of expression, through Drama, dance, body language, conversation, storytelling, drawing and use of visual materials to find suitable ways to engage children with diverse profiles and requirements. Although Article 13 stresses that expression can take many different forms through the use of diverse media, the appropriateness of and access to these media is rarely debated.

Being listened to

There are five principles for listening to children, namely, recognizing children's many languages; allocating communication spaces; making time; providing choice; and subscribing to a reflective practice (Lancaster, 2006). Many innovative ideas for listening to children's contributions come from the Mosaic study that has developed techniques to listen to the perspectives of three- and four-year-old children on their nursery provision e.g., based around children's drawings, their photographs and tape recordings (Clark and Moss, 2001). The notion of a developmentally appropriate practice is not at odds with maximizing the fit between approaches to encourage participation and the age and maturity of the child.

The suitability of procedures designed to enable children with intellectual and communicative difficulties to express their views and participate requires further examination. Although adults are obliged to use different modes of expression, through art, drama and play, children with different levels of intellectual and social maturity may experience participation as another burden that is likely to marginalize them further. The variation in the participatory procedures for children with disability and other facets of diversity (e.g., minority children) may pose more obstacles than resolving dilemmas.

Views are taken into account

Clear procedures for determining the extent to which adults who engage in joint decision with children are responsive to children's views should be implemented to safeguard children's participatory rights (Fielding, 2004). Cavet and Sloper (2004) stress the need to evaluate both the experience of participation and its outcomes, especially the extent to which young people's views have been taken into account and acted upon. The impact and sustainability of young people's participation is determined by the extent to which their views are taken seriously.

There are three essential procedures for the empowerment of marginalized young people, namely mandate, information and resources (Lolichen, 2006). The concept of 'mandate' validates participation by creating a critical space for children to negotiate, express and legitimate wishes and also reflect on the implications of their choices and consequent risks. It sets the scene for opinion to be voiced and demands to be negotiated, making child's best interest a central point. 'Information' enables children to negotiate and make skilled and relevant contributions. 'Resources' can be accessed once information and skills are acquired. Children access information through conversations with their parents and peers or the media.

If young people's views are not respected, they are less likely to respect others' views and engage in democratic processes. Nurturing citizenship requires children to learn about their rights and responsibilities and to reflect on the rights and freedoms of others, as well as on the ways in which their actions affect the rights of others. Practices for learning and democracy involve the development of agency in children and capacity for judgement and expressing views and opinions and engaging in action. Agency coupled with action is likely to enable young people to participate and influence decision making and power sharing. Citizenship can be taught through an active engagement with the power structures at a school and community level.

Decision making and power sharing

Lansdown discusses children's right to expression in the context of democratic processes and makes a distinction between a 'substantive and a procedural right' (2001: 2). Substantive right involves empowering children to make decisions about matters that are important to their lives, and procedural in terms of engaging actively in democratic procedures to challenge violation of their rights and power inequalities through power sharing. She notes that the right to expression does not automatically grant children autonomy and political power, mainly because children rely on adults for nurturing them as citizens and supporting them to exercise their rights.

The distinction between empowering children to make decisions and challenging inequalities is crucial, in the light of the content and scope of Articles 12 and 13. Article 12, in particular, specifies that 'parties shall assure to the child who is capable of forming his or her own views the right to express those views freely in all matters affecting the child, the views of the child being given due weight in accordance with the age and maturity of the child'. The Article 12 addresses children's procedural right; however, to what extent it meets their substantive rights in terms of capability and empowerment towards participation is unclear.

A Contextual Approach to Children's Rights

Santos argues that rights, including children's rights, should be understood from the perspective of local cultures, languages and locations where the translators have knowledge and an understanding of different cultures. Considering children's local cultural perspectives does not mean accepting a form of cultural relativism as a guiding principle to children's rights. The implementation of 'transcultural criteria' or indicators of multiple citizenships would allow an exercise in plurality where local issues are offered multiple interpretations (Santos, 2001: 211), enabling the transference of children's rights into local contexts.

Children's rights, as an international legal framework, often fail to account for the context of children's lives. De-contextualizing rights makes them irrelevant and thus obsolete. The right to participation, protection and provision should not be reduced to universal codes of conduct because, if they do, they become ineffective and potentially misleading. For example, a number of national and international campaigns against child labour have accounted for neither the societal and cultural context of children's life, nor children's views. Specifically, a campaign targeting child labour in a garment factory in Bangladesh resulted in children losing their job and undertaking jobs under more dangerous conditions. This well-intended campaign caused more problems than what it actually solved. Rather than making decisions about what we think is good for the child labourers' life, perhaps, we could have obtained their views about their circumstances, and implemented context-specific, culture-driven policies and systems of support. Making decisions about children's life without listening to their views and accounting for their contexts can have devastating consequences (see Chapter 3 for a discussion on hybridized rights).

To balance cross-cultural and context-specific conceptions of children's rights, the practices of difference should play a central role in continually negotiating principles of equality and difference. The construction of 'local, national and transnational relations based on the principle of redistribution (equality) and the principle of recognition (difference)' will 'emerge as counter-hegemonic globalization' (Santos, 2001: 187). These relations can be sustained in a new transnational political culture whose archetype is 'subjectivity and sociability', based on the cultural and social interactions of groups of people in different places all over the world. This new culture will not rely on grand narratives but on a 'cosmopolitan law' to ascertain the particularities, regional resources and 'diversified economies' of people's lives (Mander and Goldsmith, 1996: 18).

Emancipation, Governance and Regulation

The globalized world becomes increasingly volatile and unstable, increasing the vulnerability of subordinate social groups, especially displaced and refugee children and their families. Against this background, social life and relational structures are judged by their marketability, likely to result in a society that is 'ungovernable and ethically repugnant' (Santos, 2001: 187). The dominance of free markets has increasingly destabilized nation-states and has replaced governance with over-regulation. The State assumes the role of coordinating private sector initiatives, e.g., subcontracting of private services. The increasing privatization of basic services, such as health, education, and the 'corporatisation of governance' have placed restrictions on the basic human rights in both children and adults (Lolichen, 2006).

The remit of nation-states is changing, and governance is being gradually replaced by over-regulation. With childhood and family life becoming over-regulated, an important question is what legitimizes knowledge and decision making about children's well-being. Moreover, who will be making decisions about children's lives when the political class is replaced by corporate leaders and administrators (Lyotard, 1979)?

For Santos, emancipation can be realized in terms of three broad rationalities, namely, instrumental–technical rationality, moral–practical rationality and aesthetic–expressive rationality. He argues that the last two rationalities have been made peripheral, with the instrumental–technical rationality gaining considerable ground supported by the weight that scientific knowledge is thought to bear. The technical–instrumental rationality has been influenced by the Enlightenment principles, such as normalization and objectivity and certainty. As Dahlberg and Moss observe, where instrumental rationality prevails, the ethical becomes technical, and power and responsibility become detached from each other (2005). Bauman has also critiqued modernity's ethics, commenting that ethics have been replaced with order, rules and regulations, reducing them into a prescribed code of behaviour (1993).

The moral–practical and aesthetic–expressive rationalities, both important sources of interpersonal and communal relations and identity formation, have been marginalized. Santos stresses the importance of reviving these traditions to counteract the marginalization of children and their families. With market shaping social relationships and public services, the gap between the included and the excluded is not only an ideological but a spatial and a social one. Zones of exclusion impact on children at a micro (poverty, families under pressure, lack of trust in the neighbourhood) and macro (capacity building for participation in decision making, education and employment) level. The right to childhoods should have at its heart a social contract that ensures the fulfilment of the most basic expectations for children and their families in terms of provision, protection and participation. This contract should not be based on processes of responsibilizing individuals to engage in corresponding duties because it should not assume equality among them. A focus on the moral–practical and aesthetic–expressive rationalities may offer possibilities for children's rights to be emancipatory.

An Ethical Praxis

The right to childhoods is framed by an ethical praxis that brings together rights legislation, care and capability building to enable children participate, take responsibility, challenge injustice and inequality. Most importantly, an ethical framework may transform rights from being a universal code into a living reality, a language of respect and citizenship. An ethical praxis should not be confined to merely following the law because laws, intentionally or unintentionally, may deviate from what is ethical. Ethics cannot rely on abstract notions of justice and truth but emerge from everyday problems whose solutions have to make sense to children's particular contexts and local requirements. Ethics involve standards of right and wrong which are culture-specific, and prescribe what humans ought to do in terms of rights (as a law), obligations, respect, justice, equality and citizenship.

The right to childhoods is situated within an ethical praxis that exudes a relational quality by facilitating norms to emerge from transcultural conversations and a common understanding. There are three sets of norms and values that emerge from Gould's cosmopolitical democracy that may set the basis for children's rights as an ethical praxis. The first refers to intersociative norms where values are generated in relationships of care, concern, empathy and solidarity. The second set of values is posited through common choices or co-agency, whether based on common goals and projects or on shared needs and interests. The third set of norms is generated through consensus or common conversation (2004: 65; slightly paraphrased). The right to childhoods as an ethical praxis, is based on ethics that are generated in relationships of care and concern, where children are encouraged to be moral and social agents who understand their shared world with its global and local dimensions. This approach relies on knowledge of what is common and what is different in all young people without engaging in essentialist interpretations of children's life and marginalizing difference.

Children's rights as a universal code of conduct is static; thus, relying on the rights legislation alone does not allow for capacity building and judgement capable of setting standards open to question. An ethical praxis framework is likely to support children to challenge inequality, participate in decision making, exercise responsibility and respect and develop citizenship. Feelings, views, laws, social and cultural norms and notions of equality may deviate from interpretations of ethics. Thus, it is important for children to develop capacities to re-examine the standards of equality, care, justice, respect and citizenship to ensure that they are reasonable, based on local knowledge which takes into account the culture and the social–political reality of their life.

There is a need for fundamental changes in the way that society as a whole approaches children's rights. What supports and sustains the right to childhoods is an acceptance of children as respected members of a social group, who are capable of exercising their democratic rights and responsibilities at a local level with global implications. The social and political structures that support or hinder children and their families to develop the intellectual, social and emotional capital that is required to become active citizens should be debated publicly. In the next part, the type of education and pedagogies that have the potential to support young people to acquire knowledge for rights and citizenship in an era of radical doubt is discussed.

Notes

[1] Universalism refers to the notion that there are objective, universal criteria to judge different cases, and that the principles that underpin societal organization are universal and applicable across contexts. Particularism, on the other hand, accepts that difference exists and that the criteria applied to judge a case are shaped by the cultural, social and political parameters of people's surroundings and experiences. Thompson and Hoggett argue that universalism and particularism share the same basis, in that universalism 'provides a fair standard by which to treat particular cases, and, on the other, particularism derives its moral force from an underlying universalism' (1996).

[2] Historically, cosmopolitanism was perceived as being elitist, idealistic, imperialist and capitalist. The term cosmopolitan denoted a person with diverse cultural influences. It has been used as a praise for individuals who have opened up themselves to diverse cultural experiences and practices, or as a denigration, depending on how much diversity and difference is valued. The term has been also used to differentiate between the culturally sophisticated and those who hold parochial views. A current understanding of cosmopolitanism is as an entity that has been shaped by a border-crossing mentality; it 'pushes us to make border-transcending new beginnings' (Beck, 2006). Also, see *The Political Philosophy of Cosmopolitanism*, by Gillian Brock and Harry Brighouse. Cambridge University Press, 2005.

[3] The Committee on the Rights of the Child (CRC) is a body of independent experts that monitors the implementation of the Convention on the Rights of the Child by its State parties under the aegis of the Office of the United Nations High Commissioner for Human Rights. The website is: www.ohchr.org/english/bodies/crc/index.htm

[4] Organizations include many voluntary sector groups: CRAE (Children's Rights Alliance for England: www.crae.org.uk) is an alliance of voluntary and statutory organizations; ARCH (Action on Rights for Children: www.arch-ed.org); CRIN (The Child Rights Information Network) is a global networking organization that disseminates information about and supports the implementation of the UNCRC (www.crin.org). Moreover, The Children's Legal Centre publishes ChildRight, a journal on children's rights: www.childrenslegalcentre.com. The 'Inspiring

Schools' publications and website www.participationforschools.org.uk contain material and case studies on young people's participation.

[5] By liberal views here I mean those that are promoted and sustained in a liberal society, which is defined as 'one based on recognition of the equal dignity of each individual, and the vulnerabilities inherent in a common humanity' (Nussbaum, 2004: 18).

Part IV

Knowledge for Rights and Democracy

What type of knowledge is required to develop capabilities in young people to exercise human rights, democracy and citizenship? What type of knowledge can ensure a viable future for all? An assumption that underpins these questions is that the future is likely to be fundamentally different for our children and grandchildren. These questions imply that knowledge, democracy, rights and citizenship are intertwined. They also imply that democracy is changing and not disappearing completely, and that it can still be salvaged, albeit in a different form. Educators, policy makers and academics have deployed a range of claims about the future of knowledge, and what there is to be known. These claims have emerged from different contexts (e.g., pedagogic, political, legal), different epochs (e.g., Enlightenment, postmodern era), different academic traditions (e.g., humanism, psychology, anthropology, sociology) and different policy contexts (e.g., UK SEN Code of Practice, UNCRC, UNESCO).

In this section, the concept of a learning society and pedagogies for a viable future aligns with the Deweyan idea of education for democracy. Learning society is not an economic but a political and moral entity, where the purpose of learning is for participation and democracy, a 'learning democracy', and not just for employment (Ranson, 1998: 23). Knowledge for rights and democracy shifts the focus from a corporate towards a civic and cosmopolitan education to enable children and their families to exercise their rights and citizenship. This view of learning addresses the child as a whole rather than a fragmented entity that is comprised of components that are prone to dualisms such as mind and body, emotions and reason or universal and local meaning. In recent times, the principles of a market-driven economy have shaped education by situating learning in the discourses of standards, accountability and competition (e.g., Florian, 2007;

Rouse and McLaughlin, 2007). Moving towards a civic education is essential to enable young people develop a 'critical attitude towards those things that are given to our present experience as if they were timeless, natural, unquestionable' (Rose, 1999a: 20).

A critical attitude, not only as an exercise of reason but, most crucially, as a critical approach to ethics, obligation and difference and their influences on how we construct meaning may support young people to face future societies. A critical attitude enables young people to reflect on the nature of knowledge and the object of knowing, and understand the mechanisms and societal structures by which knowledge is legitimized. This form of criticality is likely to support young people to explore possibilities instead of accepting things as being self-evident, and respect the narratives that emanate from their diverse communities.

Communities of practice and learning offer young people a critical space to construct knowledge and the means for participation and decision making. The various types of social capital resources that already exist in their families and communities (e.g., parental involvement, parent–schools partnerships, close-knit communities) can be harnessed for personal and collective benefits and form communities for learning and active participation. Young people as researchers, or co-researchers, can also contribute to communities of practice, where, through research, issues that are relevant to their life are explored, and decisions are enacted and evaluated.

Chapter 10

Knowledge and Morality in an Era of Radical Doubt

A theme of the late 20th century is that there are no certainties, and thus there are no special means to construct knowledge about the human world. Lather observes that 'we seem somewhere in the midst of a shift away from a view of knowledge as disinterested and towards a conceptualization of knowledge as constructed, contested, incessantly perspectival and poly-phonic' (1991; xx). Parker also acknowledges this shift and 'the capacity to articulate doubt', which is 'the mark of the attitude of seriousness; of an ability to recognize the true depth and gravity of a situation . . . This idea of open-mindedness – the exhortation constantly to question, criticize and change – issues in a culture of radical doubt' (1997: 122).

Lyotard observes that, in a postmodern society, there are no grand narra-tives (1979). There is a consensus that grand narratives are oppressive and operate in the exclusion of others, prescribing ethical and political views in society that regulate decision making and codes of conduct. Grand narra-tives are challenged along the lines of 'whose true' and 'under what circumstances' an idea or a perspective is considered to be true. Pinker, at a Simonyi Lecture at the University of Oxford, argued that the complexity of human nature has been denied because the most influential psychologi-cal and sociological theories of the last century have focused on three grand narratives, namely the Blank Slate, the Noble Savage and the Ghost in the Machine (2003). The Blank Slate narrative argues that behaviour, language and learning are shaped entirely by the environment. The Noble Savage refers to romantic notions of childhood (e.g., Rousseau's *Emile*, 1979) argu-ing that children are born good and innocent and society corrupts them. Finally, the Ghost in the Machine argues against behavioural determinism and body–mind dualisms. These views constitute human nature a project, understood through the lens of either biological or sociological forces, and, ultimately, reducing the complexity of the interplay between biology and culture.

Lather states that postmodernism has risen as a 'response to the loss of faith in the traditional religious and political orthodoxies' (1991: 159). This loss of faith has been highlighted by the collapse of communism (a grand political narrative) and the increasing questioning of religions (e.g., Christianity) within the liberal foundations of the Western civilization. One may ask what the nature of knowledge and morality is in a society with no grand narratives, and, most crucially, what legitimates the construction of knowledge.

The Enlightenment project whose main premise was/is that, through reason and science, people will achieve knowledge and moral authority, and, eventually, become liberated, has also been under scrutiny. Moss offers a comprehensive critique of the Enlightenment project and its assumptions about knowledge as being foundationalist and universal, relying on dualistic categories of thought.

> The Enlightenment project is inscribed with certain values and assumptions: the possibility of an ordered world, certain, controllable and predictable, built on foundations of universal, knowable and decontextualized criteria and laws; knowledge as an objective mirror of the real world, unaffected by values and politics; the separation of reason and emotion, one of many dualisms; linear progress to a universal civilization without cultural differences; the superiority of the West, whose institutions and values provide the basis for this universal civilization; and one true, reason-dictated solution for every problem.(Moss, 1999, 142–143)

Within the Enlightenment project, education strives for certainty through the acquisition of knowledge that is fixed and objective and capable of encapsulating absolute truths. Uncertainty brings risks and requires individuals to have the conviction to explore possibilities that may bring more uncertainty and more risks. Expressing uncertainty has become a sign of intellectual and emotional maturity, a desire to encounter different perspectives and discourses that are not necessarily situated within normative views of knowing. Moreover, by expressing uncertainty we assume responsibility, whereas the acceptance of an 'objective true' based on universal laws, removes responsibility from the person and their cultural surroundings.

Knowledge in an era of uncertainty becomes 'heterarchical and transient and carried out in the context of application, where it includes more temporary and heterogeneous sets of practitioners, collaborating on a problem defined in a specific and localized context' (Gibbons et al., 1994: 3). This type of knowledge is relational and in contrast to that traditionally developed within academic contexts, characterized by hierarchical relationships and attempts to cluster knowledge around generalizable abstract ideas. Knowledge as a relational entity signifies a move towards an 'embedded knowledge', or knowledge that is shaped by human experience. Hardin and Hintikka argue that 'knowledge should be grounded on human experience' and bounded by people's social interactions, and the language used during these interactions (1983, x). These shifts in knowledge require its users, be they teachers or pupils, to be 'more socially accountable and reflexive', with the role of the teacher/educator and pupils being negotiated in the context of communities of practice (Gibbons et al., 1994).

Others view the Enlightenment, as a historical and cultural phenomenon that replaced dogma and religious authority with science (e.g., Colquhoun, 2006). The fundamental principle of the Enlightenment 'think for yourself' has created autonomous individuals who rely on natural sciences rather than religious authorities to make moral judgement and understand the world. Within this mindset, the hegemony of religion slowly declined, and education and democracy were flourished. Colquhoun describes the transition from modernism to postmodernism as a process of 'endarkenment'. To him, knowledge has become void of meaning and the uncertainty and doubt it has brought have created the perfect conditions for the rise of dogma and religious and secular fundamentalism (2006).

The Nature of Knowledge

The nature of knowledge has been framed by discourses that draw on distinctive traditions of philosophical, educational, psychological and political thought, and by frameworks that translate knowledge into practice. In the era of Enlightenment, knowledge, e.g., Kant's *Critique of Judgment*, was understood as a 'mental aptitude' that was characterized by originality, with some people having a greater capacity than others to gain knowledge. The notion of knowledge as a universal property was critiqued by Bourdieu, who, among others, contested the universality of knowledge by arguing for the importance of a context (habitus) in shaping knowledge and aesthetics (1984). Bourdieu's critique offers a democratic view about knowledge by stressing its emancipatory role in mitigating against inequality, hierarchies and prejudices.

Within postmodern societies, the nature of knowledge is fundamentally different from that risen within the Enlightenment project, i.e., scientific knowledge based on reason. Scientific knowledge is thought to reflect a social reality that is based on nomological, cause-and-effect relationships which do not always account for the complexity and fundamental uncertainty in the world. Scientific knowledge, or what Lyotard called the grand meta-narrative of science, has been prominent over the last two centuries and, in recent years, has received intense criticism (1979). Apple, in his critique of scientific knowledge, stated that

> the programme of making everything knowable through the supposedly impersonal norms and procedures of 'science' has been radically questioned. The hope of constructing a 'grand narrative', either intellectual or political, that will give us the ultimate truth and will lead us to freedom has been shattered in many ways. (1991: vii)

The criticism of scientific knowledge centres on the realization that science has not always benefited people, especially those who experience disadvantage and have been excluded from existing institutional arrangements and scientific advances. This raises ethical questions about the validity and usefulness of scientific knowledge, in terms of who has access and who benefits from it. Furthermore, science has been criticized as being a tool to support neoliberal ideologies and justify policies that do not have a genuine public interest. In the context of this critique, the role of knowledge is to increase individuals' human capital and accountability for the benefit of those in power (e.g., Apple, 1991).

Recently, a revival in the importance of scientific evidence in Education and Social Sciences has been observed, as a response to a state of 'crisis' in current social research. The US National Research Council has defined quality of evidence along the lines of evidence-based, scientific research. In the view of Michael Castle, a US Representative, educational research has been described as being 'broken', stressing the need for experimental research and causal analysis as the only way to conduct research.

> Congress must work to make it more useful . . . Research needs to be conducted on a more scientific basis. Educators and policy makers need objective, reliable research. (National Research Council report, 2002: 28)

Following an international symposium to discuss education for a viable future, UNESCO commissioned a report to identify new modes or types of knowledge. In his report, Moran presents the 'seven knowledges' that have the potential to shape human sciences (1999). Within this framework, knowledge is understood as a multi-dimensional construct, reflecting the nature of a society in the 21ˢᵗ century, and is underpinned by the following premises:

- knowledge is not a static entity, but fluid and changeable;
- knowledge is not given but is continually contested and revisable;
- knowledge should be relevant with the capacity to bring together the local and universal;
- knowledge should not be fragmented within different disciplines;
- knowledge should emanate from understanding 'all aspects of the human condition – physical, biological, psychological, cultural, social and historical' (Watson, 2001: 262);
- knowledge of the world and different cultures should underpin children's identity formation. Identity should not be defined by national boundaries to embrace difference and diversity;
- knowledge, and not dogma, is required to confront uncertainties;
- knowledge as a way of understanding difference to tackle fundamentalism and racism;
- knowledge, and not a moral authority located within a particular religion, is required to promote ethics and an ethical praxis through critically engaging with the world; and
- knowledge to achieve a democratic participation and genuine polyphony.

Morin's 'seven knowledges' typology challenges discipline-based knowledge, suggesting a repositioning of our perception of and attitudes towards the 'known', and the type of education required to help young people adapt to change and uncertainty (Watson, 2001: 262). The seven knowledges, as they are presented here, are likely to build bridges across different subject areas, and encourage learners to make intrinsic connections between education and everyday life.

Moreover, the view of knowledge as being contextualized, technicist, applicable and transparent, as opposed to being abstract, universal, and with a strong philosophical and moral ground, reflects Aristotle's[1] conceptualizations of knowledge as episteme and phroenesis. The distinction between episteme and phroenesis is an important one; episteme is an abstract and universal body of knowledge, that is cumulative and generalizable, whereas phroenesis is a value-centred and action-oriented knowledge, which is participatory and relational and reflects power relationships and societal structures.

Armstrong discusses the nature of knowledge by arguing that people's thinking has been constructed around two poles, i.e., mythos and logos.

Armstrong ascertains that 'myths captured the timeless and enduring, and did not try to be rational by encapsulating literal facts but offered a truth of another kind, whereas rationality and science is to guide daily practical affairs. Each was indispensable in its own way' (2000; xiv). With the advent of modernity, reason and science were seen as liberating forces to advance humanity, whereas myths and beliefs were largely discounted.

Recognizing the polarization between logos and mythos, or Aristotle's epestemi and phroenesis, we shall not be forced to choose mythos or phroenesis as a substitute to science or episteme, with the view that the latter has not entirely addressed the needs of humanity. Knowledge can be both universal and local, and a more integrative framework is required to occupy the spaces between the two poles and counteract dualistic thinking (O'Lincoln, 2002).

Knowledge is shaped by the discourse frameworks within which it is situated. A discourse, according to Worrall, 'embraces all aspects of communication – not only its content, but its author (who says it?), its authority (on what grounds?), its audience (to whom?), and its objective (in order to achieve what?)' (1990: 8). It also reflects implicit and explicit ideological positions and power structures. A communicative interaction describes social experiences and events, and also shapes the knowledge that is derived from them through the creation of cultural references.

Language is not a neutral and transparent tool that is used to transmit information about absolute truths and the 'world out there'. In Wittgenstein's Language Games, the processes and structures that shape a discourse are articulated, ultimately, explaining the ways in which knowledge is legitimized. Wittgenstein viewed language as an integral component of the social, political and cultural context within which it is used, being defined by its use. With this in mind, the use of language is relational and a form of political action. Language is central as 'both carrier and creator of a culture's epistemological codes' (Punch, 2005: 140). Interpretation and not absolute truths is the cornerstone of a postmodernist knowledge which relies on multiple interpretations bounded by power structures (Foucault, 1980).

In an era of radical doubt, one may ask whether knowledge about childhood is created through many little narratives or a grand narrative. The multiplicity and plurality of children's lives should not be contained within one grand narrative; knowledge about childhood should be local, contested, non-hierarchical and meaningful to children's and their parents' lives. It should also function both as an explanation and as a legitimization of cultural and societal practices, power relationships and the norms that shape children's everyday experiences. In market-driven societies, however, knowledge has an instrumental value as a commodity and, thus, it is legitimated by its performativity,[2] or the extent to which knowledge production and use are connected with knowledge achieving certain outcomes.

The instrumentality of knowledge

At present, education in many developed countries is defined by measurable outputs, consumer responsiveness, service efficiency, public inspection and a managerialist and audit culture and profitability. The discourses on targets, effectiveness and efficiency, rather than purpose or values dominate the educational systems in many Western countries. In the United Kingdom, the Early Learning Goals as set in the Curriculum Guidance for the Foundation Stage in England have clearly set a technocratic rather than a pedagogic agenda regarding the education of young people. The principles that underpin these frameworks are 'well-planned activity that is purposeful and capable of engaging children in learning activities', limiting their scope with regard to participation, individual integrity and ethics. Moss observes that the universality and validity of a target-orientated culture 'cannot imagine other forms of rationality, for example aesthetic rationality or ethical rationality – that you might do something because it is pleasing or judged right' (2002).

The instrumentality of knowledge is apparent in educational policy and practice that target children and their families who encounter socio-economic inequality. The alleged aim of this instrumentality is to ensure that children will break the cycle of poverty and disadvantage by being equipped to meet economic targets, viewing early years education as a means to an end. The curricular structure of instrumental learning and teaching places an emphasis on skills and knowledge that bear an economic advantage. Within this conceptualization of education, failure to learn would mean failure to actively participate in economic production and, ultimately, restriction in participatory freedoms. When pedagogy becomes instrumental, Moss argues, there is a tendency to offer management solutions to issues that are embedded in complex political and ideological contexts (2002). The process of offering management solutions to solve issues of social justice and ethics has been described by Clarke as managerialization:

> The problems which the managerial state is intended to resolve derive from contradictions and conflicts in the political, economic and social realms. But what we have seen is the managerialisation of these contradictions: they are redefined as 'problems to be managed'.(Clarke, 1998: 179)

In a knowledge-based society, Oancea observes a capacity trading instead of capacity building with professional knowledge and expertise becoming tradable commodities (2007). Capacity trading also construes improvement in services in terms of efficiency and meeting targets, not necessarily in terms of achieving children's well-being. Children's well-being is traded with 'fabrications of performance' and 'constructions of success' (Ball, 2004), suggesting a reimaged relationship between state intervention and children's services, with over-regulation becoming an important feature.

Knowledge of an instrumental nature is less likely to be embedded in ethics, in that decisions on children's well-being do not reflect the dilemmas of obligation, diversity and difference and professional accountability. Regarding accountability, Ranson observed a 'revolution' of accountability that has been articulated through five types of professional accountability, namely, professional judgement and ethics; consumer accountability based on market competition and consumer choice; contract in terms of competitive tendering; performative accountability expressed in terms of standards, a culture of audit, quality assurance; and corporate that mainly involves profitability (2003: 463–464).

The nature of knowledge as an individual or a collective endeavour, and the extent to which education is linked to all domains of human activity are rarely debated. To counteract the culture of targets and outcomes, and universal standards to education, Dahlberg and Moss argue for moving from a 'narrative of predictable outcomes' to embracing a 'narrative of uncertain possibilities' regarding education and learning (2005). Children need to be taught about the issues that affect their lives, such as the environment, poverty and social marginalization, technology, happiness, loss or diversity, rather than acquiring fragmented knowledge that aims to enhance their marketability only. As a society, our approach to knowledge reflects our vision about ethics and morality, and with the increasing categorization and subcategorization of knowledge, this vision is likely to become fragmented.

Morality and Knowledge

The Enlightenment project was to free individuals from the constraints of superstition and authority to allow them to think for themselves. Kant's main thesis was that individuals, through reason, can reach moral authority and autonomy. This thesis has been critiqued extensively, questioning whether reason alone can set the basis for a moral authority, with some arguing that 'thinking for yourself' has brought moral chaos in contemporary societies. However, what has barely been critiqued is the limited capacity of current education systems to encourage reason and critical thinking in children and young people and enable them to engage critically with the major issues that shape their lives. One should question the view that the moral chaos in contemporary societies has resulted from the enlightenment principle 'think for yourself', and explore the possibility that it might actually be the outcome of inadequate education, poverty and the rise of polarized societies.

Children and young people should be supported to develop emotional maturity to make reasoned judgements and differentiate between right and wrong. If we are to support children to act as citizens with rights and responsibilities, being non-judgemental is not an option. Law offers examples of a growing tendency to be non-judgemental and accept moral relativism as a sign of maturity and tolerance. He stresses that the capacity for moral judgement is particularly important in individualistic societies characterized by a self-serving morality (2006). Communities of learning have the potential to foster cultures of learning, where young people have opportunities for their views to be peer reviewed and cross examined. Such communities can function as a moral authority, capable of cultivating and sustaining young people's capacity for critical reflection and moral judgement.

MacIntyre and Rowan Williams see narratives and stories as the context within which moral judgement flourishes (cited in Law, 2006). However, narratives and discourses do not (and should not) reside within religious traditions only. They can also be found in philosophical and academic traditions and communities. Narratives of art and religion that are produced within academic institutions and practices have been criticized for being elitist and not relating to children's lives, perpetuating exclusion rather than inclusion. Knowledge and the development of a moral self are not independent of the context within which they are construed. Law suggests that children 'should learn to think critically about the tradition in which they find themselves' (2006: 136). Children's moral judgement reflects the circumstances that surround their life, and is meaningful when it emanates from their context, rather than being a distillation of top-down, abstract ideas. The narratives and discourses that originate in traditional canons as well as those from religious or academic contexts are equally important as long as they are embedded in the traditions of children's communities and reflect children's lived experiences.

One may argue that the distinction between an abstract objective truth and knowledge that is context-bound may lead to relativistic interpretations of what constitutes evidence, resulting in an 'everything goes' type of mentality, where judgement has no place in a morally relativist universe. However, a contextual approach to knowledge does not necessarily result in a lack of judgement and scrutiny of interpretation. On the contrary, contextualizing interpretations is likely to maximize their accuracy and offer individuals opportunities to make judgements that are relevant to their life.

Moreover, through research and peer review occurring within communities for practice, the concepts of right and wrong can be judged. Moral judgment relies on individuals' capacity for scrutiny and critical reasoning, as well as an understanding of the mores or customs and traditions that surround their lives. The pressure to choose between objective and contextual knowledge or external religious moral authority and relativism is a myth (Law, 2006). Equally, to approach moral judgement as a matter of a personal choice or, as Law observes, to privatize it, is likely to impede a holistic understanding of the moral dilemmas of the world young people occupy. Another way is possible, by raising children as 'citizens now' with rights and responsibilities to be in a position to form moral judgements. And, as I argue in this section, fostering responsibility and critical thinking in young people requires a civic education[3] with a strong liberal orientation.

Chapter 11

Civic and Corporate Education

Basically we are always educating for a world that is or is becoming out of joint, for this is the basic human situation, in which the world is created by mortal hands to serve mortals for a limited time as home . . . To preserve the world against the mortality of its creators and inhabitants it must be constantly set right anew.

Arendt, 1954/1993

The shifting views about knowledge and morality require education and pedagogies in the 21st century to move away from taking dogmatic views about knowledge, and foster young people's ability to construct and contest knowledge within their communities. As Arendt argues, we should accept that we are educating young people for a world that is 'out of joint'. Thus, a new form of criticality should question the drive of current educational systems to reach sameness and a consensus at all cost on the knowledge and skills that young people require. Plurality brings antagonism; however, this is a true reflection of the world. The world is not predictable and controllable and thus education should not be geared towards the possibility of an ordered world. Education for democracy and citizenship should embrace 'the possibility of difference' where conflict and dissent should be tolerated (Bergdahl, 2008).

Education for achieving a cosmopolitan citizenship and democracy (Osler, 2006) and education for increasing market competitiveness (e.g., OECD, 2004) are two distinct entities, with the former offering the tools to exercise human rights and the latter as a mode of enhancing economic productivity. In this chapter, the discussion on education for a viable future and a civil society[1] distinguishes between civic and corporate education. A civic education incorporates pedagogies for an ethical praxis, diversity and difference, and aims at developing young peoples' capacity to exercise rights and deliberative democracy. In contrast, a corporate education focuses on markets and choice, reproducing what is known as the Haykean order.

The tension between a civic and a corporate education is reflected mainly in the differences between professional and bureaucratic accountability.

It is a tension between the intrinsic excellence and professional ethics that underpin professional accountability, and the external, administrative and corporate structures that define bureaucratic accountability. MacIntyre differentiates between the 'internal goods of excellence' such as ethics, honesty and an intrinsic sense of responsibility and the 'extrinsic goods of effectiveness' such as profitability, competition and managerialist values (1982). These competing discourses on professionalism and accountability delineate the fundamental differences between civic and a corporate education. Webb argues that professional power is being eroded by 'state governments and the corporate community' (2005: 191). This view is reflected in children's services where children are the customers and the professionals are the service providers. Within this mindset, using 'specialist knowledge as criterion and personal judgement' is replaced by consumer choice, competition and financial gain (Oancea, 2007: 20). A possible solution to this tension is to retain scrutiny and accountability without taking a narrow view of managerial accountability based on targets and efficiency. A professional accountability that relies on honesty and ethics can be exercised through a civic education to create what Dahlberg and Moss (2005) and Readings (1996) refer to as 'loci of ethical praxis'.

A Civic Education

A civic education aims at developing children's understanding of the principles that underpin the creation of a civil society in contrast to a market-based society. A civil society is not entirely dependent on state and market influences, and has a strong participatory democracy and community involvement. Moreover, it is underpinned by the principles of democracy and participation, community cohesion, local engagement in civic matters and governance, and strives to achieve collective goals. A civic education is expected to prepare young people for the society we would aim for, 'a society of democracy, equity and justice, a society at peace and in harmony with its natural environment, a society that can think as one as well as within its constituent parts' (Watson, 2001: 262). A civic education, or education for democracy, is dialogic, critical, socially engaged and sensitive to the dynamics of power.

Two important principles that underpin civic education are divergence and difference. These principles oppose the idea that knowledge should be possessed in equal amounts by all children, favouring a heterogeneous approach where difference is recognized in educational policy and practice. Although rights-based educational policies have played an important role in combating marginalization and stigma and legislating access to education, education should account for and respect human variation and promote a culture of difference. Recognizing difference has the potential to free education from pedagogies that are steeped in gender, race and social class, and redistribute social and cultural capital. Within civic education, gender, disability or ethnicity can be accommodated by removing illiberal school practices that enforce gender and ethnic inequality.

A civic education is a liberal and authoritative education. Law draws a distinction between an authoritative and authoritarian education. He offers a detailed discussion on authoritarian education methods such as punishment, rewards, emotional manipulation, social pressure, repetition, control and censorship, tribalism and brain washing used to reproduce certain types of knowledge (2006). In contrast, a civic education relies on critical thinking as the basis for moral authority, where children are given opportunities and the tools to reflect on their own beliefs and scrutinize received wisdom. Law offers a list of capabilities to be cultivated within the boundaries of authoritative education, including the capacity to

- reveal and question underlying assumptions in any given point of view;
- predict and consider possibilities regarding the moral consequences of a decision or action;
- understand fallacies and inconsistencies in reasoning;
- gather and interpret evidence fairly and impartially;
- draw reasoned arguments to make a point clearly and concisely;
- develop debate and public speaking techniques and the communication skills required;
- develop emotional maturity and disentangle emotive from reasoned responses;
- develop empathy and perspective taking to view an issue from others' point of view; and
- question the appropriateness and implications of your actions. (2006; paraphrased)

Craft's notion of 'possibility thinking' as the capacity to think about different possibilities is at the heart of a civic education (2002: 3). Through a curriculum that has a philosophy and humanities as well as a technical orientation, children are likely to appreciate cultural differences and develop critical thinking and emotional intelligence. Such a curriculum is geared towards children's multi-dimensional development and involves emotional, spiritual, technological and economic understandings of an inquiry. Children should also be supported to develop the capacity for novelty, to link ideas together and apply knowledge across different contexts. Time should also be built into the curriculum for children to engage in exploration of materials and ideas, especially through play. Play in young children fosters 'insight ability and divergent thinking', in that cognitive capacities such as reasoning and creating possibilities (imaginary thought and supposition) are involved in children's pretend play (Russ, 2003: 291) (see Chapter 4 for a discussion on children's play).

Critical thinking involves the development of 'a critical attitude towards those things that are given to our present experience as if they were timeless, natural, unquestionable: to stand against the maxims of one's time, against the spirit of one's age, against the current of received wisdom (Rose, 1999a: 20). This type of critical thinking stresses the importance of understanding the multiplicity and plurality in people's perspectives and ways of life, and interrogates dominant views about the 'truth' and the mechanisms that legitimate it. To articulate the process by which knowledge is legitimated, Santos coined the phrase 'hegemonic globalisation', that is 'the successful globalisation of a particular local and culturally specific discourse to the point that it makes universal truth claims and "localises"' all rival discourses' (2001: 188).

Critical thinking can be encouraged within a framework of a personalized learning. Personalized learning is learner-centric in terms of offering choices and opportunities to learners on what to learn, how to learn, where to learn and why, and providing closer relationships between service providers such as schools/universities and learners. An important dimension of civic education is pupils' voice and participation, viewing participation as a right and as a mechanism for exercising rights. A criticism of personalized learning is that it relies heavily on choice. Choice, however, is a contested term and individuals with disabilities as well as those who experience multiple layers of disadvantage are less likely to exercise it.

Some educators are positive about personalized learning, recognizing its potential to support education for a civic society[5] (Fielding, 2004). Others argue that the rhetoric of a personalized learning with its emphasis on community cohesiveness and citizenship masks its economic focus (e.g., Taylor, 2005). These clashing views reflect a wider uncertainty about what education for a civic society should entail, with a growing interest in education that places learners at its centre.

Within personalized learning, the curriculum is expected to reflect the learners' needs, debating whether it should focus on specific subjects or cover areas that have a direct impact on young people's everyday lives. Pinker states that humans have developed capacities in areas that posed challenges to our evolutionary ancestors such as speaking and listening, reading emotions and intentions, making friends and influencing people (2003). However, the human mind is less competent to solve challenges, such as reading and writing or calculation that are posed by a rapid moving technology and modern life. Pinker suggests that education should provide children with new 'cognitive tools' to understand the complexities of modern life. To this end, Pinker argues for education that focuses selectively on certain curriculum areas.

However, we should not judge the importance of one subject matter over another, but identify areas, such as the destruction of the environment, diversity in society, human rights, that are central to a civic education agenda. It is important to avoid current discipline fragmentation and take a multi-disciplinary approach towards understanding important phenomena that define our very sense of being human as well as the future of humanity. A civic education should be geared towards preparing young people to meet the challenges posed by an increasingly complex society.

A Corporate Education

Education has always been the battlefield for different political agendas. Increasingly, business, the private sector enterprise, charity bodies and religion have a role to play in shaping education, moving it from the public sphere to the corporate sector (Ranson, 2003). In contrast to a civic education, the principles that underpin a corporate education are choice, marketization and corporatization, and a view of young people as investment and resources. Externally imposed interests that are stimulated by profit, business/financial needs and religion are likely to influence the workings of schools and the professionalization of teachers. Professional accountability has turned into a neoliberal accountability where teachers are forced to operate in an open market to provide service to customers. Much emphasis has been placed on standards and even early years education is measured against how well a child, especially those from deprived backgrounds, adapts into the school life. This raises questions regarding the role of schools and teachers within a corporate education, and to whom and for what schools are accountable, and how these accountabilities are defined.

A corporate education is an important tool for the knowledge-based economy. For some, the knowledge economy 'carries a powerful democratic impulse' in that talent, 'creativity and intelligence and not birthright'

are important for success (Leadbeater, 2000). For others, within a knowledge society, creativity and knowledge have been corporatized to justify the
new trend for workers to work harder and harder in poorly-paid employment, which bears little connection to creativity and self advancement
(Banaji et al., 2007; Buckingham and Jones, 2001). It is argued that, in the
new economy age, creativity, flexibility and problem solving skills are the
minimum requirements. For the workforce of the future, the greatest challenge would be to 'stay afloat' to deal with diverse demands in the face of
change (Banaji et al., 2007). This view is also reflected in Seltzer's and
Bentley's discussion on 'skills paradox':

> While skills requirements are rising, more qualifications are not necessar-
> ily helpful. Because of the premium on new ideas and flexibility, people
> who have built up detailed knowledge over time find themselves at a dis-
> advantage if they do not know how to apply what they know in different
> ways. The new basic skills are about how people think and act, not just
> what they know. (1999: 10)

The knowledge-based economy requires a flexible workforce that can
learn new skills fast at all time. Life-long learning has become an important
drive of a corporate education. The Organisation for Economic Cooperation and Development recognizes four central features in the concept
of life-long learning:

- life-long learning covers the whole life cycle and comprises all forms of
  formal and informal learning;
- the learner is central to the process;
- the motivation to learn is fundamental to life-long learning and is fostered through 'learning to learn'; and
- personal goals for learning may change over time and will encompass all
  aspects of our life. (OECD, 2004: 1)

The OECD agenda implies a dialogue between learners and service providers in order to achieve learners' own goals and potential. The centrality
of the learner in the learning process however does not sit comfortably with
the growing emphasis on the creation of a flexible workforce/learners that
is responsive to the shifting needs of market economies. Life-long learning,
as it stands, offers clashing possibilities by bringing together economic and
personal development models that articulate learning as both a work-based
training and retraining to enable individuals contribute to the economy

(human capital), and a capability building for individuals to achieve cohesive communities and social justice. The OECD model stresses that these purposes of learning can coexist and work in synergy, in that learning to sustain employability is likely to contribute to alleviating socio-economic disadvantage and maximize community cohesion. The OECD model also suggests that learning is not only for employment but a life-long endeavour that has the potential to enhance every aspect of life. However, the onus for life-long learning rests with the individual and, thus, failure to identify learning opportunities and engage with them may result in social exclusion.

Bernstein observes that life-long learning has created a highly pedagogized society, one that encourages individuals to train and retrain to respond flexibly to the requirements of free markets (2000). As Seltzer and Bentley stated in the Demos report 'The Creative Age', 'knowledge has become the primary resource of the new economy, and as a result, the way people acquire and use it have taken on a new significance' (1999: 1). Masschelein argues that 'learning to learn as activity does not create or produce a common world, but is conducive to further individualization'. The point of contest is that learning to learn is not relational and not 'about knowing' but 'about taking part in the process, being absorbed and included in the stream of information and exchange' (2001: 15).

Within corporate education, knowledge is not local but global and functions as the 'raw materials'. It is important to differentiate between knowledge and information at this point; the 'raw materials' refer to information which has to be converted to knowledge, in what Sen describes as 'valued functionings' or economic profit (2006). In computer-mediated spaces, such as the internet, a plethora of information is available; however, the challenge is to process the information meaningfully and make judgements about its validity. Information is no longer a scarce commodity; in contrast, knowledge is. Converting information to knowledge requires time and capacity for incremental learning, critical engagement, flexibility, creativity and problem solving and, most crucially, 'new forms of personal discipline and self-reliance' (Seltzer and Bentley, 1999: 1–2).

Within the Hayekian marketplace philosophy, human variation along the ability–disability continuum that does not have a competitive edge is less likely to contribute to the new kind of individuality embodied in the 'entrepreneurial citizen' (Marginson, 1997: 64) (see Chapter 3 for a discussion on the rise of the entrepreneurial child). Distinguishing between education as a response to competing markets, and education for citizenship and democracy is of paramount importance, especially for special needs education. Young people who, for various reasons (e.g., disability), do not fit into the economy model of education are likely to become disaffected and marginalized. In the past, narrow education agendas and a utilitarian perspective on learning have constituted persons with disability a consumer of education, being offered limited opportunities to develop and pursue personal interests and participate actively in their communities.

In a market-driven economy, education becomes the means to an end and is geared towards the development of a workforce, offering reduced possibilities for personal and social development. It is appealing to take a pragmatic approach towards unemployment and socio-economic disadvantage and offer education with a technicist agenda. However, important issues such as the breakdown of communities and the rise of a consumerist culture require pedagogies to support children develop a social and emotional maturity. To maximize the potential in 'how people think and act' requires pedagogies that build resilience, playful/creative attitudes and a sense of self-efficacy, as well as an understanding that knowledge should be open to interrogation and scrutiny. Most crucially, it requires pedagogies that are geared towards citizenship and rights within a framework of ethics, care and responsibility.

Pedagogies for Rights and Democracy

Education is a universal right (Article 26 of the United Nations Universal Declaration of Human Rights, 1948). As such, rights can be invoked in terms of right to education (entitlement and access to education), rights in education (equitable classroom practices) and education as enabling young people to ascertain rights (exercising rights) (Gutmann and Thompson, 2004) to achieve what Slee refers to as 'putting the public in policy making'(1996).

Within the rights discourse, a distinction is made between education as a right and education as a promotion of human rights. The rights movements have not resolved the dilemmas of access and equity, as well as building capacity for persons with disability to exercise their rights and participate fully in social and cultural life. At present, the rights-based legislation focuses on entitlement and access to education; however, this has not been sufficient in promoting children's rights. Within the framework of inclusion, as stated in the Salamanca framework of action, education was approached as a human right; however, the type of education that prepares young people to exercise rights and citizenship was not delineated. Failure to account for difference as a part of the human nature places restrictions on education in general and special needs education in particular, in their capacity to support young people for social justice and citizenship. A rights legislation has the potential to challenge marginalization and stigma; however, it is important to stress that some rights-based laws and policies, that were created to support individuals with disabilities, have also served to marginalize them (Minow, 1990).

It is commonly accepted that once we fulfil the right to education in terms of access, equity, social justice, citizenship and democracy will follow (Sen, 2000). Access to education is a critical first step, and despite many legislative frameworks, access is denied to a large numbers of children worldwide. However, it is important to note that the right to education is located within the purpose and role of education (Florian, 2007). Within the circles of the World Bank, education is viewed as a means for developing individuals and nations to become competitive in a global economy to achieve national prosperity. In this context, education may not offer a remedy to social injustice and inequality, and is less likely to stimulate capability building towards exercising human rights. A market-orientated education is characterized by a rather technocratic instrumentality and is not compatible with the Deweyan concept of education for democracy (Dewey, 1916).

To counteract the market model of education, a cosmopolitan education is proposed to set the scene for building capacity for democratic participation, respect and citizenship (Appadurai, 2001; Waldron, 2003). Jeremy Waldron advocates a cosmopolitan education, arguing that the cosmopolitan and the parochial are not very distant from each other. He stresses that the purpose of a cosmopolitan education is to support children develop a cosmopolitan citizenship that emphasizes universal moral concerns for humans and transcends national boundaries, cultures and religions. As societies become increasingly diverse through migration and displacement of populations, technology and globalization, the boundaries between national and cosmopolitan identities are blurred, in that young people move from local to global communities, and consider possibilities beyond the group/clan boundaries.

In a globalized world, pedagogical practices operate at a local level whereas educational policy has a global base, causing tensions between international and local bodies of knowledge. Pedagogies for rights and democracy need to deparochialize notions of respect, participation and citizenship, through a cosmopolitan education, whereas, at the same time, retain the significance of local contexts and knowledge by decoding rights at a global level and negotiating meanings and identities within their local contexts.

Through education, children should be given the opportunity to develop a critical appreciation of the issues that affect their life in order to express, deepen and validate their knowledge and understandings of the world at a local and global level. Individual open mindedness, emotional and social intelligence and capacity to open to possibility are essential to enable young people to participate actively in a civic society. A civic education that encapsulates pedagogies for an ethical praxis encourages children to think about social institutions and show collective responsibility, care and respect, which underpin pluralism and democracy.

Pedagogies for an ethical praxis, diversity and difference

Readings (1996) and Dahlberg and Moss (2005) have argued for reconceptualizing education as 'loci of ethical practices' where pedagogy is contextual, relational and based on ethics, care and obligation. Readings argued for 'a rephrasing of teaching and learning as sites of obligation, as loci of ethical practices . . . I want to insist that pedagogy is a relation, a network of obligation' (Readings, 1996: 158). This view of pedagogy stresses the important role that relations and obligation play in constructing knowledge, where the learners are not seen as autonomous individuals but human beings who learn within 'an open network of obligations that keeps the question of meaning open as a locus for debate' (Readings, 1996: 162). Teaching and learning, occurring within a network of obligation, relationships and ethics, carry a strong impetus for young people who are different and, possibly, marginalized as a result of being different.

Ethics, relations and obligation

Pedagogies for an ethical praxis have the potential to lay the foundation for a civic and cosmopolitan education. They aim at supporting children to develop as social agents and as personal beings through self-awareness, empathy and emotional maturity. To develop as a personal being is not a project towards becoming an autonomous individual, but one that requires awareness of the cultural and societal norms, stressing the importance of a context in shaping selfhood. This has important moral implications in that responsibility, intention and commitment are culture and context specific. Personal development demands an understanding of the 'maxims and rules . . . subject to public assessment as to their compatibility with local moral orders' (Harre, 1983: 262). An example of this is the Swedish preschool curriculum which places a strong emphasis on ethics and values, stating

> The foundation on which these values rest expresses the ethical attitude which shall characterise all pre-school activity. Care and consideration towards other persons, as well as justice and equality, in addition to the rights of each individual shall be emphasised and made explicit in all pre-school activity.(Swedish Ministry of Education and Science, 1998: 6)

Forming and sustaining networks of obligation and an ethical praxis support young people to develop as personal and social beings. Harre argues that self-awareness is a prerequisite for morality and acceptance of responsibility (1983). He emphasizes the importance of the conversations and little narratives for young people to develop as personal and social beings, reflecting

> The fundamental human reality is a conversation, effectively without beginning or end, to which, from time to time, individuals may make contributions. All that is personal in our mental and emotional lives is individually appropriated from the conversation going on around us and perhaps idiosyncratically transformed. The structure of our thinking and feeling will reflect, in various ways, the form and content of that conversation.(1983: 20)

Children and young people moderate their cultural and conversational expressions to tune in the culture that surrounds them. Through conversation, children use cultural artefacts as a vehicle for personal expression, and understand what legitimates personal and social action. Children's personal lives are construed by appropriating the conversations and narratives that 'idiosyncratically transform' them. At present, education, at its best, is geared towards children's intellectual development, the celebration of reason, which is steeped into the Enlightenment ideals. Descartes' notion of 'I think therefore I am' defines existence in intellectual terms, marginalizing the role of emotionality and social understanding. It is more inclusive to consider the possibility of 'I am and therefore I think, I feel, I am capable of a relational understanding of the world (animate and inanimate objects)', experienced in an interactive manner and not as separate or competing entities.

Empathy and emotional intelligence are central for children to be part of an ethical praxis. They are cultivated within education where care and respect are not instrumental but located within a 'network of obligation' (Readings, 1996). When defining the role of education in economic terms, objective criteria can be used to evaluate its effectiveness. However, it is not easy, nor is desirable, to construct objective criteria to evaluate the process of preparing children for personal and social life. A lack of objective criteria offers fluidity and opens up possibilities, but may also accentuate conflict in multi-cultural societies, in that the ways in which empathy, friendships and relationships are construed differ across cultures.

In an era of increasing breakdown of families and communities, it is particularly important for schools to undertake the responsibility for preparing young people for social and personal life (see Chapter 6 for a discussion on the role of schools/education to support children's happiness). To this end, schools should take a less technocratic agenda by introducing subjects in humanities, philosophy and literature to foster the development of emotional and social intelligence to enable children form meaningful relationships, and display empathy and social reciprocity. Preparing for both public and personal life can maximize the social and cultural capital of children in terms of becoming adults who are able to form communities of care and tolerance.

Diversity and difference

Pedagogies for diversity and difference are likely to offer young people the knowledge, skills and values they would need to 'critically negotiate and transform the world in which they find themselves' (Giroux, 1991: 509). Most importantly, such pedagogies set a critical and a discursive space to debate otherness and understand the processes and mechanisms that devalue the 'other', and how they are perpetuated and internalized through power structures.

Educating young people for rights and democracy should entail pedagogies for diversity and difference that show

> an openness to the difference of the Other, to the coming of the Other. It involves an ethical relationship of openness to the Other, trying to listen to the Other from his or her own position and experience and not treating the other as the same. (Dahlberg and Moss, 2005)

The universal characteristics of humanity are not fixed but variable, depending on the social, cultural and political contexts within which people find themselves. Children's commonalities and differences are not conflicting entities, but an acknowledgment of diversity. It is easy to group characteristics together and form categories; the problem lies in thinking that these categories are immutable and representative of all children across cultures. The politics of cultural differences aim at 'trashing the monolithic and homogeneous in the name of diversity, multiplicity and heterogeneity; to reject the abstract, general and universal in light of the concrete, specific and particular; and to historicize, contextualize and pluralize by highlighting the contingent, provisional, variable, tentative, shifting and changing . . . what makes these gestures novel' (West, 1990: 93).

Equitable educational practices require teaching and learning to be ethical and to account for diversity and difference. Feminist scholars have argued for the need to account for gender differences when considering practices of teaching and learning. Others have looked at class distinctions to understand the ways in which class and economic divisions perpetuate disadvantage and exploitation and the role that education plays in that (Apple, 1991). Moreover, anti-racist and post-colonial research has argued for accounting for racial differences in education. Research on difference aims at deconstructing normative understandings of learning and promoting educational policies and practices that account for difference.

To view learners as a homogeneous group who, through standardized teaching and learning, acquire knowledge is no longer acceptable. In some educational systems, difference is construed as deficit; examples of this view abound in bilingual literacy studies where, in some classrooms, a learner and his/her community are seen as being deficient (e.g., Frederickson and Cline, 2002). Educating students as citizens requires recognition of difference. Dewey referred to difference as a critical component of a just society. With this in mind, we need to reconcile the value of difference and strive to create equity in education.

Pedagogies for diversity and difference rely on acknowledging difference and human variation and offer the impetus to fight against representations of disability as being deviant or deficient. Minow observed that what problematizes difference is not difference per se, but what we make of it, and how we understand it and respond to it (1990). To define normal as usual and good is to approach human variation and difference as not usual and thus not normal and, possibly, not good (Nussbaum, 2004). The dilemmas of difference are dilemmas of access and equity in education, and are situated between exclusionary and inclusionary educational policies and practices. Within the special needs education, the difference discourse is supported; however, as Florian argues, special education should reimage difference (2007). This may be achieved by positioning difference and diversity within the context of rights for access and equity in education and engaging in democratic practices at schools (e.g., listen to the voice of young people with disabilities and offer a forum for political participation).

The pedagogies for difference are likely to place learning within pluralism through curricula that educate young people about the responsibility for participation in social and cultural life. To this end, young people should be encouraged, through the development of critical thinking, to consider societal and cultural changes and the politics of representation, especially those who operate outside dominant cultures and discourses. Most crucially, as Giroux states, 'to offer students possibilities for being able to make judgments about what society might be, what is possible or desirable outside existing configurations of power' (1991: 508).

On the politics of cultural difference, Giroux stresses the importance for young people to understand 'how cultural, ethnic, racial, ideological differences enhance the possibility for dialogue, trust and solidarity' (1991: 508). He refers to these possibilities as 'border crossing' and the pedagogies that support them as 'border pedagogies'. Pedagogies for democracy, difference and an ethical praxis are border pedagogies, in that they may form the basis for citizenship and democracy. I would like to expand Giroux's notion of cultural difference to include human variation, as a result of biological, social and cultural forces, and individual differences along the ability–disability continuum.

Pedagogies for diversity and difference are likely to support young people to become 'border crossers' to gain an understanding of power relationships, structures of dominance and what sustains them, and thus challenge difference as a marker of deficit and inferiority. Ideas of justice and equality, and disability issues should be approached from the canon of difference to enable young people to understand the impact of biological and sociological determinism, and question dominant ideologies (e.g., ability as a fixed and normative human characteristic, programmes for social engineering).

Furthermore, educating for pluralism and democracy requires young people to approach solutions to problems as raptures or points of departure, by questioning the epistemological bases of the problem itself and seek other possibilities. The self-righteous declarations of 'celebrating diversity' should be replaced by respecting difference and accepting the dilemmas of difference. The notion of 'celebrating otherness' can be tokenistic because we truly celebrate something that we understand and relate to it. Diversity has many facets and although ethnicity, religion or nationality are dominant in the discourses of diversity, other aspects of otherness such as disability and the mechanisms that underlie provision for individuals with disabilities are rarely debated.

Pedagogies for ethics, diversity and difference: a framework for action

The implementation of pedagogies for rights, ethics and difference can be explored through a 'future scenario planning'. Future scenario planning originates in the commercial sector, and has been applied in public services to 'predict' the future, not in a statistical sense, but more in terms of a narrative/scenaria of many possible futures (Schwartz, 1998). A future scenario planning has been described as a process towards creative predictions in an attempt to become responsive to change and uncertainty.

One possibility or future scenario is to maintain the status quo, which is to admit that some educational systems fail to account for difference. Another possibility is to move towards a civic education to meet the educational requirements of learners with diverse profiles. To maintain the status quo is not an option in that, as market economies shape educational policy and practice, the state becomes more interactive rather than proactive. Moreover, the education user has become a consumer, with an emphasis being placed on young people to develop entrepreneurialism to exercise choice and demand customization. The second possibility, i.e., to enable education to become responsive to the needs of learners with diverse profiles within a critical pedagogy, is a more viable model for a future pedagogy.

Pedagogies for ethical praxis, difference and democracy can be encouraged through

- challenging the current curriculum in schools. A key proponent of this view is the Royal Society of Arts (RSA), which commented: 'We still have a curriculum model close to the one that prepared students for the much more stable and certain society of the 1950s where we knew what a 'subject' was, and what you 'ought' to know about it. Employers are now looking for, but not finding, people who know how to manage themselves in a range of situations, who can recognize problems and know how to resolve them, who know how to communicate (Gigerenzer and Lane, 2002);
- reimaging special needs education to critically engage with concepts of needs and individual differences, by locating differences in learning within the social, cultural and political contexts that surround children's life;
- adaptation of complex materials or differentiation. Special needs education has based on teaching strategies developed alternative views about

teaching and learning, differentiating the curriculum in ways that would enable persons with disabilities to learn and participate. Lewis and Norwich (2005) advocated teaching strategies to be differentiated along a continuum of intensity, meaning that it is the application and not the teaching strategy that is differentiated. This is consistent with research stating that special education strategies that have been effective for children with difficulties can also be useful for all students (Cook and Schirmer, 2003, for a review);

- personalized learning to respond to learners' personal needs, which has the potential to support young people's personal development. However, we should be aware that increasing specialization and personalization are not always conducive to pedagogies that are responsive to diversity because they may lead to fragmentation;

- a forum where education policy that is relevant to the interests of children and young people with SEN/disabilities can be appraised critically and proactively. This would require schools to examine and evaluate policy options and share current practice through organizing events for policy makers, professionals, parents, voluntary associations and academics/researchers to attend;

- classroom practices that support learners to read and write in a polyphonic language, a language that is not exclusive of otherness. This may be achieved by placing an emphasis on critical thinking and interrogating knowledge to strive for agency;

- challenging abstract and universal bodies of knowledge that bear little relevance to young people's everyday life, especially those in the periphery of the dominant cultures. To this end, learners should be encouraged to read and write within their traditions and critically engage with them, whereas, at the same time, they are offered a space for subjectivity to develop as personal and social beings (Harre, 1983);

- reading and interpreting texts from different traditions and discourses, as well as offering opportunities to learners to interrogate their own histories and the histories of their communities, especially for individuals and groups who have been historically marginalized;

- challenging the neutrality of knowledge by stressing that constructions of knowledge are inseparable from positions of power and the mechanisms that legitimize it;

- understanding the political and economic interests of outside agencies and their involvement in decisions about school curriculum;

- becoming aware of the possibility of clashing cultures between school and home, especially for learners who come from minority or non-dominant cultures;

- enabling learners to express their views, especially when experiences and voices become multilayered and diverse, where conflicting views and accounts of reality can fragment young people's identity. Also, respect their silence.

Chapter 12

Communities of Practice and Learning

Communities for learning and civic participation play an important role in a globalized world where diversity and difference shape the nature and purpose of knowledge and the capacity of educational systems to support young people become cosmopolitan citizens.

Traditional ways of schooling have not always been adequate to enable young people acquire knowledge for rights and democracy. In a knowledge-based society where the pursuit of knowledge is not restricted to a specific locality (school, university) or developmental phase of a person's life (childhood, adulthood), the role of communities of learning and practice to support young people build capabilities for critical analysis and reflection is paramount.

Lave and Wegner (1991) and Wenger (1998) stipulated that learning occurs within communities of practice, stressing their crucial role in the formation of young people's identity as learners. They defined a community of practice as 'a set of relations among persons, activity and the world, over time and in relation with other tangential and overlapping communities of practice', particularly noting that a 'community of practice' refers to 'participation in an activity system about which participants share understandings concerning what they are doing and what that means in their lives and for their communities' (Lave and Wegner, 1991: 115).

Communities of learning and practice involve joint enterprise, in terms of individuals engaging in joint inquiry; mutuality that relies on norms and relationships in the community and the cultural and social capital they generate; and a shared repertoire, in terms of shared artefacts, discourses and a capacity for reflection and self awareness (Wenger, 2000: 231). In such communities, learning occurs through engagement with practice by being immersed in the structures, discourses and processes of a community, e.g., how its members talk, act, model certain behaviours, patterns of collaboration and attitudes towards outsiders (Lave and Wegner, 1991). Wenger conceptualized learning as being relational, delineating participation in systems of learning through 'engagement, imagination and alignment' (2000: 231). Engagement refers to young people working together towards a joint goal with their experience being shaped by others. Imagination refers to how young people map the world and construct their identity through storytelling and creative practices. And alignment refers to the extent to which local activities are aligned with other processes to ensure a long-term impact.

In a community of practice, learning is not confined within the boundaries of school curriculum but is acquired and judged through dialogue that allows polyphony in terms of multiple perspectives and stories to be told. This view of learning is different from the one that is judged through conformity to prescribed norms and practices seen as being objective and valid (Dahlberg et al., 1999). Learning for new members was described as a process of 'legitimate peripheral participation' (Lave and Wegner, 1991: 29). The notion of legitimacy refers to the expectations for new members to participate in the activities of the community, whereas peripheral refers to the gradual increase of the demands for their time, commitment and responsibility, giving the newcomers time to adjust. The notion of peripherality is empowering in terms of supporting young people to move towards an active participation, but also can be disempowering in that members are in the periphery of activities which may make them feel not included (Bathmaker and Avis, 2007).

Communities of practice and learning have the potential to generate social capital, but also rely on social capital in order to become established. Formal and informal sources of social and cultural capital are thus essential. Involving parents in their children's education and encouraging young people to participate as researchers or co-researchers at school and their communities are feasible ways of generating social and cultural capital to support the formation of such communities. Genuine participation of young people within communities of practice should be encouraged through engagement in public inquiry, e.g., research projects, as a means of generating evidence and supporting decision making. As I discuss in this chapter, engaging in research can have a transformative potential for young people and their communities because it offers a platform to go beyond simply having a voice. And, as Thomson and Gunter remind us, we should be 'sceptical of an automatic linkage between voice/rights and transformative educational agendas' (2006: 853).

Children, Families and Social Capital

Social capital has been defined as something that exists within the relational bonds of human societies, a 'durable network of . . . relationships'

(Bourdieu, 1984: 248); a 'social structure' (Coleman, 1994: 302) or 'social networks' (Putnam, 2000: 19). Social capital refers to the density and quality of both formal and informal social networks and diverse groups and associations in which people are involved. Social capital, such as bonding and bridging, has the potential to bond people together and promote a sense of shared identity, bridge schools with the wider community through collaborative workings (e.g., home–school partnerships, inter-agency collaboration), and link people to opportunities and structures of support and learning. The bonding capital is generated within close-knit communities and is likely to form homogeneous groups, whereas the bridging capital is likely to emanate from socially diverse groups. An important aspect of the relational character of the social capital is the quality of the interpersonal relationships, and the trust and reciprocity that sustain them. The main principle that underlies the notion of a social capital is that social relationships are a resource, a currency that can be traded, used, or exchanged for the collective benefit of communities.

Schools and communities with a social capital are more likely to support practices of learning and counteract individualism and community fragmentation. The nature and patterns of social relationships between the family, school and the local community influence children's school performance, in that differences in school performance can be explained by differences in the social capital generated in these relationships (Coleman, 1994). In contexts such as faith based schools, for example, where there is a social 'closure' or strong relationships between schools and parents/ communities, children's academic achievement is higher than is in non-denominational schools (Paterson, 2000). Although communities or groups with a strong social closure generate social capital, social closure has implications for diversity and the process of building links between communities that do not share norms or values.

It is important to differentiate between forms of social capital that facilitate the creation of cohesive communities and those that encourage the creation of cliques and zones of exclusion. Certain forms of social capital, such as bonding, are the by-product of consensus, typically generated within homogeneous groups with a common culture and norms; however, this type of social capital may not encourage diverse views to be aired. Bonding is likely to bring together like-minded individuals and this can have both positive and negative implications. Positive in terms of creating a common space for individuals to interact and develop a shared identity, and negative in terms of creating zones of exclusion, maximizing the benefits of the few at the expense of the many (Putnam, 1998) (see Chapter 5 for a discussion on zones of exclusion in young people's friendships). Linking, on the other hand, has the potential to link people or groups of differential power. As such, young people and their families, especially those who experience disadvantage and limited opportunities, may be enabled to network with others, not as a tokenistic gesture, but as a genuine participation opportunity. Linking social capital has the potential to support diversity and difference.

Child development is shaped by social capital. Trust, networks, and norms of reciprocity within a child's family, school, peer group and the larger community influence their opportunities and choices, and hence their education and development (Putnam, 2000). In traditional social capital theories, children have been approached as passive recipients of social capital from their families, schools and communities. However, children are also active in generating their own social capital. For example, children, who access technology, tend to use it as a platform of common interests and lifestyles to build links with peers and gain access to the popular culture. Moreover, in computer-mediated social sites, young people interact with each other and form virtual networks. The type of social capital that is generated through these networks can be bridging or linking, rather than bonding, which is more likely to occur within the context of their family, including extended family.

Children who experience community fragmentation and civic disengagement due to poverty, ethnic tensions, social disadvantage, residential mobility or displacement, are less likely to accumulate social capital and be afforded choice and opportunity. In such a context, communities of practice and learning that rely on meritocracy and academic achievement are less likely to flourish. An interesting relationship between manifestations of meritocracy, such as hard work and education and social/financial capital emerged when data collected from young people in Britain were analyzed (YPSA, 2003).

In the YPSA study, young people were asked about factors they considered to be important to doing well in life. Two factors, namely, getting a good education and hard work, emerged as being 'essential' or 'very important to doing well in life' by substantial proportions. Both factors were perceived as being influenced by a person's own actions and capabilities. Fixed attributes such as race and gender, were not seen as very important to doing well in life, although views about the role of race and ethnicity regarding success and failure were found to associate with household income. Compared to those in the lowest income quartile, young people from the highest income quartile thought race or gender were 'not at all important in doing well in life'.

At first glance, young people in Britain perceive success as being based on merit and achievement rather than being influenced by class, gender or ethnicity. However, when the influence of socio-economically advantageous households was explored, the results were less straightforward. While the majority of young people (60 per cent) thought that socio-economic advantage was not important, around 40 per cent stated that family wealth, and the social capital it generates, was important to doing well in life. At the same time, getting a good education and working hard were seen as very important factors. These views are not in conflict, in that although getting a good education and working hard suggest individual effort and initiative, they are embedded in socio-economic advantage. Getting a good education and working hard are influenced by the opportunities offered to young people and the choices they are afforded. Choice and opportunity are more likely to be exercised by individuals who have access to social/cultural and financial capital. With this in mind, although a direct link between meritocracy and ethnicity/gender was not found, it appears that meritocracy is influenced by socio-economic advantage.

Moreover, young people's views about socio-economic advantage were differentiated along household income. Young people from less affluent backgrounds were more likely to agree that socio-economic advantage plays an important role in achieving in life, compared to those from more affluent households. It appears that young people with a socio-economic advantage were more likely to attribute success to meritocracy, e.g., individual initiative, hard work, than to family influence and support. Meritocracy is constructed along factors, such as hard work, that can be controlled by a person, showing determination and agency to actualize one's own potential. In contrast, young people from less well-off families viewed factors, such as gender, ethnicity or money, that are external to an individual and thus beyond her or his control, to determine success in life.

In delineating the ways in which social capital influences children's experiences, their families and communities, it is important to differentiate between social, cultural, financial and human capital and explore how they affect the experience of childhood. Childhood embodies human capital, but also requires certain forms of social and cultural capital to flourish. Traditionally, social and cultural capital has been located within middle class practices. However, non-dominant forms of social capital, such as close links with families and communities, informal networks, can support the well-being of children and their families. Some ways of generating social and cultural capital include parental involvement, school–parents partnerships, and young people functioning as researchers/co-researchers; and these have the potential to bring together family, school and community cultures and practices.

Generating social capital through parental participation

Increasingly, schools are expected to adapt their structures to become strategic in engaging the wider community. Developing a collaborative ethos with shared goals and responsibilities towards children's education and care can be achieved by encouraging parental participation. Desforges and Abouchaar argue for a 'whole-community, strategic approach to parental involvement' (2003: 89), and unless this approach is embedded in the school's teaching and learning strategy and development plan, the link between educational outcomes and parental involvement is likely to be weak. The question remains how to support parents to build upon their strengths and existing forms of social capital to contribute to their children's education and well-being.

Parental involvement and its influence on children's educational outcomes have been approached from a social capital point of view. The World Bank has recognized the social and economic benefits of social capital, stressing that schools are more effective when parents are actively involved, with 'teachers being more committed and students achieving higher test scores' (1999). The interaction between social capital and school, parents and community partnerships has been explored extensively (e.g., Catts and Ozga, 2005; Coleman, 1988). In a study on social capital and home–school partnerships, Catts and Ozga identified several home–school dimensions of social capital, including contacts between schools; families and the wider community; parental participation and communication; teachers' collaboration with other professionals; and responsiveness of school staff to particular issues, including diversity.

Practices of learning and the systems that support learning should be calibrated according to the family needs to account for types of social/cultural capital such as cultural practices and rituals with regard to child rearing, friendship networks, understandings of disability, knowledge of the system and access to resources and people's personal and generational histories (Gardner et al., 2003). With this in mind, employing 'workers with sufficient credibility and trustworthiness in relation to the clients' cultural background' is crucial for engaging parents and building relationships based on trust and respect (Moran et al., 2004: 95).

In a study on family learning and community development, Ranson and Routledge stress the need to move from the 'external and instrumental' to the 'internal goods' present in families and communities, and build on them to support parents function as active citizens and advocates of their children's rights (2005: 69). The internal goods, or indicators of social and cultural capital that exist in families have the potential to offer parental support that is relevant to their family values. Identifying social capital indicators in families is consistent with a strengths-based approach to service provision. Although social capital does not have measurable, concrete objectives, the overarching aim is to build upon the strengths the parents bring into school–home partnerships.

Moran, Ghate and van der Merwe argue that parental support systems with a clearly articulated model of change and improvement work best (2004). Social capital building schemes should provide a clearly articulated model by incorporating systems and practices that are already tested and employed in the family/community setting. However, Gewirtz et al. warned that social capital building practices should be 'ethically acceptable' to be effective in developing meaningful forms of parental participation and engagement (2005: 670).

Moreover, parent learning and mentoring schemes should respect the diversity in the ways with which parents become involved in their children's education. Diversity in parents' patterns of involvement has been observed in different ethnic groups (Crozier and Davies, 2007; Diamond, Wang and Gomez, 2004). Parents from some ethnic groups may see their role as supporting 'behind the scene' by maintaining a supportive and a secure family setting to model values and appropriate behaviour, whereas in other cultures parents' involvement may be 'up-front and direct', by maintaining a visible presence in schools.

Russel and Granville also found that the perceptions and expectations about parental involvement, and the roles and responsibilities that parents expect the school to assume vary widely (2005). They found that the majority of parents want to be more actively involved with their children's education; however, patterns of communication, language and information requirements are likely to set barriers to their involvement. Also, the requirements of parents vary; some need advocacy or information about child development issues, whereas others may need guidance about special needs and disability issues, and educational provision.

Raffaele and Knoff (1999) and Epstein (2002) have argued for parental involvement to be proactive and based on respect of the values and contributions that parents make. In order to 'capitalize' on strengths that may already exist in families and communities, parental involvement practices should take into account parents' personal circumstances, build upon parents' strengths, and challenge views that certain types of social capital are more valid than others. Supporting parents to build upon their strengths and become involved with their children's education can set the scene for the formation of communities of practice and learning.

Young people as researchers: researching difference

Communities of practice and learning also rely on the social capital that is generated through young people's active participation as researchers or co-researchers. To participate actively in communities of learning, young people should be given opportunities to engage in inquiry, to seek evidence and, through critical analysis, interpret and make sense of the circumstances that surround their life.

Much of current research and policy making relies on adults' views about children's requirements. Traditionally, children have been left out of planning and decision-making processes, and have been treated as objects of research and passive recipients of interventions (Lolichen, 2006). Recently, there is a growing awareness of the benefits from engaging young people in research, and conducting research with them rather than on them (e.g., Christensen and James, 2000). There is potential for genuine participation when supporting young people to engage in all phases of a research project, including setting up the research agenda. Most crucially, research as participation is likely to have a transformative effect on young people, through the process of translating research findings into policy and practice.

A transformative research addresses questions about the lives of people who have been marginalized or discriminated against (Banks, 2006). Research on difference is also geared towards offering valid and meaningful accounts of young people's lives, especially those who experienced disadvantage and marginalization, by trying to see the world through their eyes (Ragin, 1994). This has the potential to demystify the structures that surround groups that have experienced powerlessness, raising awareness among them by articulating/representing their situation under a new light.

To view young people as researchers, or co-researchers, promotes a democratic involvement of children in all phases of decision making. The act of obtaining knowledge about a situation has the potential for change and transformation. Moreover, becoming involved in all phases of research encourages young people to own the research, actively interrogate evidence and offer their views about social and educational policies and practices as they relate to their own life (Fielding, 2001; 2004). Finally, through research, young people are likely to understand the politics of participation, and challenge tokenistic gestures towards it.

There is a limited research on young peoples' views on research methods/ tools and, most importantly, their topics of interest. Young people as research- ers require methodological tools and, most crucially, the relevant discourses that can be developed through reading others' work and engaging critically with others' ideas. Understanding young people's type and degrees of research involvement has important implications, especially with regard to researching difference. Edwards and Alldred discussed the purposes and outcomes for young people engaging in research along the lines of

- research as personal education, where learning takes place;
- research as therapy, pointing to the therapeutic advantage of talking about certain issues; this may be relevant to sensitive issues such as loneli- ness or trauma;
- research as empowerment, approaching research as a process with a trans- formative power, having the capacity to stimulate sustained change. (1999)

Engagement with research enables young people to negotiate different, and at times, conflicting identities, such as a consumer of education, a citi- zen, or resources who exercise choice and manage themselves and their communities responsibly. Despite its pragmatism, the purpose of engaging young people in research should not be instrumental and should not intend to simulate a market culture and business thinking. Rather, young people are expected to rethink and realign power structures, and achieve maxi- mum participation in social systems of learning. Through research, young people are likely to form values and develop strategies towards self manage- ment, capacity to take initiatives, reflexivity, adaptability and flexibility to change (Bragg, 2007).

Teachers' professional identity and boundaries shift by being involved in research carried out by students. In such a context, children are active in offering and challenging professional's views on teaching and learning, and both students and staff co-construct pedagogy and engage with debates on what good teaching is. To act as researchers creates a 'new form of internal policing in which students become their own critics rather than a hierarchy in which students are told what to do, helping them become self-managing agents of their own lives and enhancing their reflexivity' (Bragg, 2007: 352).

It is important to stress that although research has the potential to empower, young people should be proactive in terms of choosing the research activity themselves and ensuring a key input in setting the research agenda. Research, as a bottom-up activity, has the potential to become transformative because it originates within young people's micro settings. Young people should be aware of the dangers from 'over-formalising and over-pressurising the process of hearing the views of children, particularly those with learning disabilities', and ignoring their right/choice for 'silence, privacy and non-response' (Bragg, 2007: 352). Bragg challenges the assumption on the will to participate when young people engage in research, arguing that a top-down participation is likely to create a new normativity, and thus those who choose not to participate can become marginalized, rather than being seen as exercising their right to not participate. Top-down participation may also reinforce elitism in schools where the more able young people are those who are chosen to participate in research activities at the expense of the less able students (2007).

Lack of participation should not be equated with failure to participate, but with the right to not participate. The young people view their own time, i.e., time away from adult control, as a precious resource and are keen to ensure that it will not be used by adults' demands (Christensen et al., 2000). When discussing opportunities for participation against young people's free time, the issue of alternative costs and benefits emerges. Some young people are happy to 'trade' adult-controlled time, in terms of engaging in consultation instead of being in a lesson; however, they may be less willing to offer their leisure time for consultation/research purposes.

Fielding has expressed dilemmas about the practices that underlie children's voice, and the judgements we make about these practices. The intensity of children's voice ranges from being passive and 'audible through the products of past performance' to becoming 'the initiating force in an inquiry process which invites teachers' involvement as facilitating and enabling partners in learning'. On a continuum of participation, students as researchers may become involved in the capacity of students as data source, students as active respondents, students as co-researchers or researchers' (2004: 201).

Thomson and Gunter developed a discursive framework regarding pupils' involvement in research, juxtaposing two discourses, i.e., standards and improvement discourse and rights discourse (2006). The standards and improvement discourse considers pupils' involvement as researchers 'as desirable because it is likely to lead to more effective change', whereas the rights discourse views it as 'a right to determine the nature, scope and conduct of research they do, and to be involved in making recommendations and be involved in their implementation' (2006: 845). Researching diversity and difference in particular should be underpinned by a view of difference as a part of human nature, and by 'commitments to democratic agency' (Fielding, 2001: 123).

Children's experience of school and learning is shaped by their positioning in friendship circles and the cultural practices (e.g., music, popular culture) in their everyday life (Thomson and Gunter, 2006). Thus, researching and understanding difference is likely to offer them a lens to look at their social interactions and the power structure and pressures that define them. Furthermore, researching difference is likely to give young people a space to debate and make sense of their multiple and perhaps contradicting views about themselves and others. Their views, and the language they use to articulate them, are not neutral; thus, researching difference may help young people to understand the multiplicity of their experiences and position themselves in relation to the rights of others and their communities. In so doing, young people as researchers need to operate within communities of practice with a strong ethical basis.

Researching difference

To understand the diverse and complex landscape of childhood requires us to support children and young people to research difference. In researching difference, young people explore issues that affect their lives, and hopefully stimulate a shift in adults conversing with them rather than talking about them. In so doing, young people are expected to engage with the dilemmas about access, normalcy and discrimination, and challenge the limited rights that individuals with disability exercise. Researching difference has the potential to challenge the boundaries between personal crisis and social barriers, and promote a view that difference and disability are 'not about the medical condition of people, it is about social justice, about fairness and about opportunities to participate in everyday life' (Blunt and Wills, 2000). Understanding difference and disability through research may untangle beliefs and socially pervasive practices that are discriminatory, perpetuating themselves through inflexible institutional structures.

Moreover, researching difference is expected to challenge theoretical and methodological assumptions that underpin constructions of childhood, children's rights and participation, and changes in family and education. Most crucially, it may challenge the assumptions that underlie human variation, and the spaces between ability and disability, the positionality of researchers (e.g., insider, outsider), their relationship with the researched and their influence on power structures.

Researching difference is not a new concept; it has been long established in multicultural education, as it emerged out of the civil right movements in the 1960s and 1970s. However, young people researching difference offers a new dimension, which is likely to explore childhood issues through children's perspectives and voices and through the lens of difference. As with multicultural education research, researching difference has an emancipatory quality, because it encourages individuals who have been marginalized or neglected to express their views about issues that concern their lives. Multicultural education research has generated knowledge that challenges structural inequalities and institutionalized discrimination (Banks, 2006). In a similar vein, researching difference in childhood focuses on children from diverse racial, ethnic, linguistic, ability/disability and social perspectives and gives them the tools to tackle issues that are pertinent to their experiences of growing up.

Research on difference share the same characteristics with multi-cultural research, as articulated by Banks:

- seeks to describe the cultures and experiences from the perspectives of the group being studied (emic rather than etic perspective);
- seeks to describe the experiences, values and perspectives of marginalized groups in accurate, valid and sensitive ways;
- constructs concepts, theories, paradigms, explanations and narratives that challenge established and institutionalized knowledge. Develops counternarratives to mainstream accounts and narratives;
- views scientific knowledge as having both subjective and objective components that are interactive;
- seeks to reveal the ways in which research is influenced by the lives, cultures and positionality of researchers;
- assumes that scientific knowledge should enhance justice and equality within society. (2006: 776)

Participation in decision making can be contrived unless children are supported to engage in research, in terms of formulating and testing hypotheses and problem solving. UNICEF stressed the need for developing processes to evaluate children's participation through research where children are active players (2004). Questions to be tackled during research on difference include the following:

- Who has the legitimacy to define childhood and children's spaces?
- What is the power structure between children and adults?
- How do cultural/social and political contexts affect children's experiences of growing up?
- How can adults best support children and young people to participate actively?

- Who does benefit from the ways in which the intersections between childhood, poverty and inequality are construed?
- How would involving young people transform the dynamics of children–adults interactions?
- How can we ensure that young people do not suffer as a result of engaging in research?

Researching difference is expected to engage individuals who have been marginalized to have a voice and be listened to, aiming at generating knowledge to rework the social structures towards human emancipation. Emancipation relies on discourses of difference, rather than normalizing discourses, in that norms and standards pose obstacles to individuals and groups whose narratives are not dominant. Researching difference also requires a new research paradigm to counteract dominant deficit paradigms. To this end, a human variation paradigm to underpin research on difference in childhood is discussed, highlighting difference as strength. The human variation perspective, due to either biological or environmental factors, manifested in race, language, ability–disability, offers a framework to construct meaning about children's diverse worlds.

Children and their families who experience disadvantage tend to be described as being culturally and socially deficient and in need for remedy and compensation. In the 1960s, the 'deficit within communities' paradigm was seen as being liberating, an attack against the individual pathology paradigm which supported biological determinism and had dominated education for many decades. However, it was soon understood that the social/cultural deficit paradigm was supporting a form of environmental determinism. Both nature and nurture deficit worldviews have been inadequate and damaging in understanding childhood. The cultural difference paradigm is inclusive in terms of approaching differences in children's cultures and social context as strengths. The human variation paradigm expands cultural differences to also include biological differences in children's capabilities and possibilities.

How to research difference: a mini case study

In the Needs Analysis study, young people with experiences of bullying were involved as co-researchers (Hartas and Lindsay, 2007). Although they did not set up the research agenda per se, they became involved in discussing issues regarding bullying at their school and offered strategies towards resolving bullying with the view to present these strategies to their schools. These young people engaged in research that tackles an aspect of difference (pupils being perceived as different) and its implication (pupils being bullying as a result of being perceived as different). As co-researchers, young people engaged in decision making, and showed confidence in presenting these decisions to their schools.

A framework for researching difference, construed as human variation, was introduced to them to facilitate their research work. They were encouraged by the main researchers to

- think about situations that involve interactions with their peers, and reflect on them;
- gain a holistic view of the context, meanings and interpretations, the ways in which language is used, systems and mechanisms that legitimize certain points of views and actions during these peer interactions and delineate the overall context of bullying;
- capture understandings about how norms, language and cultural practices construct meaning from the inside. This was useful for them to reflect on the underlying causes of bullying;
- understand the ways young people come to understand, account for, take action and otherwise manage their day-to-day situations (Miles and Huberman, 1994).

In this mini study, the young people engaged with everyday issues that affect their life at school, i.e., bullying. They offered interpretations about their and others' points of view during their discussion on the underlying causes of bullying. An intolerance to difference, be it racial, religious, physical appearance or intellectual capacity/disability was stated as being the underlying reason for bullying. Some young carers stated that they have been bullied for looking after family members with disabling conditions, especially siblings with disabilities attending the same school (see Chapter 6 for a discussion on the effects of bullying on children's happiness).

The centrality of language and its use when researching difference is acknowledged by requiring these young people to use the tools of discourse analyses (supported by the main researchers) to interpret their every day experiences and construct or deconstruct their 'little narratives'. In this way, they were able to expose multiple meanings and views about bullying during their focus group discussions. Reflecting on the underlying causes of bullying, for example, the young people identified a number of triggers of bullying, namely

- good academic standing and overall intelligence (e.g., 'being jealous for being clever and answering questions in class');

- physical appearance (e.g., 'I've been bullied and it's all down to the way people look. Some people get the mick taken out because they look different; I was bullied myself in Y3 and Y4, because I am quite tall and a bit fat');
- sports ability/sports competition (e.g., 'I liked to play football and I was told I was rubbish and I talked to my dad who spoke to school to sort it. I would go home and cry; during football a boy tripped me off so I cannot finish the game');
- boredom (e.g., 'bullies are bored and they wanted something to do');
- religious discrimination (e.g., 'she was cyber bullied because she is a Christian, she got mates and they all send her pictures of Jesus with his tummy torn');
- racial discrimination (e.g., 'I saw a friend of mine being bullied because she is coloured and a bit of a junky and she gets physical abuse'); or
- disability (e.g., 'they want to take the mick out of someone who cares for her disabled brother. They do not know what it is like to look after someone like that').

In many cases, young people talked about bullying starting without any provocation, with the person being bullied not knowing what has triggered it (e.g., 'I don't know really, it started and went on throughout Y7'). Some young people observed that

> sometimes not even the bully realises what he is doing . . . they start joking and then it gets out of control . . . the next thing that happens is that they steal beer and then go to court to pay a couple of thousand pounds in fine.

Young people perceived bullying as a random act of violence (physical or psychological), and as a dynamic rather than a static entity, a situation that can escalate and get out of control easily, with the victim and the bully not always realizing its ramifications.

After exploring difference and its implications regarding bullying, through conversation in focus groups, young people offered strategies to resolve conflict at a classroom and school levels. These include

- act quickly when bullying occurs (e.g., 'you need to do something quickly before it gets worse');
- do not keep silent (e.g., 'bullies threaten you not to tell, but you have to tell if you want it to stop');
- get help from friends (e.g., 'there's this kid in assembly and he takes the mick and I have these friends and I don't do anything but they stick up for me they go up and call him stuff');

- resolve the conflict through conversation (e.g., 'I say, hey, I do not like being bullied and you do not like being bullied so why don't you treat me with the same respect and she was speechless and I said why not be friends and not enemies'; 'you sit down on a round table to talk and decide what stories are over the top, and then you find out that what started as a joke and got out of hand'; 'sit down on the table and just talk, and this is important because sometimes you may not have realized what you have done and through talking it becomes clear. The attacker might think that he did just a little bit of hurting and not realize the damage'; 'Talk about bullying with the matron or a teacher and try to understand both the victim and the bully'; 'Bring the bully and the victim to talk to each other');
- do not use bullying as a 'blanket' term (e.g., 'sometimes people go over the top, for minor things'; 'in an all-boys school everybody throws an apple, that is not bullying; if the school had both boys and girls, boys may change the focus to other things like cigarettes or beer to make the girls like them);
- be aware that bullying is widespread (e.g., 'There is bullying in this school, although you have to pass the 11 plus to get here, because you can be tough and bully and have the brains of a very clever person and bullying happens in these schools even more);
- use avoidance tactics (e.g., 'keep away from the bullies, avoid them, do not sit close to them in the classroom');
- remove the bully physically/socially (e.g., 'change classrooms or sit outside until break, and if constantly bullying you, they need to be excluded for a week or so');
- support the victims (e.g., 'have a group session that they talk about it and get some advice. There is a school council and we have a book with all our thoughts and give it to a teacher and read things in assembly sometimes');
- support the bully (e.g., 'the bullies also need support because they are insecure, give them anger management classes try to make friends because they may not feel accepted by the others; give the bully something to do that they can feel good about'; 'I talk to them and say – I know that things may go wrong in your family but you cannot take on other people – ');
- warn the bully (e.g., 'if you keep being a bully you will go to jail when you grow up . . . you will be one who uses drugs and guns and goes to jail');
- expand the curriculum (e.g., 'instead of having too many literacy lessons just have a bullying lesson, and ask children to write down their thoughts about how bullies think; It is only in assembly that we talk about bullying but they do not stop bullying; During PHSE (Personal Health and Social

Education) we mostly talk about how to be safe and about drugs but not about bullying, need to include more about bullying');

- ease the transition to secondary school (e.g., 'Y7 should have more freedom in that they need time to settle down; Or, on the other hand, to apply more discipline, to be harsh to Y7 to set things straight from the start, so they know that there are detentions');
- understand the behaviour of the bully (e.g., 'some people seem quite rough and they get upset and hide their emotions, so they need to talk about to understand their emotions so they do not take it on others; Need to take into account background circumstances: if the parents have divorced that may make a good person behaving bad, it should be a bit light handed then, for a short time until it goes away');
- teachers should act quickly (e.g., 'you move out of the class to another classroom, and this should happen right away instead of waiting at the end of 12 weeks, because by then it may be too late');
- offer mentorship (e.g., 'a mentor is important because speaking to one you trust, it is easier than speaking to your teachers');
- ensure transparency in rules (e.g., 'more openness and discipline is needed so people know how to behave');
- modify the nature of reward: offer competitive rewards and rewards with a personal meaning for good behaviour (e.g., 'there are rewards for people who behave nicely. Yes, there are a book token or a sticker or a certificate but these are not really good stuff, I would rather have like an iPod; There must be a prize not just a piece of paper that is meant to look nice; A reward that means something to you');
- avoid manipulation of the reward system (e.g., 'I know of a person who just became good towards the last month of the year and then he got rewards after rewards and then got the biggest reward');
- regulate the detention system (e.g., 'instead of getting after school detention which is not very bad, and it builds up, it is lunch time detention, and then it is after school and then builds up to Saturdays, then it is internal and then it is external for 2 weeks and then you are kicked out. But then it is difficult to know what type of detention should match the bullying situation');
- invoke a sense of justice in the bully (e.g., 'I 'd walk away from them tell them to pick on someone their own size');
- ensure methods are effective (e.g., 'it is important to come up with one method that works. It is like the mythical creature with many heads that you cut one and another is popping up. You have to cut things from the root');

- involve the parents (e.g., 'My mum always listen to me because she has been bullied herself and my brothers too; If a boy was the bully, bring his parents and if he keeps doing it, go through again until he gets the idea'); and
- record bad behaviour (e.g., 'I'd get a clipboard and follow him for 2 weeks and report good and bad behaviour').

As this mini case study illustrates, researching difference in childhood has the potential to make explicit young people's diverse values and perspectives, especially those that challenge mainstream views of childhood along the lines of vulnerability. The young people in this study felt empowered to make decisions about what they thought might work in terms of tackling bullying, and took the initiative to present their strategies to their schools.

Research on difference shares similar assumptions with a pluralistic research that 'recognizes multiple social constructs within educational contexts and includes multiple perspectives and voices of the school community in its research' (Grant et al., 2004: 187). Like pluralistic research, its intention is to 'seek equity and transform power relationships', and account for the interplay between knowledge and power (ibid.: 187). To this end, research on differences in childhood acknowledges the multiplicity of children's social/political and cultural contexts and is likely to generate knowledge that can have a positive impact on young people who experience adversity and disadvantage.

Notes

[1] See *Nicomachean Ethics by Aristotle, 350 BC*, translated by W. D. Ross.
[2] The term performativity was originally coined by Lyotard (1984) and refers to outcomes or target-related measures of performance upon which a corporate form of accountability is based. The targets are predefined, and performativity becomes an instrument of control, in that it overrides a professional accountability based on ethics (see Ball 2004; Oancea, 2007).
[3] Civic education incorporates a critical pedagogy that is understood here as educational theory and practices of teaching and learning that are likely to empower the individual to engage critically with social issues, structures and processes, especially those that perpetuate oppressive social conditions. A critical pedagogy is seen as having the potential to raise learners' social consciousness about issues such as civic engagement and participation in their communities, cultures of consumption and their impact on children's everyday experiences and political participation. A critical pedagogy has its roots in critical theory of the Frankfurt School whose main representatives are Max Horkheimer, Paulo Freire and Henry Giroux.

[4] The term civil society has been originally used to separate the state from other social institutions such as family, the economy, education and the legal system (Thomas and Loxley, 2001). A civil society encapsulates social rights, civil rights and political rights. Social rights involve a right to education, health services and welfare (access to public services). Social rights rely on a distributive justice to ensure that access to services is mediated by an assessment of individuals' needs to delineate the factors that determine eligibility and equality of treatment. Civil rights refer to equal representation before the law, and political rights involve equal rights to vote and participate to political decision making (ibid., 2001).

[5] Civic society refers to a society that is bounded by human rights, global justice and a form of democratic globalization. In contrast, neoliberal societies put in place mechanisms for self-regulation and self-legitimation. In this book, the term civic society is used to separate a corporate or market-driven society that is based on individual liberty and free market, from a society where distributive justice is exercised, and individuals engage with social and political practices, a society with a strong communitarian ethos.

Epilogue

The concept of childhood is multiple, diverse and fluid. Childhood is not a social artefact but the outcome of the interplay between biology and society/culture as mediated by technology. A child, as a social artefact, is the child that is not 'real', at its best, and the child that is misrepresented and misrecognized, at its worst. Constructions of childhood that do not represent, or even ask, who the child is, are often observed in policy making in the form of a mismatch between programmes and the views that children have about themselves (McDonald, 2007). At a policy level, children are ascribed identities that do not always reflect their views of who they are and what they want. These misconstructions reflect a culture of contempt for children and their parents, and a reduced capacity to respond to difference ethically.

Childhood is politicized, and its continuous reinvention highlights our ambivalence about the current and future state of childhood, and, most crucially, the role that a society plays in educating, socializing, misrepresenting or criminalizing children. Many children grow up isolated and less cared for, in an era when family and community are disintegrating, and nation-states are dissolving, being replaced by international corporate structures. Worldwide, a large number of young people face institutionalized violence, commodification and fundamentalism, and experience marginalization within their increasingly fractured communities.

Some of the current debates on childhood assume that children occupy a terrain that is separate from that of adults', and focus on issues that appear to affect children only. However, adults also face similar dilemmas. Issues such as globalization, the decline of nation-states, the shifting boundaries of the human nature as propelled by advances in genomics and bio-engineering, and changes in citizenship have an impact on both adults and children. With the family moving into the public arena, an increasing pressure is placed on parents to offer the conditions for a secure attachment between parents and children to occur. Although the role of parents and families is crucial in children's well-being and happiness, the positive impact of good parenting can hardly be sustained in a culture that is characterized by individualism, division and polarization. As Kraemer observes, emotional intelligence, empathy and thoughtfulness towards others may not be the most adaptive attributes in a society that is characterized by thoughtlessness (1999), raising immense implications with regard to children's social and moral status.

The new political thinking, encapsulated in the economic doctrine of neoliberalism, reflects a world that is dominated by economic rather than ideological or ethical concerns. Against this background, ideology as a political doctrine, and as a complex system of culture, religion and morality, is no longer relevant. With the decline of ideology, the notion of citizenship also changes, from being originally conceived as an allegiance to a nation with well-defined borders, to becoming a flexible and fluid citizenship that crosses borders (e.g., digital citizenship). A flexible citizenship fits a citizen who responds fluidly and opportunistically to the dynamics of a borderless market economy (Ong, 2006).

Moreover, a new form of citizenship, i.e., biological citizenship, emerges to embody individuals' biowelfare and biovalue (Ong, 2006; Rose and Novas, 2003). Historically, social and biological determinism has denied the complexity of the human nature. At present, we seem to be moving towards an era where the human nature may be reconfigured. Technology (e.g., biogenetics) gives us, possibly, the tools to re-engineer our bodies and minds. The body itself, as a biological entity, has become an object for exploration, and as Rose states, biology is not a destiny but an opportunity, whereby, through bio-engineering, the boundaries of their human nature may shift. The possibility of human nature being reconfigured has generated heated debates on the biopolitics or the politics of children's well-being and happiness.

This book did not attempt to reconcile contradictory views on what the child is. Childhood exists in many sizes and colours; children are unequal and different with abled and disabled bodies and minds, and with diverse experiences to share. The right to childhoods is about the right of children to be recognized as a distinct social group, and as equal citizens. As discussed, current frameworks of children's rights offer ahistorical and apolitical views of children's experiences and place in the world. Children's rights rarely translate into living rights, and, for a large number of children, the basic rights for protection and survival, let alone participation in public life, are not met. As the number of refuge and displaced children increases due to state violence (e.g., war on terror) and the politics of fear (e.g., overriding individual liberties in the name of security, the demonization of immigrant children and their families), children's biowelfare, especially for those who experience multiple layers of disadvantage, is increasingly under attack.

This offers a dystopic view about the present and future of childhood, in that for many children the struggle is (and, possibly, will be) about sheer survival, the preservation of a bare life, rather than what Masschelein refers to 'the life of someone' (2001: 18).

Or, perhaps, the future images of childhood may not be as gloomy as they are depicted here. Children are resilient and capable of showing competence and agency. Children, even those who operate under difficult circumstances, can be assertive and have a voice, albeit within the context of their interactions with family and peers because their voices are less likely to reach those in positions of power. Nevertheless, resilience and powers of representation in children and their families can be fostered within communities of practices where new forms of criticality and collectivity are likely to emerge. Communities of practice, be they computer-mediated environments or more conventional places, are likely to offer new spaces and possibilities for young people to enable their political participation at a local and global level. A new form of collective responsibility, or subpolitics, emerges whereby through cross-border activism, often mediated by the internet, young people become responsive to local challenges in ways that have global implications.

Communities of practice can also offer civic fora for young people to develop a criticality through conversations, peer reviews and engagement in inquiry as researchers, and exercise agency in setting agendas and engaging in decision making. This form of criticality is not constrained within the learning society discourses, which approach learning as reflexive thinking and problem solving for the purpose of offering solutions to existing problems, but embraces the capacity to explore 'the possibility of freedom'. Learning in a learning society is underpinned by a technical rationality that focuses on survival, achieved through individuals learning how to manage risks and deal with uncertainty. However, this view of learning has limited emancipatory potential in that it seems that the more technicist knowledge we acquire the less control we have over technology, and its intended and unintended outcomes, and over societal and institutional structures. In contrast, the knowledge that is acquired within communities of practice is likely to have a transformative capacity because it goes beyond learning for survival or learning to overcome personal crises; it is learning as a means of exploring other possibilities.

It may be the case that educating young people for democracy and critical thinking goes against preparing them for a learning society. Reflexive problem solving defined in terms of generating alternatives and making rational choices is not the same as knowledge for ascertaining rights as a citizen. In post-industrial economies, knowledge and creativity are judged by their capacity to solve technical problems to ensure the satisfaction of sophisticated consumer demands. In contrast, the capacity to ascertain rights requires a continuous critique and interrogation of what is there to be known and why. It also requires 'a radical questioning of the given order of things, a questioning which is not directed by needs but finds its origin in the appearance of a meaning which transcends these needs' (Masschelein, 2001: 16). Knowledge for rights and democracy is about young people's continuous critical engagement with the world, and most importantly, the realization that other ways of living are possible, different from the existing order of things.

Santos (1995) argues that the 'future promised by modernity has no future', stressing the need to create alternative futures and make a 'paradigmatic transition' by developing a 'new epistemology' (479–481). Paradigmatic transitions require the possibility of freedom and the individual and collective capacity for radical questioning, critical reflection and argumentation. Above all, they require a dialogue between status quo and change, and critiques on the nature of change, especially when change is likely to bring alienation from our sense of continuity that is historical and embedded in traditions of humanism and liberal thought.

Appendix

Research Evidence

In this book, data from the Needs Analysis study (Hartas and Lindsay, 2007) were used to support the discussion of issues regarding young people's access to services and their physical, social and virtual spaces, bullying and friendships and the participation of young people as co-researchers. In addition, the results from analysing the 2003 Young People's Social Attitudes (YPSA) were used to highlight issues of young people's attitudes towards family, friends, social capital and participation in civic life.

The Needs Analysis Project

The Needs Analysis project included 54 young people, comprising 17 young carers (young carers group), 19 young people who have experienced bullying (have been bullied themselves and/or have witnessed bullying – bullying group) and 18 young people with learning difficulties/disabilities – LDD (LDD group). The LDD group consisted of 15 children from special schools and 3 from mainstream schools. The majority of the young carers (12 out of 17) have assumed caring responsibilities for siblings, with five of them looking after parents with disabling conditions. The young people who cared for siblings were part of a wider, informal support system, including parents and other more able siblings, reducing their caring responsibilities. Among the five young people with caring responsibilities for their parents, a couple of them did not share any responsibilities with siblings or their extended family, being the sole carers. Regarding the bullying group, 15 out of the 19 participants reported to have been bullied themselves.

Focus groups were employed as a means of qualitative data collection. The main assumption that underlies focus groups is that knowledge is socially constructed, generated through social interactions, i.e., generative group interactions, where negotiating points of view and sharing perspectives take place (Punch, 2005). A major advantage of focus groups is that the moderator is able to observe the process whereby people make private contributions public by formulating their views and attitudes through conversations with the rest of the groups. Instead of offering short answers to questions, the groups in this study were encouraged to engage in conversation with each other and, collectively, construct diverse views about the issues raised. As such, motivation is an important attribute to ensure that the contribution is genuine and sustained. Moreover, an atmosphere of mutual respect, where the individuals involved, including the moderator, are non-judgemental is required. Consensus was never the goal of these focus groups.

Another advantage of a focus group is that it contextualizes the discussion and creates a public forum by encouraging the participants to think beyond their own lives and thoughts. In other words, participants move beyond the private sphere and, in so doing, they are more likely to address possible inconsistencies in their thoughts and offer a better quality of data. Moreover, focus groups were considered to be an effective method for data collection on issues that affect young people who experience challenges in the form of caring responsibilities for family members, bullying or learning difficulties. By avoiding a question–response format, young people were offered the social and critical space to talk about their life in a non-threatening and non-judgemental way. This is particularly important in the light of concerns regarding the limited opportunities that young people have for genuine participation and involvement, especially for participating as co-researchers. For this study, focus groups were deemed to be appropriate because they brought together young people who share common experiences (e.g., bullying, young carers) who are likely to be forthcoming and join in the conversation. Research studies show that group conversations work best if members know each other and share similar characteristics and experiences, in that as the sociability among group members increases the child–adult tension is diffused.

As a method of data collection, focus groups brought together around six people for approximately 1 hour and 30 minutes, depending on the needs of the participants. For children and young people who experienced complex needs, smaller focus groups took place, 3–4 people. The participants selected for the focus group had common characteristics as defined by the research questions and goals. For this project, the focus group discussion started by setting the ground rules in terms of discussing issues regarding anonymity, stressing its voluntary nature. The goals of the focus group were discussed, as well as the moderator's responsibilities and expectations from the participants. Moreover, the participants were informed that they were not expected to disclose anything above their comfort level, and that if they wanted to talk privately they could contact the moderator to discuss the issue further. As a moderator, it was crucial to ensure that everyone in the group had opportunities to express their views, raising awareness about the possibility of bias is in terms of, implicitly or explicitly, favouring certain responses over others.

YPSA Project

In addition to the Needs Analysis study, data were provided from the 2003 Young People's Social Attitudes (YPSA) survey of 12 to 19 years old in the United Kingdom. The YPSA survey was funded by the DfES and was carried out by the National Centre for Social Research. This survey covered areas such as friendships and social networks, participation and decision making, family issues/patterns and involvement with household chores and social trust. For the purpose of the data collection, face-to-face interviews were conducted with 653 young people by the National Centre for Social Research.

LIVERPOOL JOHN MOORES UNIVERSITY
LEARNING SERVICES

References

Aarnikko, H., Kyttä, M. and Myllymäki, T. (2002). Lasten näkökulma tienpidossa. [Children's viewpoint in road management]. *Esiselvitys. Tiehallinnon Selvityksiä* 53/2002. Helsinki: Tiehallinto.

Ackerman, L., Feeny, T., Hart, J. and Newman, J. (2003). *Understanding and Evaluating Children's Participation: A Review of Contemporary Literature.* UK: Plan.

Agamben, G. (1998). *Homo Sacer: Sovereign Power and Bare Life.* Stanford, CA: Stanford University Press.

Ainley, P. (1998). Rhetoric and reality: learning and information theory. In S. Ranson (ed.), *Inside the Learning Society.* London: Cassell.

Ainscow, M., Booth, T. and Dyson, A., with Farrell, P., Frankham, J., Gallannough, Howes, A. and Smith, R. (2004). *Improving Schools, Developing Inclusion.* London: Routledge.

Alanen, L. (1992). *Modern Childhood? Exploring the 'Child Question' in Sociology,* Publication Series A, Research Reports 50. Jyväskylä: University of Jyväskylä, Institute for Educational Research.

Alderson, P. (2000). School students' views on school councils and daily life at school. *Children and Society,* 14, 121–134.

Altman, I. and Churchman, A. (eds) (1994). *Women and Environment.* New York: Plenum Press.

Amnesty International United Kingdom (1999). *In the Firing Line: War and Children's Rights.* London: Amnesty International United Kingdom.

Appadurai, A. (2001). Deep democracy: urban governmentality and the horizon of politics. *Environment and Urbanization,* 13(2), 23–43.

Apple, M. W. (1991). The politics of curriculum and teaching, National Association of Secondary School Principals (NASSP). *Bulletin,* 75 (532), 39–50.

Arendt, H. (1954/1993). *Between Past and Future.* London: Penguin Books.

Arendt, H. (1998). *The Human Condition.* Chicago: University of Chicago Press (2nd Edition).

Argyle, M. (1987). *The Psychology of Happiness.* New York: Methuen.

Argyle, M. and Martin, M. (1991). The psychological causes of happiness. In F. Strack, M. Argyle and N. Schwarz (eds), *Subjective Well-being: An Interdisciplinary Perspective* (pp. 77–100). Oxford: Pergamon Press. Member of Maxwell Macmillan Pergamon Publishing Corporation.

Armstrong, K. (2000). *The Battle for God: Fundamentalism in Judaism, Christianity and Islam.* London: Harper and Collins.

Aynsley-Green, A. (2007). Future potential. *The Guardian,* 24 December.

Ball, S. J. (2004). Performativities and fabrications in the education economy: towards the performative society. In D. Gleeson and C. Husbands (eds), *The*

LIVERPOOL JOHN MOORES UNIVERSITY
LEARNING SERVICES

Performing School: Managing, Teaching, and Learning in a Performing Culture (pp. 210–226). London: Routledge Falmer.

Banaji, S., Burn, A. and Buckingham, D. (2007). *The Rhetorics of Creativity: A Review of the Literature*. London: Arts Council of England.

Banks, J. (2006). Improving race relations in schools: from theory and research to practice. *Journal of Social Issues*, 62(3), 607–614.

Bathmaker, A. M. and Avis, J. (2007). How do I cope with that?: the challenge of 'schooling' cultures in further education for trainee FE lecturers. *British Educational Research Journal*, 33(4), 509–532.

Baudrillard, J. (1983). *Simulations* (Translated by Paul Foss, Paul Patton and Philip Beitchman). New York: Semiotext(e), Inc.

Bauman, Z. (1993). *Postmodern Ethics*. Oxford: Blackwell.

Bauman, Z. (2000). *Liquid Modernity*. Cambridge: Polity Press.

Beck, U. (1992). *Risk Society: Towards a New Modernity*. London: Sage.

Beck, U. (1998). *Democracy without Enemies*. Cambridge: Polity Press.

Beck, U. (1999). *World Risk Society*. Cambridge: Polity Press.

Beck, U. (2006). *The Cosmopolitan Vision*. Cambridge: Polity Press.

Beck, U. (February, 2008). A God of One's Own: Individualisation and Cosmopolitanisation of Religion. A lecture at the London School of Economics and Political Science. A lecture on 13 February 2008. London: LSE.

Beck, U. and Beck-Gernsheim, E. (2002). *Individualization. Institutionalized Individualism and Its Social and Political Consequences*. London: Sage.

Beilharz, P. (2003). The globalisation of nothing: a review symposium of George Ritzer's 'The Globalization of Nothing'. *Thesis Eleven*, 76, 103–105.

Bergdahl, D. T. (2002). The systemic paradigm of consensus in the scientific statements of Lacan. *Social Text*, 12(6), 121–48.

Bernstein, B. (2000). *Pedagogy, Symbolic Control and Identity, Theory, Research Critique*. Baltimore, MD: Rowan and Littlefield Publishers.

Blanden, J. and Machin, B. (2007). *Recent Changes in the Intergenerational Mobility in Britain*. London: The Sutton Trust.

Blunt, A. and Wills, J. (2000). *Dissident Geographies: An Introduction to Radical Ideas and Practice*. Harlow: Pearson Education.

Booth, T. and Ainscow, M. (2000). *The Index for Inclusion*. Bristol: Centre for Studies on Inclusive Education.

Borland, M., Hill, M., Laybourn, A. and Stafford, A. (2001). *Improving Consultation with Children and Young People in Relevant Aspects of Policy-Making and Legislation in Scotland*. The Scottish Parliament: Edinburgh.

Bourdieu, P. (1984). *Distinction: A Social Critique of the Judgement of Taste*. Cambridge, MA: Harvard University Press.

Bourdieu, P. (1988). *Homo Academicus*. Cambridge: Polity Press.

Boyd, D. (2006). Friends, friendsters, and top 8: writing community into being on social network sites. *First Monday*, 11(12).

Bragg, S. (2007). 'Student voice' and governmentality: the production of enterprising subjects? *Discourse*, 28(3), 343–358.

British Medical Association (2001). *Consent, Rights and Choices in Health Care for Children and Young People*. London: BMA.

Brock, G. and Brighouse, H. (eds) (2005). *The Political Philosophy of Cosmopolitanism.* Cambridge: Cambridge University Press.

Brooks, L. (2006). *The Story of Childhood: Growing up in Modern Britain.* London: Bloomsbury.

Bruce, T. (1997). *Time to Play in Early Childhood Education.* London: Hodder and Stoughton.

Buckingham, D. and Jones, K. (2001). New labour's cultural turn: some tensions in contemporary educational and cultural policy. *Journal of Educational Policy,* 16 (1), 1–14.

Bunting, M. (2006). Behind the baby gap lies a culture of contempt for parenthood. *The Guardian,* 7 March.

Burgess, R. (1986). *Sociology, Education and Schools: An Introduction to the Sociology of Education.* London: Batsford.

Burr, R. and Montgomery, H. K. (2003). Children and rights. In M. Woodhead and H. K. Montgomery (eds), *Understanding Childhood: An Interdisciplinary Approach.* West Sussex: The Open University/John Wiley & Sons.

Butler, J. (1993). *Bodies that Matter: On the Discursive Limits of 'Sex'.* New York: Routledge.

Buxton, N. (2007). Dogmatic assumptions underlie non-religious world views too. *The Guardian,* 14 April.

Catts, R. and Ozga, J. (2005). *What is Social Capital and How Might It be Used in Scotland's Schools?* London: Department for Education and Skills.

Cavet, J. and Sloper, P. (2004). Participation of disabled children in individual decisions about their lives and in public decisions about service development. *Children and Society,* 18, 278–290.

Chawla, L. (ed.) (2001). *Growing Up in an Urbanising World.* London: Earthscan/UNESCO.

Children and Young People Unit (CYPU) (2001). *Listening to Listen: Core Principles for the Involvement of Children and Young People.* London: Department of Health.

Children's Society (2007). *The Good Childhood Inquiry.* London: Children's Society.

Christensen, P. and James, A. (2000). *Research with Children.* London: Falmer Press.

Christensen, P., James, A. and Jenks, C. (2000). Home and movement: children constructing 'family time'. In S. Holloway and G. Valentine (eds), *Children's Geographies: Playing, Living, Learning* (pp. 139–155). London: Routledge.

Clack, A., McQuail, S. and Moss, P. (2003). *Exploring the Field of Listening to and Consulting with Young People* (*Research Report 445*). London: Department for Education and Skills.

Clark, A. and Moss, P. (2001). *Listening to Young Children: The Mosaic Approach.* London: National Children's Bureau.

Clarke, J. (1998). Thriving on chaos? Managerialisation and the welfare state. In J. Carter (ed.), *Postmodernity and the Fragmentation of Welfare.* London: Routledge.

Clinton, H. (1973). Children under the law. *Harvard Education Review,* 43, 508–516.

Coad, J. and Lewis, A. (2004). Engaging children and young people in research. *Literature Review for the National Evaluation of the Children's Fund* (*NECF*). London: NECF.

Cohen, D. and Prusak, L. (2001). *In Good Company: How Social Capital Makes Organizations Work.* Boston, MA: Harvard Business School Publishing.

Coleman, J. (1994). Social capital, human capital and investment in youth. In A. Petersen, J. T. Mortimer (eds), *Youth Unemployment and Society* (pp. 34–50). Cambridge: Cambridge University Press.

Coleman, J. C. (1988). Social capital in the creation of human capital. *American Journal of Sociology*, 94, 95–120.

Coleman, J. C. (1994). *Foundations of Social Theory*. Cambridge, MA: Harvard University Press.

Colquhoun, N. (2006). The Era of 'Endarkenment'. Accessed from www.edge.org. 15 March 2008.

Committee on the Rights of the Child (1997). General discussion on the rights of children with disabilities. *UN/CRC/C/66, Annex V*. Geneva: United Nations.

Committee on the Rights of the Child (2002). Concluding observations of the Committee on the Rights of the Child: United Kingdom of Great Britain and Northern Ireland. *UN/CRC/C/15/Add.188*, Geneva: United Nations.

Committee on the Rights of the Child (2005). General Comment No.7 (2005): Implementing child rights in early childhood. *UN/CRC/GC/7*. Geneva: United Nations.

Concu, A. and Gaskins, S. (2006). An integrative perspective on play and development. In A. Concu and S. Gaskins (eds), *Play and Development: Evolutionary, Sociocultural and Functional Perspectives* (pp. 3–17). New Jersey: Lawrence Erlbaum Associates.

Cook, B. and Schirmer, B. (2003). What is special about special education? *The Journal of Special Education*, 37(3), 200–205.

Cooke, B. and Kothari, U. (2001). Participation: the new tyranny? In B. Cooke and U. Kothari (eds), *Participation: The New Tyranny*. New York: Zed Books.

Craft, A. (2002). *Creativity and Early Years Education: A Lifewide Foundation*. London: Continuum.

Crozier, G. and Davis, J. (2007). Hard to reach parents or hard to reach schools? A discussion of home–school relations, with particular reference to Bangladeshi and Pakistani parents. *British Educational Research Journal*, 33(3), 295–313.

Csikszentmihalyi, M. (1996). *Creativity*. New York: HarperCollins.

Csikszentmihalyi, M. (2006). The Free Market. Accessed from www.edge.org. 15 March 2008.

Csikszentmihalyi, M. and Larson, R. (1984). *Being Adolescent*. New York: Basic Books.

Csikszentmihalyi, M. and Mei-Ha Wong, M. (1991). The situational and personal correlates of happiness: a cross-national comparison. In F. Strack, M. Argyle and N. Schwarz (eds), *Subjective Well-being: An Interdisciplinary Perspective* (pp. 193–212). Oxford: Pergamon Press. Member of Maxwell Macmillan Pergamon Publishing Corporation.

Dahlberg, G. and Moss, P. (2005). *Ethics and Politics in Early Childhood Education*. London: RoutledgeFalmer.

Dahlberg, G., Moss, P. and Pence, A. (1999). *Beyond Quality in Early Childhood Education and Care: Postmodern Perspectives*. London: FalmerRoutledge.

Damon, W. (1983). *Social and Personality Development. Infancy through Adolescence*. New York: Norton.

Dench, G., Gavron, K. and Young, M. (2007). *The New East End: Kinship, Race and Conflict*. London: Profile.

Department for Education and Skills (2001). *The Special Educational Needs Code of Practice.* London: DfES.

Department for Education and Skills (2003). *Every Child Matters.* London: DfES.

Department for Education and Skills (2003). *14–19: Opportunity and Excellence.* Norwich: HMSO.

Department for Education and Skills (2004). *Five Year Strategy for Children and Learners.* London: DfES.

Department of Health (2001). *The Expert Patient: A New Approach to Chronic Disease Management for the 21ˢᵗ Century.* London: Department of Health.

Department of Health (2003). Strengthening accountability: involving patients and the public. *Policy Guidance, Section 11 of the Health and Social Care Act 2001.* London: DOH.

Desforges, C. and Abouchaar, A. (2003). *The Impact of Parental Involvement, Parental Support and Family Education on Pupil Achievement and Adjustment: A Literature Review.* London: Department for Education and Skills.

Dewey, J. (1916). *Democracy and Education.* New York: Macmillan.

Diamond, J., Wang, L. and Gomez, K. (May, 2004). African–American and Chinese–American parent involvement: the importance of race, class, and culture. *Research Digest.* FINE Network: Harvard Family Research Project.

Diamond, P., Katwala, S., and Munn, M. (2004). Introduction: the new politics of the family. Family Fortunes: The New Politics of Childhood. Accessed from www.Fabian.org.uk. 23 February 2008.

Dieleman, A. J. and Van der Lans, J. (eds) (1999). *Heft in eigen handen. Zelfsturing en sociale betrokkenheid bij jongeren.* Assen: Van Gorcum.

Donahue, M. and Bryan, T. (1984). Communicative skills and peer relations of learning disabled adolescents. *Topics in Language Disorders,* 4(2), 10–21.

Donahue, M., Hartas, D. and Cole, D. (1999). Research on interactions among oral language and emotional/behavioral disorders. In D. Rogers-Adkinson and P. Griffith (eds), *Communication Disorders and Children with Psychiatric and Behavioural Disorders* (pp. 69–98). San Diego: Singular Publishing Group.

Du Bois-Raymond, M. (2001). Negotiating families. In M. Du Bois-Raymond, H. Süncker and H. Krüger (eds), *Childhood in Europe* (pp. 63–90). New York: Peter Lang.

Du Gay, P. (1997). *Production of Culture/Cultures of Production,* Milton Keynes: Open University Press.

Edwards, R. and Alldred, P. (1999). Children and young people's views of social research. *Childhood,* 6(2), 261–281.

Eerola-Pennanen, P. (2002). Lapset ja yksilöllistyminen. [Children and individualisation]. Licentiate thesis. Jyväskylän yliopisto, Yhteiskuntatieteiden ja filosofian laitos.

Ehrenreich, B. and Hochschild, B. (eds) (2003). *Global Woman: Nannies, Maids and Sex Workers in the New Economy.* New York: Metropolitan Press.

Epstein, J. L. (2002). *School, Family, and Community Partnerships: Your Handbook for Action.* Boston: Corwin Press, Inc. A Sage Publication Company.

Esping-Andersen, G. (1990). *The Three Worlds of Welfare Capitalism.* Cambridge: Cambridge University Press.

The Evangelical Magazine (1799). *The Evangelical Magazine.* Volume VII. January to December 1799. London: T. Chapman publication.

European Commission (2003). PROGRAMMING MANDATE ADDRESSED TO CEN, CENELEC and ETSI IN THE FIELD OF SERVICES. Brussels: EU.

Fass, P. (2003). Children and globalization. *Journal of Social History,* 36(4), 963–977.

Feinberg, J. (1980). *Rights, Justice, and the Bounds of Liberty: Essays in Social Philosophy.* Princeton, NJ: Princeton University Press.

Fielding, M. (2001). Beyond the rhetoric of student voice: new departures or new constraints in twenty-first century schooling? *Forum,* 43(2), 100–110.

Fielding, M. (2004). 'New wave' student voice and the renewal of a civic society. *London Review of Education,* 2(3),197–217.

Fielding, M. (2007). The human cost and intellectual poverty of high performance schooling: radical philosophy, John Macmurray and the remaking of person-centred education. *Journal of Education Policy,* 22(4), 383–409.

Fielding, M. and Bragg, S. (2003). *Students as Researchers: Making a Difference.* Cambridge: Pearsons.

Fleer, M., Anning, A. and Cullen, J. (2004). A framework for conceptualising early childhood education. In A. Anning, J. Cullen and M. Fleer (eds), *Early Childhood Education: Society and Culture* (pp. 175–186). London: Sage.

Florian, L. (2007). Reimaging special education. In L. Florian (ed.), *Sage Handbook of Special Education* (pp. 7–20). London: Sage.

Flutter, J. and Rudduck, J. (2004). *Consulting Pupils: What's in It for Schools?* London: RoutledgeFalmer.

Foucault, M. (1977). *Discipline and Power: The Birth of a Prison.* Harmondsworth: Penguin Books.

Foucault, M. (1980). Truth and power. In C. Gordon (ed.), *Power/Knowledge: Selected Interviews and Other Writings, 1972–1977* (pp. 109–133). London: Harvester Wheatsheaf.

Foucault, M. (1997). Technologies of the self. *The Essential Works of Michael Foucault,* Vol. 1. New York: The New York Press.

Franklin, B. (December, 1994). Children's Rights to Participate. Paper presented at the European Conference on Monitoring Children's Rights, University of Gent.

Franklin, B. (2002). Children's rights and media wrongs: Changing representations of children and the developing rights agenda. In B. Franklin (ed.), *The New Handbook of Children's Rights. Comparative Policy and Practice* (pp. 15–42). London: Routledge.

Frederickson, N. and Cline, T. (2002). *Special Educational Needs, Inclusion and Diversity.* Maidenhead, Berkshire: McGraw-Hill/Open University Press.

Freeman, M. (1992). Taking children's rights more seriously. *International Journal of Law and the Family,* 6, 52–71.

Freeman, M. (2000). The future of children's rights. *Children and Society,* 14, 277–293.

Frones, I. (1994). Dimensions of childhood. In J. Qvortrup, M. Bardy, S. Sgritta and H. Wintersberger (eds), *Childhood Matters: Social Theory, Practice and Politics* (pp. 145–164). Aldershot: Avebury.

Gabel, S. and Peters, S. (2004). Presage of a paradigm shift? Beyond the social model of disability towards resistance theories of disability. *Disability and Society*, 19(6), 585–600.

Gallagher, D. (2007). Challenging orthodoxy in special education: On longstanding debates and philosophical divides. In L. Florian (ed.), *Sage Handbook of Special Education* (pp. 515–536). London: Sage.

Gardner, F., Ward, S., Burton, J. and Wilson, C. (2003). The role of mother–child joint play in the early development of children's conduct problems: a longitudinal observational study. *Social Development*, 12(3), 361.

Gewirtz, S., Dickson, M., Power, S., Halpin, D. and Whitty, G. (2005). The deployment of social capital theory in educational policy and provision: the case of Education Action Zones in England. *British Educational Research Journal*, 31(6), 651–673.

Gibbons, M., Limoges, C., Nowotny, H., Schwartzman, S., Scott, P. and Trow, M. (1994). *The New Production of Knowledge: The Dynamics of Science and Research in Contemporary Society*. Stockholm: Sage Publications.

Gigerenzer, G. and Lane, A. (2002). *Reckoning with Risk: Learning to Live with Uncertainty (Report number 153.43 GIG)*. London: RSA.

Gill, T. (1999). Play, child care and the road to adulthood. *Children and Society*, 13(1), 67–69.

Gill, T. (2007). Cotton wool revolution. *The Guardian*, 30 October.

Giroux, H. A. (1991). Democracy and the discourse of cultural difference: towards a politics of border pedagogy. *British Journal of Sociology of Education*, 12(4), 501–519.

Gleeson, B. (1999). *Geographies of Disability*. London: Routledge.

Gordon, C. (1991). Governmental rationality: an introduction. In G. Burchell, C. Gordon and P. Miller (eds), *The Foucault Effect: Studies in Governmentality*. Hemel Hempstead, England: Harvester Wheatsheaf.

Gordon, T., Holland, J. and Lahelma, E. (2000). *Making Spaces. Citizenship and Difference in Schools*. London: Macmillan Press.

Gould, C. C. (2004). *Globalizing Democracy and Human Rights*. Cambridge: Cambridge University Press.

Grant, C., Elsbree, A. and Fondrie, S. (2004). A decade of research on the changing terrain of multicultural education research. In J. Banks (ed.), *Handbook of Research on Multicultural Education, Second Edition*, San Francisco, CA: Jossey-Bass/A Wiley Company.

Gray, J. (1999). *False Dawn: The Delusions of Global Capitalism*. London: Granta Books.

Greenham, S. (1999). Learning disabilities and psychosocial adjustment: a critical review. *Child Neuropsychology*, 5, 171–196.

Grenot-Scheyer, M. (2004). Friendships and other social relationships of children with and without disabilities: considerations and strategies for families and school personnel. TASH Connections, On-line Newsletter (Invited paper), www.tash. org, Baltimore, MD.

Gupta, A. and Ferguson, J. (1997). Beyond 'culture': space, identity, and the politics of difference. In A. Gupta and J. Ferguson (eds), *Culture, Power, Place. Explorations in Critical Anthropology* (pp. 33–51). Durham: Duke University Press.

Gutmann, A. and Thompson, D. (2004). *Why Deliberative Democracy?* Princeton, NJ: Princeton University Press.

Habermas, J. (1984). *The Theory of Communicative Function.* London: Heinemann.

Habermas, J. (1990). *Moral Consciousness and Communicative Action,* Cambridge, MA: MIT Press.

Hall, D. E. (2004). *Subjectivity.* New York: Routledge.

Hallgarten, J., Breslin, T. and Hannam, D. (2004). *I Was a Teenage Governor.* London: IPPR and Citizenship Foundation.

Hanssen, B. (2000). Ethics of the other. In M. Garber, B. Hanssen and R. L. Walkowitz (eds), *The Turn to Ethics.* London: Routledge.

Hardin, S. and Hintikka, M. (1983). *Discovering Reality.* Dordrecht: D. Reidel.

Harre, R. (1983). *Personal Being.* Oxford: Basil Blackwell.

Hart, R. A. (1992). *Children's Participation: From Tokenism to Citizenship, Innocenti Essays.* Florence: UNICEF International Child Development Centre.

Hartas, D. and Lindsay, G. (2007). The Needs Analysis Study. University of Warwick: Centre for Educational Development Appraisal and Research.

Heap, S. and Ross, A. (eds) (1992). *Understanding the Enterprise Culture: Themes in the Work of Mary Douglas.* Edinburgh: Edinburgh University Press.

Heiman, J. (2000). Students with learning disabilities in Higher Education: academic strategies profile. *Journal of Learning Disabilities,* 36(3), 246–256.

Hengst, H. (2000). Die Arbeit der Kinder und der Umbau der Arbeitsgesellschaft. In H. Hengst and H. Zeiher (eds), *Die Arbeit der Kinder. Kindheitskonzept und Arbeitsteilung zwischen den Generationen* (pp. 71–97). Weinheim: Juventa.

Herr, S. S., Gostin, L. O. and Koh, H. H. (eds) (2003). *The Human Rights of Persons with Intellectual Disabilities.* New York: Oxford University Press.

Heshusius, L. (2004). Special education knowledges: the inevitable struggle with the 'self'. In D. J. Gallagher (ed.), *Challenging Orthodoxy in Special Education: Dissenting Voices* (pp. 283–309). Denver, CO: Love Publishing.

Heymann, J. (2006). *Forgotten Families: Ending the Growing Crisis Confronting Children and Working Parents in the Global Economy.* Oxford: Oxford University Press.

Hodges, E. V. and Perry, D. J. (1999). Personal and interpersonal antecedents and consequences of peer victimization. *Journal of Personal and Social Psychology,* 76(4), 677–685.

Horelli, L. and K. Vepsä (1995). *Ympäristön lapsipuolet [The community's step-children].* Helsinki: ITLA.

Hughes, P. and MacNaughton, G. (2002). Preparing early childhood professionals to work with parents: the challenges of diversity and dissensus. *Australian Journal of Early Childhood,* 24, 45–56.

Hunt, A. (2003). Risk and moralization in everyday life. In R. Ericson and A. Doyle (eds), *Risk and Morality.* London: University of Toronto Press.

Hutchings, K. (2007). Feminist ethics and political violence. *International Politics,* 44, 90–106.

Hutt, S. J., Tyler, S., Hutt, C., Christoperson, H. (1989). *Play, Exploration and Learning: A Natural History of Pre-School.* London and New York: Routledge.

Hyder, T. (2005). *War, Conflict and Play.* Maidenhead, Berkshire: McGraw-Hill/Open University Press.

International Labour Organisation (ILO) (2006). *Labour and Social Trends in Asia and the Pacific*. Bangkok. Accessed from www.ilo.org/public/english/region/asro/bangkok/14arm/download/labour.pdf. 23 February 2008.

Jans, M. (2004). Children as citizens: towards a contemporary notion of child participation. *Childhood*, 11(1), 27–44.

John, M. (1996). Voicing: research and practice with the silenced. In M. John (ed.), *Children in Charge: The Child's Right to a Fair Hearing*. London: Jessica Kingsley.

Kasturi, S. (2002). Constructing childhood in a corporate world: cultural studies, childhood and Disney. In G. S. Cannella and J. L. Kincheloe (eds), *Kidworld: Childhood Studies, Global Perspectives and Education*. New York: Peter Lang.

Kavale, K. A., and Forness, S. R. (1996). Social skill deficits and learning disabilities: a meta-analysis. *Journal of Learning Disabilities*, 29, 226–237.

Kelly, P. (2001). Youth at risk: processes of individualisation and responsibilisation in the risk society. *Discourse: Studies in the Cultural Politics of Education*, 22(1), 23–33.

Kiili, J. (1998). Lapset ja nuoret hyvinvointinsa asiantuntijoina. Raportti hyvinvointi-indikaattoreiden kehittämisestä. [Children and young people as experts on their own welfare]. Jyväskylä: Yhteiskuntatieteiden ja filosofian laitoksen yhteiskunta-politiikan työpapereita.

Kilkelly, U., Kilpatrick, R. and Lundy, L. (2005). *Children's Rights in Northern Ireland, Northern Ireland Commissioner for Children and Young People*. Belfast, NI.

Kirby, P. and Bryson, S. (2002). *Measuring the Magic? Evaluating Young People's Participation in Public Decision-Making*. London: Carnegie Young People Initiative.

Knowles, C. (1999). Cultural perspectives and welfare regimes, In P. Chamberlayne, A. Cooper, R. Freeman and M. Rustin (eds), *Welfare and Culture in Europe: Towards a New Paradigm in Social Policy*. London: Jessica Kingsley.

Knuttson, K. E. (1997). *Children: Noble Causes or Worthy Citizens*. Aldershot: Arena/UNICEF.

Kobayashi, A. and Ray, B. (2000). Civil risk and landscapes of marginality in Canada: a pluralist approach to social justice. *Canadian Geographer*, 44(4), 401–417.

Kopomaa, T. (2000). *The City in Your Pocket. Birth of the Mobile Information Society*. Helsinki: Gaudeamus.

Kouvonen, A. (2002). *Part-Time Work and Deviant Behaviour among Finnish Adolescents*. Helsinki: National Research Institute of Legal Policy, Publication No. 191.

Kraemer, S. (1999). Promoting resilience: changing concepts of parenting and child care. *International Journal of Child and Family Welfare*, 3, 273–287.

Kudlick, C. (2003). Disability history: why we need another 'other'. *The American Historical Review*, 108(3), 1–26.

Lancaster, Y. P. (2006). *RAMPS: A Framework for Listening to Children*. London: Daycare Trust.

Lansdown, G. (1995). *Taking Part: Children's Participation in Decision Making*. London: Institute of Public Policy Research.

Lansdown, G. (2001). *Promoting Children's Participation in Democratic Decision Making*. Florence: UNICEF Innocenti Research Centre.

Lansdown, G. (2005). *The Evolving Capacities of Children: Implications for the Exercise of Rights*, Florence: UNICEF Innocenti Research Centre.

Lather, P. (1991). *Getting Smart: Feminist Research and Pedagogy with/in the Postmodern*. London: Routledge.

Lave, J. and Wegner, E. (1991). *Situated Learning: Legitimate Peripheral Participation.* Cambridge: Cambridge University Press.

Law, S. (2006). *The War for Children's Minds.* London: Routledge.

Lawson, N. (2006). *Where Idealism and Pragmatism Meet. New Statesman.* London: New Statesman Ltd.

Lazos, H. D. (2002). *Playing in Time: Ancient Greek and Byzantine Games.* Athens: Aiolos Publishing.

Leadbeater, C. (2000). *Living on Thin Air: The New Economy with a Blueprint for the 21ˢᵗ Century.* London: Penguin.

Leffler, E. and Svedberg, G. (2005). Enterprise learning: a challenge to education? *European Educational Research Journal,* 4(3), 219–246.

Levinas, E. (1989). Ethics as first Philosophy. In S. Hand (ed.), *The Levinas Reader.* Oxford: Blackwell.

Lewinsohn, P. M., Redner, J. and Seeley, J. (1991). The relationship between life satisfaction and psychosocial variables: new perspectives. In F. Strack, M. Argyle and N. Schwarz (eds), *Subjective Wellbeing: An Interdisciplinary Perspective* (pp. 141–192). Oxford: Pergamon Press.

Lewis, A. and Norwich, B. (eds) (2005). *Special Teaching for Special Children? Pedagogies for Inclusion.* Maidenhead: Open University Press.

Lewis, A. and Porter, J. (2007). Research and pupil voice. In L. Florian (ed.), *Sage Handbook of Special Education* (pp. 222–232). London: Sage.

Lindsay, G. (2007). Educational psychology and the effectiveness of inclusive education/mainstreaming. *British Journal of Educational Psychology in Practice,* 77, 1–24.

Lister, R. (2004). Ending child poverty: a matter of human rights, citizenship and social justice. In P. Doran (ed.), *Ending Child Poverty in 2020: The First Five Years* (pp. 59–67). London: Child Poverty Action Group.

Lister, R. (2005). *Children, Well-being and Citizenship.* Paper presented to Social Policy Association Annual Conference, University of Bath, 27–29 June.

Livingstone, S. and Bober, M. (2004). Taking up online opportunities? Children's uses of the internet for education, communication and participation. *E–Learning,* 1(3), 395–419.

Liwski, N. (2006). Introductory remarks to the UN Committee on the Rights of the Child Day of General Discussion, 2004. In *Implementing Child Rights in Early Childhood.* The Hague: Bernard van Leer Foundation/UNICEF/UN Committee on the Rights of the Child.

Lolichen P. J., (2006). *Children as Informed Participants in Governance.* Accessed from www.workingchild.org. 20 December 2007.

Louv, R. (2005). *Last Child in the Woods: Saving Our Children from Nature Deficit Disorder.* Ontario, Canada: Algonquin Books of Chapel Hill.

Lundy, L. (2007). 'Voice' is not enough: conceptualising Article 12 of the United Nations Convention on the Rights of the Child. *British Educational Research Journal,* 33(6), 927–942.

Lyotard, J-F. (1979/1984). *The Postmodern Condition: A Report on Knowledge* (Translated by G. Bennington and B. Massumi). Minneapolis, MN: University of Minnesota Press.

MacIntyre, A. (1982). *After Virtue,* London: Duckworth.

Mäenpää, P. (2000). Digitaalisen arjen ituja. Kännykkä ja urbaani elämäntapa [The mobile phone and the urban way of life]. In T. Hoikkala and J. P. Roos (eds), *luvun elämää. Sosiologisia teorioita vuosituhannen vaihteesta* (pp. 132–152). Helsinki: Gaudeamus.

Malaguzzi, E. (1993). For an education based on relationships. *Young Children*, 11/93, 9–13.

Mandela, N. (February, 1999). *Opening address by President Nelson Mandela in the Special Debate on the Report of the Truth and Reconciliation Commission (TRC)*. Retrieved from http://www.info.gov.za/speeches. 20 March 2008.

Mander, J. and Goldsmith, E. (1996). *The Case Against the Global Economy: And for Turn Toward the Local.* San Francisco, CA: Sierra Club Books.

Marginson, S. (1997). *Markets in Education.* St. Leonards, NSW: Allen & Unwin.

Marquand, D. (2003). *Decline of the Public: The Hollowing-out of Citizenship.* Cambridge: Polity Press.

Masschelein, J. (2001). The discourse of the learning society and the loss of childhood. *Journal of Philosophy of Education*, 35(1), 1–20.

Matthews, H., Limb, M. and Taylor, M. (2000). The 'street as thirdplace'. In S. Holloway and G. Valentine (eds), *Children's Geographies. Playing, Living, Learning* (pp. 63–79). London: Routledge.

Mayall, B. (1994). *Children's Childhoods: Observed and Experienced.* London: Routledge.

Mayall, B. (2002). *Towards a Sociology for Childhood: Thinking from Children's Lives.* Maidenhead, Berkshire: McGraw Hill/Open University Press.

Mayall, J. (2000). Democracy and International Society. *International Affairs*, 76(1), 61–75.

McClure, G. (2001). Suicide in children and adolescents in England and Wales 1970–1998. *The British Journal of Psychiatry*, 178, 469–474.

McDonald, K. (October, 2007). *The Importance of Identity in Policy: The Case for and of Children.* Paper presented at the SPRC Workshop, Australia: University of New South Wales.

McDowell, L. (2004). Work, workfare, work/life balance and an ethic of care. *Progress in Human Geography*, 28(2), 145–163.

McLaughlin, E. (2007). The equality chameleon: reflections on social identity, passing, and groupism. *Social Policy & Society*, 6(1), 69–79.

McNay, L. (2000). *Gender and Agency: Reconfiguring the Subject in Feminist and Social Theory.* Cambridge: Polity Press.

McNeish, D. (1999). Promoting participation for children and young people: some key questions for health and social welfare organisations. *Journal of Social Work Practice*, 13, 191–204.

Melber, A. (2006). MySpace, MyPolitics. *The Nation*, 30 May. Retrieved 7 April 2007 from http://www.thenation.com/docprint.mhtml?i=20060612&s=melber.

Michalos, A. (1985). Multiple discrepancies theory (MDT). *Social Indicators Research*, 16(4), 347–413.

Mitchell, W. and Sloper, P. (2001). Quality in services for disabled children and their families: what can theory, policy and research on children's and parents' views tell us? *Children and Society*, 15, 237–252.

Miles, M. B. and Huberman, A. M. (1994). *Qualitative Data Analysis: An Expanded Sourcebook*. Thousand Oaks, CA: Sage Publication Company.

Miljeteig, P. (1994). *Children's involvement in the implementation of their own rights: present and future perspectives*. Paper presented at Symposium on the Social and Psychological Implications of the UN Convention of the Rights of the Child, International Society for the Study of Behavioural Development XIIIth Biennal Meetings, Amsterdam.

Mill, J. S. (1993–1859;1861) *Utilitarianism, on Liberty, Considerations on Representative Government*. London: Everyman.

Minow, M. (1990). *Making All the Difference: Inclusion, Exclusion and American Law*. Ithaca, NY: Cornell University Press.

Minow, M. (1995). Children's rights: where we've been, and where we're going. *Temple Law Review*, 68, 1573–1584.

Mishna, F. (2003). Learning disabilities and bullying: double jeopardy. *Journal of Learning Disabilities*, 36(4), 336–347.

Mohanty, C. T. (2003). *Feminism without Borders: Decolonizing Theory, Practicing Solidarity*. Durham and London: Duke University Press.

Montgomery, E., Krogh, Y., Jacobsen, A., and Lukman, B. (1992). Children of torture victims: reactions and coping. *Child Abuse and Neglect*, 16, 797–805.

Moran, E. (1999). Les sept savoirs necessaires a l'education du futur. *UNESCO*, Paris.

Moran, P., Ghate, D. and van der Merwe, A (2004). *What Works in Parenting Support? A Review of the International Evidence*. London: DfES.

Morris, J. (1998a). Still Missing? *The Experience of Disabled Children and Young People Living Away from their Families*, Vol. 1. London: The Who Cares? Trust.

Morris, J. (1998b). *Still Missing? Disabled Children and the Children Act*, Vol. 2. London: The Who Cares? Trust.

Moss, P. (1999). Early childhood institutions as a democratic and emancipatory project. In L. Abbott and H. Moylett (eds), *Early Childhood Transformed* (pp. 142–152). London: Routledge.

Moss, P. and Petrie, P. (2002). *From Children's Services to Children's Spaces: Public Policy, Children and Childhood*. London: Routledge.

Nasman, E. (1994). Individualization and institutionalization of childhood in today's Europe. In J. Qvortrup, M. Bardy, S. Sgritta and H. Wintersberger (eds), *Childhood Matters: Social Theory, Practice and Politics* (pp. 165–188). Aldershot: Avebury.

National Research Council (2002). *Scientific Research in Education. Committee on the Scientific Principles for Education Research* (R. J. Shavelson, and L. Towne (eds)). Washington, DC: National Academy Press.

Noddings, N. (2003). *Happiness and Education*. Cambridge: Cambridge University Press.

Nussbaum, M. (2004). *Hiding from Humanity: Disgust, Shame and the Law*. Princeton, NJ: Princeton University Press.

NUTEK (2000). *Swedish Business Development Agency*. Stockholm: NUTEK.

Oancea, A. (2007). Research policy and education research: accountability phobia, or a clash of interpretations? *Research Intelligence*, 100, 20–21.

O'Lincoln, T. (2002). Veiled threats? *Politics and Culture*, 2, 3–7.

O'Malley, P. (1996). Risk and responsibility. In A. Barry, T. Osborne and N. Rose (eds), *Foucault and Political Reason: Liberalism, Neo-Liberalism and Rationalities of Government*. London: University College London Press.

O'Neill, B. (2006). Watching you watching me. *New Statesman*, 2 October.

O'Neill, O. (1988). Children's Rights and Children's Lives. *Ethics*, 98(3), 445–463.

Ong, A. (1999). *Flexible Citizenship: The Cultural Logics of Transnationality*. Durham, NC: Duke University Press.

Ong, A. (2003). *Buddha Is Hiding: Refugees, Citizenship, the New America*. Berkeley, CA: The University of California Press.

Ong, A. (2006). Mutations in Citizenship. *Theory, Culture & Society*, 23(2–3), 499–505.

Ong, A. and Collier, S. (eds) (2005). *Global Assemblages: Technology, Politics, and Ethics as Anthropological Problems*. Malden, MA: Blackwell Publishing.

Organisation for Economic Co-operation and Development (OECD) (2004). *Life-long Learning: Policy Brief*. OECD.

Osler, A. (2006). Changing leadership in contexts of diversity: visibility, invisibility and democratic ideals. *Policy Futures in Education*, 4(2), 128–144.

Oxley, H., Dang, T., Forster, M., Pellizzari, M. (2000). Income inequalities and poverty among children and households with children in selected OECD countries. Child well-being, child poverty and child policy in modern trends and determinants. In K. Vleminckx and T. Smeeding (eds), *Child Well-being, Child Poverty and Child Policy in Modern Nations: What do We Know?* Bristol: The Policy Press.

Paley, V. (2004). *A Child's Work: The Importance of Fantasy Play*. Chicago, IL: The University of Chicago Press.

Park, A., Phillips, M. and Johnson, M. (2004). *Young People in Britain: The Attitudes and Experiences of 12 to 19 Year Old*. London: DfES.

Parker, S. (1997). *Reflective Teaching in the Postmodern World*. Buckingham: Open University Press.

Paterson, L. (2000). Citizenship in Scotland. *Scottish Journal of Adult and Continuing Education*, 6(1), 95–104.

Pearl, R., and Bay, M. (1999). Psychosocial correlates of learning disabilities. In V. L. Schwean and D. H. Saklofske (eds), *Handbook of Psychosocial Characteristics of Exceptional Children* (pp. 443–470). New York: Kluwer/Plenum.

Pellegrini, A. (2003). Perceptions and functions of play and real fighting in early adolescence. *Child Development*, 74(5), 1522–1533.

Pellegrini, A. D. (1998). Bullies and victims in school: a review and call for research. *Journal of Applied Developmental Psychology*, 19, 165–176.

Pellegrini, A. D. and Blatchford, P. (2000). *The Child at School: Interactions with Peers and Teachers*. New York: Oxford University Press.

Penn, H. (2002). The Word Bank's view of early childhood. *Childhood* 9(1), 118–132.

Pennanen, H. (2000). Neljäsluokkalaisten koululaisten iltapäivät Helsingissä: todellisuus ja toiveet.[School children's afternoons in Helsinki, grades 1–4: reality and ideals]. Helsinki: Helsingin kaupungin opetusviraston julkaisusarja B15:2000.

Peters, M. (2001). Education, enterprise culture and the entrepreneurial self: a Foucauldian perspective. *Journal of Educational Enquiry*, 2(2), 58–71.

Pettit, G., Bates, J., Dodge, K., Meece, D. (1999). The impact of after-school peer contact on early adolescent externalizing problems is moderated by parental monitoring, perceived neighborhood safety, and prior adjustment. *Child Development*, 70(3), 768–778.

Philo, C. (2000). The corner-stones of my world. Editorial introduction to special issue on spaces of childhood. *Childhood*, 7(3), 243–256.

Pinker, S. (2003). How to get inside a student's head. *New York Times*, 31 January.

Prinstein, M. J., Boergers, J., and Vernberg, E. M. (2001). Overt and relational aggression in adolescents: social–psychological adjustment of aggressors and victims. *Journal of Clinical Child Psychology*, 30, 479–491.

Punch, K. (2005). *Introduction to Social Research: Qualitative and Quantitative Approaches.* London: Sage.

Putnam, R. (1998). Foreword. *Housing Policy Debate.* 9(1), v.

Putnam, R. (2000). *Bowling Alone.* New York: Simon and Schuster.

Putnam, R. D. (1993). *Making Democracy Work. Civic Traditions in Modern Italy.* Princeton, NJ: Princeton University Press.

Putnam, R. D. (1995). Bowling alone: America's declining social capital. *The Journal of Democracy*, 6(1), 65–78.

Qvortrup, J. (1994). Introduction. In J. Qvortrup, M. Bardy, G. Sgritta and H. Wintersberger (eds), *Childhood Matters: Social Theory, Practice and Politics* (pp. 1–24). Aldershot: Avebury.

Raffaele, L. M. and Knoff, H. M. (1999). Improving home–school collaboration with disadvantaged families: organizational principles, perspectives, and approaches. *School Psychology Review*, 28, 488–466.

Ragin, C. (1994). *Constructing Social Research: The Unity and Diversity of Method.* Newbury Park, CA: Pine Forge Press. A Sage Publication Company.

Ranson, S. (ed.) (1998). *Inside the Learning Society.* London: Cassell.

Ranson, S. (2003). Public Accountability in the age of neo-liberal governance. *Journal of Educational Policy*, 18(5), 459–480.

Ranson, S. and Routledge, H. (2005). *Including Families in the Learning Community: Family Centres and the Expansion of Learning.* Rowntree Foundation.

Raundalen, M. et al. (2003). Our common responsibility: the impact of war on Iraqi children. Toronto: War Child Canada.

Readings, B. (1996). *The University in Ruins.* Cambridge, MA: Harvard University Press.

Rigby, K. (2000). Effects of peer victimization in schools and perceived social support on adolescent well-being. *Journal of Adolescence*, 23, 57–68.

Rigby, K. (2003). Consequences of bullying in schools. *Canadian Journal of Psychiatry*, 48(9), 583–590.

Roberts, C. M. and Smith, P. R. (1999). Attitudes and behaviour of children toward peers with disabilities. *International Journal of Disability, Development and Education*, 46(1), 35–50.

Robinson, J. (2000). Power as friendship: spatiality, femininity and 'noisy surveillance'. In J. Sharp, P. Routledge, C. Philo and R. Paddison (eds), *Entanglements of Power: Geographies of Domination/Resistance* (pp. 67–92). London: Routledge.

Robinson, K. and Diaz, C. (2006). *Diversity and Difference in Early Childhood Education: Issues for Theory and Practice.* Maidenhead, Berkshire: McGraw-Hill/Open University Press.

Roche, J. (1999). Children: rights, participation and citizenship. *Childhood*, 6(4), 475–493.

Roland, E. (2000). Bullying in school: three national innovations in Norwegian schools in 15 years. *Aggressive Behaviour*, 26, 135–143.

Rosaldo, R. (1989). *Culture and Truth*. Boston, MA: Beacon Press.

Rose, N. (1996). The death of the social? Re-figuring the territory of government. *Economy and Society*, 25(3), 327–356.

Rose, N. (1999a). *Governing the Soul: The Shaping of the Private Self*. New York: Free Association Press.

Rose, N. (1999b). Inventiveness in Politics. *Economy and Society*, 28(3), 467–493.

Rose, N. and Novas, C. (2003). Biological Citizenship. In A. Ong and S. Collier (eds), *Global Anthropology* (pp. 439–463). London: Blackwell.

Rouse, M. and McLaughlin, M. (2007). Changing perspectives of special education in the evolving context of educational reform. In L. Florian (ed.), *The Sage Handbook of Special Education* (85–105). London: Sage.

Rousseau, Jean-Jacques (1979). *Emile, or On Education*. (Translated by Allan Bloom). New York: Basic Books.

Rubin, K. H. (1973). Egocentrism in childhood: a unitary construct? *Child Development*, 44, 102–110.

Russ, S. (2003). Play and creativity: developmental issues. *Scandinavian Journal of Educational Research*, 47(3), 291–303.

Russell, J. (2005). We have a responsibility to look out for all children, not just our own. *The Guardian*, 26 November.

Russel, K. and Granville, S. (2005). *Parents' Views on Improving Parental Involvement in Children's Education*. Edinburgh: Scottish Executive.

Sachs, A. (1997). Human rights in the twenty-first century: real dichotomies, false antagonisms. In T. Cromwell, A. D. Pinard, and H. Dumont (eds), *Human Rights in the 21st Century: Prospects, Institutions and Process* (pp. 7–19). Montreal: Editions Themis/Canadian Institute for the Administration of Justice.

Santos, B. de S. (1995). *Towards a New Common Sense: Law, Science and Politics in the Paradigmatic Transition*. London: Routledge.

Santos, B. de S. (1998). *Reinventar a Democracia*. Lisboa: Gradiva.

Santos, B. de S. (2001). Nuestra America: reinventing a subaltern paradigm of recognition and redistribution. *Theory, Culture and Society*, 18, 185–217.

Santos, B. de S. (2004). *The World Social Forum: A User's Manual*. Madison, WI: University of Wisconsin Madison Press.

Schank, R. (2006). *No More Teacher's Dirty Looks*. Accessed from www.edge.org. 20 March 2008.

Schwartz, P. (1998). *The Art of the Long View: Paths to Strategic Insight for Yourself and Your Company*. New York: Doubleday.

Seabrook, J. (2007). Children of the market. *The Guardian*, 17 June.

Seltzer, K. and Bentley, T. (1999). *The Creative Age: Knowledge and Skills for the New Economy*. London: Demos.

Sen, A. (2000). *Development as Freedom*. New York: Anchor Books.

Sen, A. (2006). *Identity and Violence: The Illusion of Destiny*. London: Penguin Allen Lane.

Sennett, R. (1998). *The Corrosion of Character: The Personal Consequences of Work in the New Capitalism*. New York: Norton.

Sevenhuijsen, S. (1998). *Citizenship and the Ethics of Care: Feminist Considerations on Justice, Morality and Politics.* London: Routledge.

Shakespeare, T. and Watson, N. (2001). The social model of disability: an outdated ideology? In *Research in Social Science and Disability* (pp. 9–28), Vol. 2. Kidlington, Oxfordshire: Elsevier Science Ltd.

Shayer, M. (2006). Children are falling behind in maths and science. *The Edge*, 2. Swindon: ESRC.

Shier, H. (2001). Pathways to participation: openings, opportunities and obligations. *Children and Society*, 15, 107–117.

Sinclair, R. (2004). Participation in practice: making it meaningful, effective and sustainable. *Children and Society*, 18, 106–118.

Slee, R. (1996). Clauses of conditionality. In L. Barton (ed.), *Disability and Society: Emerging Issues and Insights* (pp. 436–452). London: Longman.

Sloper, P. and Lightfoot, J. (2003). Involving disabled and chronically ill children and young people in health service development. *Child: Care, Health, and Development*, 29, 15–20.

Smidt, S. (2006). *The Developing Child in the 21st Century: A Global Perspective on Child Development.* London: Routledge.

Smith, F. and Barker, J. (1999a). Learning to listen: involving children in the development of out of school care. *Youth and Policy*, 63, 38–46.

Smith, F. and Barker, J. (1999b). From 'Ninja Turtles' to 'The Spice Girls': children's participation in the development of out of school play environments. *Built Environment*, 25(1), 35–43.

Smith, F. and Barker, J. (2000). Contested spaces: children's experiences of out of school care in England and Wales. *Childhood*, 7(3), 317–335.

Smith, P. K. and Shu, S. (2000). What good can school do about bullying: findings from a survey in English schools after a decade of research and action. *Childhood*, 7, 193–212.

Stables, A., Morgan, C. and Jones, S. (1999). Educating for significant events: the application of Harre's social reality matrix across the lower secondary-school curriculum. *Curriculum Studies*, 31(4), 449–461.

Stephens, S. (1992). Children and the UN Conference on environment and development: participants and media symbols. *Research on Children in Norway*, 2(3), 44–52.

Stephens, S. (1994). Children and environment: local worlds and global connections. *Childhood*, 2(1–2), 1–21.

Stephens, S. (1995). *Children and the Politics of Culture: Rights, Risks and Reconstructions.* Princeton, NJ: Princeton University Press.

Stiker, H-J. (1997/1982). *A History of Disability* (Translated by William Sayers). Ann Arbor, MI: University of Michigan Press.

Stone, E. (2001). *Consulting with Disabled Children and Young People.* York: Joseph Rowntree Foundation.

Storr, A. (1988). *Solitude: A Return to the Self.* New York: Random House.

Super, C. M. and Harkness, S. (1986). The developmental niche: a conceptualization at the interface of child and culture. *International Journal of Behavioral Development*, 9(4), 545–569.

Swedish Ministry of Education and Science (1998). *Curriculum for Preschool.* Stockholm: Swedish Ministry of Education and Science.

Taylor, K. (2005). Thought crime. *The Guardian*, 8 October.

Thomas, C. (2004). How is disability understood? An examination of sociological approaches. *Disability and Society*, 19(6), 569–583.

Thomas, G. and Loxley, A. (2001). *Deconstructing Special Education and Constructing Inclusion*. Buckingham: Open University Press.

Thomson, P. and Gunter, H. M. (2006). From 'consulting pupils' to 'pupils as researchers': a situated case narrative. *British Educational Research Journal*, 32(6), 839–59.

Thompson, S. and Hoggett, P. (1996). Universalism, selectivism and particularism: towards a post-modern social policy. *Critical Social Policy*, 16(1), 21–43.

Titchkosky, T. (2003). Governing embodiment: technologies of constituting citizens with disability. *Canadian Journal of Sociology*, 28(4), 517–542.

Tomlinson, S. (1982). *A Sociology of Special Education*. London: Routledge and Kegan Paul.

Toumlin , S. (1990). *Cosmopolis: The Hidden Agenda of Modernity*. Chicago, IL: University of Chicago Press.

Tronto, J. (1993). *Moral Boundaries: A Political Argument for the Ethics of Care*. London: Routledge.

UNICEF (2007). *Child Poverty in Perspective: An Overview of Child Well-being in Rich Countries*, Innocenti Report Card 7. Florence: Innocenti Research Centre, www.unicef.org/irc. 20 March 2008.

United Nations (UN) (1989). *Convention on the Rights of the Child*. Geneva: United Nations.

United Nations (UN) (2008). Annual Report 2008. Covering Activities in 2007. UN: Office on Drugs and Crime.

Utting, D. (1995). *Family and Parenthood: Supporting Families, Preventing Breakdown*. York: Joseph Rowntree Foundation.

Van der Veen, R. (2001). Naar een leefwereldbenadering van burgerschap. Inleiding op het thema burgerschap. *Sociale Interventie*, 10(4), 5–11.

Vanhuysse, P. and Sabbagh, C. (2005). Promoting happiness, respecting difference? New perspectives on the politics and sociology of education in liberal democracy. *British Educational Research Journal*, 31(3), 391–403.

Veenhoven, R. (1991). Questions on happiness: classical topics, modern answers, blind spots. In F. Stack, M. Argyle and N. Schwarz (eds), *Subjective Well-being an Interdisciplinary Perspective* (pp. 7–26). Oxford: Pergamon Press. Member of Maxwell Macmillan Pergamon Publishing Corporation.

Verhellen, E. (1994). *Convention on the Rights of the Child*. Leuven/Apeldoorn: Verhellen and Garant Publishers.

Verhellen, E. (1997). *Convention on the Rights of the Child*. Leuven: Garant.

Walberg, H. J. (1984). *Improving the Productivity of America's Schools, Educational Leadership*, 41(8), 19–27.

Waldron, J. (2003). Teaching cosmopolitan right. In K. McDonough and W. Feinberg (eds), *Citizenship and Education in Liberal–Democratic Societies – Teaching for Cosmopolitan Values and Collective Identities*. Oxford: Oxford University Press.

Ward, R. (2006). Beat stress by nurturing the silence within. *Times Education Supplement*, 28 July.

Watson, D. M. (2001). Pedagogy before technology: re-thinking the relationship between ICT and teaching. *Education and Information Technologies*, 6(4), 251–266.

Webb, T. P. (2005). The anatomy of accountability. *Journal of Education Policy*, 20(2), 189–208.

Wells, K. (2007). Risk, respectability and responsibilisation: unintended driver responses to speed limit enforcement. *Internet Journal of Criminology*. Accessed 17 February 2008.

Wenger, E. (1998). *Communities of Practice Learning, Meaning and Identity*. Cambridge: Cambridge University Press.

Wenger, E. (2000). Communities of practices and social learning systems. *Organization*, 7(2), 225–246.

West, C. (1990). The new cultural politics of difference. *October*, 53, 93–109.

Wilton, R., Schuer, S. (2006). Towards socio-spatial inclusion? Disabled people, neoliberalism and the contemporary labour market. *Area*, 38(2), 186–195.

Withers, G. and Batten, M. (1995). *Programs for At-risk Youth: A Review of the American, Canadian and British Literature since 1984*. Camberwell: Australian Council for Educational Research.

Women's Budget Group (WBG) (2005). *Women's and Children's Poverty: Making the Links*. London: Women's Budget Group.

Woodhead, M. (2006). Changing perspectives on early childhood: theory, research and policy. Paper presented for *Education for All Global Monitoring*. UNESCO.

Woolcock, M. and Narayan, D. (2000). Social Capital. *World Bank Research Observer*, 15(2), 228–230.

The World Bank Group (1999). Entering the 21st century: World Development Report 1999/2000. The World Bank.

World Health Organisation (WHO) (2001). *World Health Report*. Geneva: World Health Organisation.

Worrall, D. (1990). *Radical Culture. Discourse, Resistance and Surveillance, 1790–1820*. Detroit, MI: Wayne State University Press.

Young People's Social Attitudes (YPSA) (2003). *Young People's Social Attitudes*. University of Essex: UK Data Archive.

Zeiher, H. (2001a). Children's islands in space and time: the impact of spatial differentiation on children's ways of shaping social life. In M. de Bois-Reymond, H. Sünker and H-H. Krüger (eds), *Childhood in Europe. Approaches – Trends – Findings* (pp. 139–159). New York: Peter Lang.

Zeiher, H. (October, 2001b). *Children's Access to Space and use of Time*. Paper presented at the COST Children's Welfare Meeting. Norway: Trondheim.

Index

Lightning Source UK Ltd.
Milton Keynes UK
04 January 2011

165173UK00001B/45/P